KU-754-710

Dedicating this book to my whole entire heart and soul, my granny Mary, who is no longer with me. I wouldn't have been able to write this book without her lifelong love, support, and belief in me.

Granny – I did it!! I hope I have made you proud.

# CONTENTS

# INTRODUCTION

Black and Great. Where do I begin?

Growing up as an only child in a West Indian household, I was blessed to have a family that believed in me and encouraged me. No dream was seen as too big. No limits were placed on what I could or couldn't be. It didn't seem like much at the time but now as a twenty-nine-year-old in a world that can sometimes feel stifling for me as a Black woman, it's everything. Neither my parents nor anyone in my immediate family attended university but despite this (and probably because of this), excelling in my education was important to them. So, I studied hard, securing the top grades and simultaneously, I threw myself into just about every after school extra-curricular activity you can think of, from debating club to basketball, to trampolining, to drama club and more (I was doing the most). Throughout school, it was common amongst my peers and teachers to speculate on what I would be when I grew up.

'Rene's going to become the first Black Prime Minister,' some of them said, because of my passion for evoking change in my roles as the head girl, head of school council and the winner of the regional public speaking competition.

'She's going to become a famous actress or singer.' This came from singing the lead in the school choir, securing the lead roles in the school plays and going on to perform in theatres. Shakespeare was my speciality.

Other potential careers included being a journalist or a historian, which came from my love of writing and passion for history, where I academically excelled the most.

It was great that my teachers and peers thought so highly of me but internally, I was in turmoil. I didn't know what I wanted to be when I grew up. I know that it was the same for a lot of people growing up, but for me and maybe for other Black kids, it came from not really having a blueprint, not seeing visible role models and more importantly, not knowing how to pursue certain avenues. How could I pursue a career in politics, let alone aspire to become Prime Minister, when I hardly saw any Black people, especially from my socio-economic background, in Parliament or as decision makers in my local community? Sure, I saw lighter Black actresses and singers doing their thing; as a young teenager, I knew the dances and lyrics to Christina Milian, Amerie, Ashanti and Samantha Mumba songs (this is really showing my age here, *cries*), but, as for Black British women of my darker skin complexion – I didn't see them anywhere on screen. The same goes for every other career suggestion. I couldn't see me. I couldn't see *us*.

As I moved through sixth form and then university, I decided upon financial services, specifically banking, as the industry I wanted to start my career in – although this another space where I saw few Black people. I interned at European and American investment banks and quickly realised how much more informed and ahead my white counterparts were. Many of them were on their third internship whilst I was on my first, they already knew people high up in the banks we were interning at, were invited to private lunches and after-work events. They spoke so clearly and confidently about their career aspirations, who they wanted to emulate. Everything came so naturally to them, like they had been doing it all since birth, whilst I overanalysed my every action, overthought my every move, feeling that everything I did would be perceived as reflective of all Black people. It was more than just race. It was class too; most of them came from money, attended the best schools and had access to resources I didn't. I was starting from zero, working my way up while they were already at ten. Because of this, when I did see Black people in those higher up positions, I desperately wanted to know how they got there. What was their story, their career journey? But for years successful Black people were never afforded the opportunity or platform to speak on their career experiences. They didn't feature on the major lists, weren't invited to talk on panels, they weren't being interviewed by the big publications. It was like we didn't matter. Thankfully, this has changed.

Fast forward to 2018, when I was in my second job post-graduation, and the realisation came yet again that I was in another job that I didn't want to pursue for much longer. Although I managed to stick it out for another year, there were two things that really kept me going during this time:

1. My ability to write about and share my career experiences, the things I had learnt, the challenges I faced and how I overcame them, so that it would help other Black students and graduates. My first ever post was on learning to be my authentic self in the workplace for my friend's blog and it got such a great response. I continued to write on other topics, such as how to stand out during your summer

internship, how to navigate workplace politics and using LinkedIn to secure your ideal job. I would receive loads of private messages on Twitter and LinkedIn with people following up for more advice based on what I had written about. I started to realise that there was a gap in careers and workplace guidance from and for people that looked like us.

2. My 'Blk & Great' website (now solely an Instagram page). I interviewed upcoming Black entrepreneurs, filmmakers, designers, authors and more because I felt like all this great work was happening in our community, but it wasn't being shouted about. I also wanted to document how these individuals were able to achieve these amazing things in the hope it would help and inspire those within our community with similar ambitions. 'Blk & Great' is an informative platform which celebrates the very best of us.

Let's go back to that period where I didn't enjoy my job – *ughhh*. Amid working, careers blogging and interviewing for my website, I reflected a lot. I reflected on how different my career path might've been if I had been exposed to the stories of Black people who had achieved success in a variety of spaces when I was growing up. I reflected on my daily experiences in the workplace, the career decisions I was making and how different things might've been if there was a resource which gave context to the things I was going through as a Black person in a majorly white environment and provided some sort of advice. These reflections and thoughts were the foundation for what you have in your hands now, the *Black and Great* book.

## Black and Great. Be inspired.

I have always loved writing. In primary school, I used to write these super imaginative stories and when I started secondary school, history fast became my favourite subject. In addition to the set homework, I would make up my own essay questions on Black historical figures such as Marcus Garvey, Martin Luther King Jr and write critical analyses of them. In more recent years, I've written about careers through a personal lens and as much as I hoped for this book to happen, at times it felt like a distant dream. If you're wondering what any of this has to do with the book, I hope it encourages you to persevere with your goals, especially the ones that may not materialise straight away. Don't give up. As the saying goes, the race is not for the swift, but for those that can endure it.

It's been a journey and I'll be honest, not always an easy one. Some days I felt super confident writing this book and other days self-doubt crept in. *Who am I to be writing this book?* were my thoughts. I'm not a prominent careers or self-development guru, I'm just me, Rene, six years out of university, still figuring all this stuff out too. Also, in sharing my experiences and providing advice on what has worked for me, I'd never want that to be interpreted as representing the experiences of all Black people in the workplace. We are such a diverse community and I hope that in reading *Black and Great*, it encourages more of us to shed light on our unique experiences.

## Black and Great. The contributors.

*Black and Great* features contributions from Black innovators, trailblazers and history makers from a variety of industries including law, music, technology, medicine, tv, academia and more. I felt that mass media representation of Black people succeeding was limited to only two or three industries and that's just not accurate. Our talents and capabilities know no bounds.

**Black and Great. 'This is the book I wish I had when I was starting out in the workplace.'**

Joelle, the brilliant commissioning editor for this book, said this during our first conversation, and since then, so many others have echoed those words to me. It means everything because this is why I wrote *Black and Great*. My fellow Black people – students, professionals like me, and those who decided not to pursue higher education – this book is for us. I've grown tired of reading career guidance that is devoid of the Black workplace experience. I know we aren't the majority in many workplaces, butw we exist. The blanket 'one size fits all' advice that some writers have provided their predominantly white audiences can't be as easily applied by us. There is no recognition of the challenges that underrepresented communities in the workplace face, that racism, classism and other forms of discrimination mean that the playing field isn't equal and we aren't all starting at the same place. Therefore, when I was writing my chapters for *Black and Great*, it was important for me to bring a Black context to topics such as salary negotiation, overcoming imposter syndrome, building your personal brand, networking and more. I hope that regardless of the career path you take or are currently on, *Black and Great* provides you with insight, guidance, comfort, and truly inspires you.

Black and Great. Essential Workplace Toolkit.
Unapologetically for us, by us.
Let's go!

*'Don't give up. I was studying art and trying to do film at the same time. I made my first film at 28 whilst others made films when they were 23. Your story is important, your ideas are important. If one route isn't available, there will be another.'*
- Sir Steve McQueen

# OVERCOMING IMPOSTER SYNDROME

When I received a phone call from the HR personnel of a European investment bank congratulating me on securing a place on their internship programme, I must admit I thought the lady was having a laugh. Seriously, I thought this was one big mistake and that the following day she would call me and say there had been a mix up. Sure, I applied for the programme (due to encouragement from a friend), but did I think I would get on to it? Hell no. I believed that only smart people secured those opportunities, those that studied maths and science, not vocational subjects like international business like I had done. Despite all my academic and extra-curricular achievements, I couldn't understand why I had been selected. Even when the internship started, I felt uneasy. Listening to some of my peers talk passionately about bonds and stocks, knowing the ins and outs of everything happening within the world of finance, whilst I just awkwardly laughed (praying they wouldn't ask for my opinion) made me question why I was on the programme. It never dawned on me that maybe I was selected for other qualities that I possessed. I remember thinking to myself – do I really deserve to be there?

That question seemed to stick with me even when I had landed other internships, graduated from university and started working full time. People would congratulate me and ask me how I did it but instead of welcoming the praise with open arms, I was quick to deflect it and brush it off. The truth was, I felt like a fraud and didn't think I was as smart as my peers. Being the only Black person in the room most of the time also seemed to validate my feeling that people who looked like me weren't good enough.

What I didn't know was that I was experiencing something called imposter syndrome. It's actually very common, especially for women. The term was coined by psychologists Pauline Clance and Suzanne Imes in 1978. They described it as a feeling of 'phoniness in people who believe that they are not intelligent, capable or creative despite evidence of high achievement'. While these people 'are highly motivated to achieve', they also 'live in fear of being "found out" or exposed as "frauds"'. This hit the nail on the head for me.

## Examples of some of my common feelings and thoughts:

**Being scared to fail:** when I'm given an opportunity, in my head I assume that person believes I know it all. As a result, I put a great amount of pressure on myself to not fail, make mistakes or let them down.

**Luck:** whenever I've been asked questions such as 'how did you secure that role?', I will never put it down to my abilities or hard work but more than likely say I was lucky. If I refer to a particular skill or talent that I have, I worry that people will question my competency if I'm then not seen to secure further opportunities.

"It's not a big deal": I've always downplayed my achievements and successes, never wanting to put them out there or accept any compliments. Imposter syndrome is based on the idea of us being good at something or achieving success in a particular area but discounting the value of this success. Why? Because we perceive that if something comes naturally to us, others won't regard it as highly, so we create this flawed image of our successes before they can.

## Imposter Syndrome whilst Black

For many of us, feeling like we weren't good enough started way before entering the workplace, it started in school. Racial stereo-typing and bias (conscious and unconscious) meant that from a young age through no fault of our own, our academic capabili-ties are massively underestimated. Although I was fortunate to have teachers throughout my years in school that encouraged and nurtured me, there was one incident that my mum reminded me of as I read this chapter to her. When I received my GCSE results (which were all A*s and As), we took the certificate to my college and a teacher there kept looking over them and then looking back at me. She did this a few times, until my mum asked what the issue was. She then responded, 'no issues, these are just incredibly good results', and she sounded surprised. I remember my mum being annoyed, because it seemed clear to her that the lady didn't think I, a sixteen-year-old Black girl, was capable of those results. According to a 2011 research study by the Department for Business, Innovation and Skills, Black applicants had the lowest predicted grade accuracy, with only 39.1% of predicted grades accurate, while white applicants had the highest, at 53%. The study also found that Black students are most likely to have their grades underpredicted.[*] In addition, the 2018–19 Department for Education exclusion statistics reveal that in some local communities in the UK, exclusion rates for Black Caribbean pupils are over five times higher than for white children.[†] The above statistics show that as Black children, we are directly and indirectly told that we aren't smart or capable and, in many ways are not deserving of an education.

That feeling of not being good enough, not belonging and otherness continues to fester as we enter and navigate the working world, being mistaken for employees in lower job levels, having our competency and skills scrutinised at every opportunity.

Growing up, our families tell us to keep our head down and *'work twice as hard'* as our white counterparts, which many of us do, so much so that according to the *Race in the Workplace: McGregor-Smith Review*, all Black and minority ethnic groups are more likely to be overqualified than white employees.[‡]

---

[*] Department for Business Innovation and Skills. 'Investigating the Accuracy of predicted A Level Grades as part of the 2009 UCAS Admission Process.' (June 2011). Retrieved from: https://assets.publishing.service.gov.uk/government/uploads/system/uploads/attachment_data/file/32412/11-1043-investigating-accuracy-predicted-a-level-grades.pdf

[†] Department for Education Exclusion Statistics. 'Permanent and fixed-period exclusion in England: 2018 to 2019.' (30 July 2020). Retrieved from: https://www.gov.uk/government/statistics/permanent-and-fixed-period-exclusions-in-england-2018-to-2019

[‡] McGregor-Smith review. 'Race in the workplace.' (28 February 2017). Retrieved from: https://assets.publishing.service.gov.uk/government/uploads/system/uploads/attachment_data/file/594336/race-in-workplace-mcgregor-smith-review.pdf

However white employees are more likely to be promoted and to be paid more. This is evident as The Colour of Power 2020 research project highlighted that of the 1,099 most powerful roles in the country, a total of just seventeen are held by Black men and women[*] and at the time of writing this book, there are currently no Black executives in the FTSE 100 top three roles.[†] When we see few examples of people who look like us or share our background reaching the top of the industries we aspire to thrive in, we start to question whether we belong and deserve to be in those spaces.

Imposter syndrome hits Black people hard because our abilities, achievements and wins are constantly under attack and being questioned. We are often treated like imposters, like frauds. Even when we're great, we're still not considered good enough.

Tennis player Serena Williams (winner of twenty-three Grand Slam singles titles, the most of any tennis player in the Open Era and the second most of all time) hit out at anti-doping authorities due to the increased frequency of random drug testing which singled her out, explaining she thought it was discriminatory.[‡]

[*] The Colour of Power. (July 2020). Retrieved from: http://thecolourofpower.com
[†] The Green Park Business Leaders Index 2021. 'Britain's Top firms failing Black leader.' (3 February 2021). Retrieved from: https://www.green-park.co.uk/news/britain-s-top-firms-failing-black-leaders-green-park-s-annual-business-leaders-index-records-no-black-chairs-ceos-or-cfos-at-ftse-100-companies/s228922/
[‡] ESPN News. 'Serena Williams hits out again at drug testing discrimination.' (25 July 2018). Retrieved from:https://www.espn.co.uk/tennis/story/_/id/24189408/serena-williams-hits-again-drug-testing-discrimination

This followed a report from *Deadspin* which revealed that according to the data in the USADA database, Serena had been tested five times in 2018 when other players had not been tested at all.[*] It was *more* than twice as often as other top American women players. Following Sir Lewis Hamilton winning his seventh Formula 1 championship, there was debate around whether he deserved his knighthood. Even though he has achieved the same number of championships as the Formula 1 legend Michael Schumacher, and currently holds the record for the most wins, pole positions and podium finishes (making him arguably the best Formula 1 driver of all time), there are many who attribute his success to having a good car, name other people who are more deserving of a knighthood and find fault with his tax status. In a YouGov poll of over 3000 respondents, only 21% believed he deserved his knighthood.[†] Sorry, but no one had this energy for Sir Andy Murray when he was awarded his knighthood (no shade, but his accomplishments pale in comparison if we want to get into it).

Whilst I can't speak for the imposter syndrome that some of those people may or may not have experienced in the above examples, you can see how easy it would be for those feelings to arise.

---

[*] Deadpsin.com 'An anti-doping agent occupied Serena Williams's property, and everyone is being squirrelly about it.' (27 June 2018). Retrieved from: https://deadspin.com/an-anti-doping-agent-occupied-serena-williams-s-propert-1826993294

[†] YouGov.co.uk. 'Do you think Lewis Hamilton does or does not deserve his Knighthood?' (29 October 2020). Retrieved from: https://yougov.co.uk/topics/sport/survey-results/daily/2020/10/29/eb760/2

### Tokenism and Imposter Syndrome

The assumption of tokenism, when it's theorised that you are only awarded certain opportunities because you are Black to tick off a 'diversity' box, can further heighten feelings of being an imposter. This was a prominent view in the midst of the most recent Black Lives Matter movement.

Former England and Manchester City star turned pundit Micah Richards hit back at claims that he and fellow football pundit Alex Scott were only given on-air opportunities because of the Black Lives Matter movement, having to justify all the hard work he put in to get to that position.[*] Similarly, when the news broke that Alison Hammond (who has been a presenter on This Morning since 2003) alongside Dermot O'Leary would be taking over from Ruth Langsford and Eamonn Holmes, she received a large amount of social media trolling to the extent that it was reported she was having 'duty of care' meetings with ITV to protect her well-being.[†] Some of the tweets I came across said 'she is only there for obvious reasons', clearly referring to the fact she's Black and 'this is what happens when you make decisions based on ticking boxes'.

[*] Standard.co.uk. 'Micah Richards hits back at claims he and Alex Scott are only on air because of Black Lives Matter.' (22 September 2020). Retrieved from: https://www.standard.co.uk/sport/football/manchestercity/micah-richards-alex-scott-hits-back-Black-lives-matter-a4552831.html
[†] Metro.co.uk. 'Alison Hammond holds duty of care meeting with ITV as trolls attack over This Morning job.' (3 December 2020). Retrieved from: https://metro.co.uk/2020/12/03/alison-hammond-holds-duty-of-care-meetings-with-itv-as-trolls-attack-over-this-morning-job-13696157/

## The Impact of Imposter Syndrome

Imposter Syndrome makes you feel stuck, because even when you want to move forward and do great things, you don't feel capable, even when you are. We undermine our expertise and all we have to offer and therefore are less likely to put ourselves forward for promotion, less likely to negotiate our salary and more likely to change jobs. Looking back on the first two years of my career, I really should have put myself forward for promotion, and when I changed jobs, I didn't even negotiate my salary, starting on a salary significantly less than what I was paid on my graduate scheme – all because I didn't feel worthy. I would see Black employees slightly more senior than me consistently killing it, and they didn't seem to get the promotion they deserved. Observing from afar, I used to think if they can't move up, I don't stand a chance. When I'd make mistakes, I'd beat myself up about it and carry those feelings home and back to work the following day and the day after that. There are some days when I'd feel amazing. I might complete a piece of work that received great feedback and praise and I'd feel on top of the world, and in that moment, remember who the f*ck I am. But all it takes is one thing for the self-doubt to creep back in; being interrupted or spoken over in a meeting, asked if it was really me that did the work, and indirectly having my intelligence questioned. Then I'd start to question myself all over. Imposter syndrome is exhausting because you constantly view yourself through this frame of being less than; it's further exacerbated by the daily microaggressions and other forms of discrimination Black people encounter at work, which serve as a constant reminder that the workplace as an institution wasn't built as a place for us to be able to thrive in. As explained in a Harvard Business Review article, 'In truth we don't belong, because we were never supposed to belong. Our presence in most of these spaces is a result of decades of grassroots activism and begrudgingly developed activism.[*]

The WORST thing about imposter syndrome is having to undertake the physical and emotional hard work on ourselves to fix an issue that we didn't self-inflict. We're not imposters. We weren't born with imposter syndrome; we were born into a society where systemic racism, classism, misogyny, and xenophobia, amongst other biases are rife and then we enter workplaces where our identities are marginalised and discriminated against. Whilst the onus should be on organisations to create inclusive cultures and a workplace experience where everyone can thrive, in the meantime, we still need to find ways to cope with and overcome these feelings.

## Tips for Conquering Imposter Syndrome

**Talk about it:** Bottling up any type of negative feeling – especially imposter syndrome – is unhealthy and not good for our mental health. A study of some African American college students in the US found that they had higher levels of anxiety and depression when they experienced significant levels of impostorism[†]. When experiencing these feelings, it's important

---

[*] Harvard Business Review. 'Stop Telling Women They Have Imposter Syndrome'. (11 February 2021). Retrieved from: https://hbr.org/2021/02/stop-telling-women-they-have-imposter-syndrome

[†] Nytimes.com. 'Dealing with Imposter Syndrome when you're treated as an imposter.' (12 June 2018). Retrieved from: https://www.nytimes.com/2018/06/12/smarter-living/dealing-with-impostor-syndrome-when-youre-treated-as-an-impostor.html

that we acknowledge and discuss them. These conversations can be with friends, family or workplace mentors, who may have shared similar experiences to you. I have a group chat with some of my closest friends who, like me, are Black women in tech, and we discuss these types of issues between us which has been massively helpful. It's great to know I'm not alone in how I feel and hear some of the coping mechanisms that have helped them.

**Celebrate and record small wins:** When you get things right, no matter how small or trivial they may seem, give yourself a pat on the back and accept the compliments. Be kind to yourself, you did that! Try to keep a document of them that you can look at every so often especially when the doubt starts to creep in. I have an Excel document which I update frequently with my achievements (I have a tab for workplace achievements and personal ones) and I also have a massive blue bag with all my school certificates from Reception all the way to Sixth Form, as well as artefacts of other achievements of mine over the years. Every so often I go through it because it reminds me of how far I've come and serves as a motivator for everything I still hope to accomplish.

**Reframe your language:** How you discuss your achievements is how they'll be viewed, so stop using words like 'only', 'merely' or 'simply' to describe them.

**Flip your mental script:** Not knowing 100% of everything and making mistakes here and there doesn't diminish your accomplishments and it certainly doesn't mean someone is going to 'find you out'. In our current form, we are not a 'finished article' and probably never will be, so give yourself that room to grow. We need to train ourselves to see the lessons in the losses when things don't go to plan instead of mentally punishing ourselves for it.

## Social media and Imposter Syndrome

Everyone is posting their wins and successes but never their failures and the things that didn't go so well (something many of us are guilty of). People only want to share their failures when they can round it off with an announcement of something great (LinkedIn). You'll be feeling good about yourself, where you're at, your accomplishments, and then you'll see a few announcements online and suddenly you're questioning if you're really doing as well as you thought. People announcing their promotions, new job with a massive salary increase, screenshots of the sales for their business – all these things which are amazing to see, can also make you feel like you're an imposter. In the process of writing this book I felt like despite being blessed with this book deal and having written for multiple publications, I still struggle to call myself a writer. I remember having a conversation with my friends and I said something like 'I'm not really a writer,' and they all jumped on me like 'yes you are, wth? You've written for . . .'. I'm not a full-time writer, I work in in product management (which played into those feelings) and comparing myself to full time writers online made me reduce my own achievements and feel like I wasn't a real writer, not like them. Comparison is truly the thief of joy and if your imposter syndrome stems from comparing yourself to others, you must remind yourself that everyone's path is so different.

**Be intentional about what you consume:** Over the last year or so, I have realised that my feelings of imposter syndrome can be easily triggered by what I watch, read, listen to and by social media or any form of content I consume. Because of this, where possible, I try to be selective and intentional with regards to how I engage with certain platforms, taking social media breaks when necessary, and being conscious of the types of books I read and podcasts I listen to. We can't control everything but let's try to be mindful of the messages we feed our brain.

That voice in our head telling us we're not good enough, we don't belong, we're frauds, it's a LIE. We are more than good enough, we are GREAT. We are BRILLIANT. As hard as it can be to believe sometimes, especially when we live in a world where we're constantly told the opposite, these are facts. We are here because we worked hard, we worked smart, we put in those hours, we gave it our all. Don't let anyone take that away from you. We DESERVE.

# RESOURCE: IMPOSTER SYNDROME

As mentioned, one of things that helps me to overcome imposter syndrome in my career is keeping track of my achievements, no matter how big or small.

I created a document saved as 'I did THAT!!' (corny, I know) with the below headings to capture my achievements. I came up with these headings because this is the most important information I wanted to capture, but it can be adjusted based on individual needs. For the most part it can also be adapted to capture non-workplace achievements too – e.g., if you completed an online course, spoke at an external panel event. I have provided an example below which I hope helps.

| Date / Period: | June to October 2021 |
| --- | --- |
| What did I achieve? | Delivered a new feature in the website to the European markets, the most requested feature by customers |
| Key numbers / metrics (if applicable) | Launched this feature to 1.5 million users<br>Increased monthly user logins to the website by 20%<br>Increased monthly user spend by 15%<br>Reduced daily calls to customer service by 10% |
| Key skills I learned / utilised? | Soft skills: Leadership (led two engineering teams to deliver the feature), communication<br>Hard skills: User experience design, Google Analytics |

| Links to any department / organisation goals? | Department goal: Increase month on month user spend |
|---|---|
| Key people or teams involved / collaborated with? | Engineering<br>Design<br>Marketing<br>Legal and compliance |

# RONKE LAWAL

*Founder of Ariatu PR*

Ronke Lawal was born in Hackney, East London. Having graduated with honours from Lancaster University and the University of Richmond, Virginia (USA) with a degree in International Business (Economics), she started her own PR and Communications business in 2004. Ariatu PR specialises in PR and Communications for clients in a range of B2C industries including lifestyle, consumer goods and the creative enterprise sector.

In 2010, Ronke was named as one of the top 400 women of the year in the UK for her work with the Islington Chamber of Commerce. In 2011, Ronke was honoured to receive a Precious Award for Inspirational Leadership. In 2018, she became a director on the board of directors at the Chartered Institute of Public Relations. She has been a mentor for The Blair Foundation, the *Success Looks Like You* initiative and the BME PR Pros initiative as well as a mentor to entrepreneurs and creatives outside of structured initiatives. In 2019, Ronke received an alumni award from Lancaster University for making a substantial contribution to her field of work and developed an outstanding reputation among her peers.

*Dear reader,*
*What a pleasure it is to write this letter to you. I imagine that by the time you have read this you will have either started your*

*career or perhaps you are even considering starting your own business. Hopefully the words that I write in this letter will encourage you to keep going and to stay focused on your journey to success.*

*I am a British-born Nigerian woman, I have used my dual identities to fuel my entrepreneurial journey. It has given me the tenacity and the courage to pursue my dreams even when at times it looked like those dreams were nightmares.*

*I was born in Hackney, East London and grew up in a council estate. It was a rough neighbourhood, but not necessarily one of the toughest in London. I have never been ashamed of where I grew up, the estate itself was definitely not always well looked after but growing up where there was a community spirit really made up for any sense of lack. Growing up in such an area made me want more for myself and my life but it also made me want more for my community – my working-class experience has never been something I have hidden even in a society that wants to erase experiences like mine.*

*When I was little, I remember wanting to be a millionaire. Not necessarily because of the things I could buy but because I saw having money as a form of power, power to break barriers and freedom to change things. Growing up in an area where the council didn't really invest in the community and seeing my parents work extremely hard made me see money as a form of freedom.*

*So, I grew up knowing that I would be an entrepreneur of some sort but I also knew that I wanted to be rich and successful. Has that changed much? Not really! I absolutely do see the power of money as a means of advancement in certain spaces, however now I am more concerned about using my gifts and being guided* by my calling. That is what you must remember as you move throughout your entrepreneurial journey, never be ashamed of your desire to make money but do not let that desire control you or lead you to forget your purpose.

I started my public relations business with this in mind; I became self-employed in 2004, whilst I was in a standard nine to five management role, a role in which many people my age would have been happy to have stayed in for many years. It was an interesting position with lots of responsibility, however I became a robot, unhappy with what my job was turning me into, I was stressed and would often take that stress home with me. My life lacked dynamism and, to some extent, purpose. This was one of the first times that the word PURPOSE would be so poignant in my life. I felt strongly that I was not following my true life's purpose and so I made a choice to start my own business. Many people thought I was crazy; I was, after all only twenty-three years old and my only starting capital was my savings. I was taking a big risk, although, thankfully back then I still lived at home so that helped. I wanted to create a life that I loved and by starting my own business I felt that I was able to do that. This is key; you have to find a way to create a life that you love in whatever path you choose whether that is a career or through your own business as an entrepreneur. However, you must be ready for the challenges that will come to the forefront. Being an entrepreneur is not easy at all, there can be so many obstacles along the way. There will be ups and downs but even during the downs you must keep your mind focused and have faith that the ups will come. But even if the downs last for long and you must change direction, remember that failing does not make you a failure. Failure is an opportunity to learn; be ready and willing to expand your mindset – learn how to adapt to change. Do not remain stagnant, do not allow the pain of failure to imprison you and keep you stuck. Rest, recalibrate and redirect.

My journey has been a unique one and yours will not be the same as mine. If you wish to work in an industry like PR, you may want to join an agency or consider working in-house and you will need to be clear about your career goals. You might have to start from the bottom and work your way up but take the time to consider why this might be a good thing. Your ego might try to discourage you from starting small, but the important thing is to start.

Seek a mentor and a sponsor and have a solid support network. The PR industry is about building relationships so make sure that you take the time to make the right connections across the sector. There will be some who say that they do not see colour as a way to overlook race and the very real issues of institutional racism. Unfortunately, at the time of writing this, there is still a serious lack of inclusion and diversity in the PR sector but that should not put you off, you must learn to be pragmatic and do the work, although it won't be easy.

The irony is that when I look back at my own professional and business career, I would have to say that I have often been my own biggest career obstacle or more accurately, my lack of self-belief has been a burden. I've had to constantly coach myself and, in all honesty, I think there have been stages in my business life where I have sabotaged my own success. I got in my own way because I felt like a fraud when I started to become successful. Perhaps you can relate to that feeling of constant self-doubt and uncertainty. It can be the most detrimental of all obstacles, many other issues can be overcome through practice, but it takes a lot to silence that voice that tries to convince you that you're a fraud with your own success and that you don't deserve great things. It may not always be silent, but I recognise it now and know what to say when it starts up again: 'I am worthy.'

Remember to work hard and play hard, you deserve to celebrate your successes. Research your sector and always be prepared. Build relationships and respect everyone you come across throughout your journey. Make sure you sleep! The mindset that you can sleep when you're dead is fundamentally flawed, make sure you take care of yourself on a holistic level as an entrepreneur. That means rest when you are tired, eat well and drink lots of water!

I believe that wherever you find yourself, it's important to find a way to live a life that you love. With work I say give everything your best shot, you may not always reach the top but try your best. If you make a mistake show yourself compassion and be willing to learn. Also remember that if you find yourself in a place that is not using your gifts or part of your purpose then know when to move on.

Keep striving, keep moving forward, learn from every mistake and be bold.

Yours truly,

Ronke

# DR SAMANTHA TROSS MBBS, FRCS, FRCS ED, FRCS ED (TR&ORTH)

*Consultant Hip and Knee Orthopaedic Surgeon*

Dr Samantha Tross is a consultant hip and knee surgeon. She is the Lead Orthopaedic Surgeon at Ealing Hospital, part of London North-West University Hospitals NHS Trust. When appointed in 2005, she became the first female of Afro-Caribbean descent to become a consultant orthopaedic surgeon in the UK.

Apart from her clinical work, she oversees the orthopaedic training of junior doctors and surgeons in her hospital. She is an examiner for medical school final examinations for Imperial College, London and University of the West Indies in Trinidad, and Associate Professor of Orthopaedics for the American University of the Caribbean.

Samantha is passionate about diversity in surgery and has delivered lectures on this topic at many UK orthopaedic conferences. She was part of the panel that produced the recently published Diversity and Inclusion Report for the Royal College of Surgeons of England. Samantha received a Black British Business Award for mentoring and raising awareness of medicine in her community. She is listed in the Powerlist of 100 Most Influential Black Britons and featured in a photographic exhibition of fifteen Black female leaders from different sectors commissioned by the Black Cultural Archives and JPMorgan.

**Tell us about yourself?** *I am a Consultant Hip and Knee surgeon. I studied medicine at University College and Middlesex School of Medicine and my basic surgical training was on the Royal London Hospital's rotation. Higher surgical training was on the Guy's and St. Thomas's rotation before undertaking advanced Fellowship Training in Toronto, Canada and Sydney, Australia. I was born in Guyana, South America and moved to England at age eleven to attend boarding school. The move occurred because my father's job with the Commonwealth Secretariat required him to take posts in Zambia and Tanzania. At the same time, my mother was awarded a scholarship to do a master's in public health at Liverpool University, England, which involved field work in what is now Sri Lanka. My parents wanted to ensure myself and my siblings' education was not disrupted by moving countries and the British education system was well respected. I remained in boarding school until age sixteen and then attended sixth form college in Birmingham, prior to entering medical school.*

**What was your motivation to get into medicine and how did you secure your first opportunity within this space?** *At age seven I declared I was going to be a surgeon when I grew up and I remained focused on this throughout my schooling. I'm not sure where the idea emanated from. My mum was a nurse, and I must have visited her at the hospital. My maternal grandmother, great aunt and childhood friend died when I was very young and being exposed to death at a young age, no doubt had an impact. I was also an avid reader and may have gotten the idea from a book because strangely I never said 'doctor', I said I was going to be a surgeon. I investigated the requirements to get into medical school and ensured I matched the criteria. This involved doing* voluntary work in a hospital or with an allied profession (mine was in a psychiatric hospital), in addition to getting the relevant A-level grades, particularly in chemistry, a necessary requirement. I wrote to the hospital expressing a desire to study medicine and need for work placement and they kindly accepted me.

Once at medical school, I loved anatomy, the study of the structures making up the human body. This coupled with the fact that surgery appeared to offer a direct cure for patients' ailments and the ward rounds (clinical review of the patients) were much faster, cemented my desire to pursue a career in surgery. I chose orthopaedic surgery as a subspecialty because of the following reasons:

- The speciality offers variety e.g. hand surgery, hip and knee surgery, foot and ankle, shoulder, spine, etc. It allows you to treat males and females, young and old.
- The first female surgeon I met was an orthopaedic surgeon.
- The patients are generally well and recover quickly.
- Unless you are a trauma surgeon, most surgery is done in daylight hours.
- Orthopaedic surgeons are generally affable and fun to be around.
- It came naturally to me, someone who enjoyed fixing things.
- In addition, it is an ever-changing specialty with constant improvements in prostheses, surgical materials, and surgical techniques. The future is exciting and incorporates artificial intelligence and robotic surgery.

**What do you see as some of the barriers that aspiring Black medics face when getting into medicine?** *I believe barriers occur* *on both sides. Bias occurs in all aspects of society and that includes the education system. Black students may not be encouraged to aspire to a career in medicine and may not be given the necessary help in their subjects or guidance with the application process. I remember my teachers suggesting I choose another profession as surgery would be difficult as a Black woman. They weren't wrong that there were unique challenges but that didn't mean I shouldn't have had the aspiration. Universities historically have institutional bias in the selection process, where if two applicants have the same CV but different names, the English-sounding one is more likely to be shortlisted. The process has become more transparent, but it is difficult to completely eradicate bias. The lack of visibility and the subtle negative stereotypes over time may erode the confidence of those without the appropriate support mechanisms, such that they do not consider the profession.*

**For a while, you were the only Black female consultant of your medical specialty in the UK – did that present any unique challenges or opportunities?** *In medical school, I was the only Black female student in my year out of 200 students and the only Black woman in my orthopaedic training programme. I recall my medical school experience being largely pleasant. I had just come from boarding school which I found emotionally traumatic, having been separated from my parents and in a different culture. I quickly learnt to integrate with other cultures, become self-reliant and developed emotional fortitude. This assisted me at medical school. As I elevated through the training programme the sexism (predominantly) and occasional racism became more noticeable, not from my peers but from the occasional* *consultant. Both are still experienced as a consultant, but I have gotten better at dealing with them and attitudes are also changing. Having mentors, who I attracted by my hard work and enthusiasm, was crucial to me navigating the training programme successfully, As I stood out, I made it work to my benefit. I do not believe it was a level playing field regarding opportunities but with determination, focus and hard work, I was able to succeed. Whilst I was training, patients often mistook me for a nurse despite introducing myself as a doctor. Attitudes have changed and I can't recall the last time I have had a negative reaction from a patient. Usually, patients come requesting to see me.*

**There is a lot of distrust between the Black community and the wider medical authorities. How do you navigate that and what do you think would be the impact of having more Black representation within medicine?** *There is distrust of the medical authorities by Black doctors, much less by the patients. It isn't helped by the cases of David Sellu, a surgeon wrongly convicted and imprisoned for gross negligence manslaughter, as well as the Bawa Garba case, where a Black female doctor who was involved in the care of a child was convicted when the child died. There were clear systematic failings in both cases. Then you have historic atrocities like the unethical Tuskegee study of untreated syphilis in Black people all led to undermining confidence in the profession. In addition, the community may have personal experiences of inequalities in their health service provision or their treatment. Having more Black representation in the healthcare system will help to counter that distrust. I have certainly had Black patients say they felt more relaxed coming to see someone who looked like them. The Royal College of Surgeons of England*

*and many of the other colleges recognise the imbalance in the healthcare system and are currently investigating and implementing ways to improve the diversity. Many studies support this action as they found diverse workforces are more open minded, flexible and successful.*

**What challenges have you experienced in your career and how have you overcome them?** *I faced racism and more often sexism and bullying but during these times, I remained focused on my goal of becoming a consultant. The reality is that in any career path, no matter your gender or race, there will be hardships to face. Being Black or female, depending on the job, means there may be more. It's not right but how you deal with those hardships is the key to your success. I set clear boundaries for myself, and I chose my battles. In some situations, I had to leave and just focus on my goal. My other and most significant challenge was overcoming self-doubt, which began to creep in over time. I overcame my challenges by building a supportive network, having mentors, and constantly reminding myself of my goal. Erasing self-doubt and building confidence took discipline and practice and remains a work in progress.*

*I'm happy to have retained my sense of self throughout it all. It would have been too much effort trying to be someone else.*

**What have been some of your career highs and lows?** *The high points of my career to date are: being the first female of Afro-Caribbean origin to become a consultant in the UK, being asked by another consultant orthopaedic surgeon to perform his mother's knee replacement operation and being the first female in Europe to be trained in robotic hip and knee replacement surgery.*

However, getting positive feedback from my patients is mostly what motivates me to keep doing what I do. Outside of the hospital arena, I have been awarded a Black British Business Award and a WinTrade Award, been profiled in many books, been the subject of a careers book used in schools, included in the Black Powerlist, involved in a photographic exhibition of fifteen female leaders across numerous sectors sponsored by JPMorgan and been the keynote speaker for the Mayor's Black history month event in 2019.

As far as low points of my career, that depends on the mindset at the time. What initially appeared as low points, in retrospect were not. One was failing my orthopaedic examination at the first attempt, the other not being successful at my first consultant job interview. What I have learnt is that failure is part of the journey, and sometimes what you think you want is not what you need. Retaking the exam improved my knowledge and confidence, as during the exam it was clear I was impressing the examiner. The unsuccessful first interview improved my interview skills so that I was successful the next time round. I ultimately ended up in a department much better suited to me.

There continue to be bumps along my journey, but I choose to see them as stepping stones rather than hurdles.

**What has been the best career advice given to you?** *The best career advice was during a period in my life as a junior doctor when the long hours and lack of social life were getting me down and I questioned whether I had chosen the right career. My consultant sat me down and said, 'Okay, so you aren't happy at the moment. What else are you passionate about?' I had no answer. He said, 'In that case, I suggest you carry on.' I had to* remind myself that I was in a profession that offers variety, is stimulating and allows the potential to sub-specialise in an area of key interest. Also, it pays well and there is certainty as it generally is a job for life.

**What advice would you give to Black students and professionals starting out and advancing in their careers?** *Take time to get to know yourself; learn your positive and negative attributes and core values. Knowing yourself will help inform your choices when choosing a career and ensure it is one most suited to you. You should not be afraid to be outside your comfort zone or to fail, as failure is an opportunity to grow and learn. Be open to feedback as not every negative comment is undeserved. Have clear goals which you are working towards and a supportive network and/or mentor are key.*

*Although societal bias is improving, it still exists. Therefore, you are likely to face inequalities. Try to seek out the positives in adverse situations and remain focused on the end goal. It's not the injustice but your reaction to it that may have a longer lasting impact. I'm not saying not to speak up if there is injustice, far from it, but ensure the repercussions of the event do not continue to personally impact you negatively thereafter.*

# PROFESSOR PATRICIA DALEY

*Professor of the Human Geography*
*of Africa, University of Oxford*

Patricia Daley is Professor of the Human Geography of Africa in the School of Geography and the Environment, University of Oxford, and Vice-Principal and Helen Morag Fellow and tutor in geography at Jesus College, Oxford. She holds a BSc in geography from Middlesex Polytechnic, an MA in African studies from SOAS University of London, a PGCE from Goldsmiths, University of London, and a DPhil in geography from the University of Oxford.

Patricia is a Pan-African feminist scholar who teaches and researches on aspects of forced migration, especially on refugees, humanitarianism, and genocidal violence in Eastern and Central Africa. Her publications include *Gender and Genocide: The Search for Spaces of Peace in Africa* (2008) and the *Routledge Handbook on South South Relations* (2019) (co-edited with Elena Fiddian-Qasmiyeh). She has also published an essay on the scholar activism of Black women in the academy in *Communities of Activism: Black Women, Higher Education, and the Politics of Representation.*

**Tell us about yourself?** *I was born in Kingston, Jamaica and grew up in Clarendon, Jamaica in what Jamaicans call the countryside – mainly because my mother, who had custody of us at* the time, migrated to the UK and so my brother and I went to live in the countryside with my grandparents.

I came to Britain when I was ten years old, and I did one year in a primary school in Hackney. After that, I went to a secondary school called Clapton Girls'. It was a little far from where we lived but my mum wanted me to go there because it had a good reputation. In my first year, I had the third highest grades in my year group and then from the second year onwards, I was top of the year. It was only later, after my mother died, that one of my cousins told me that my teachers believed I should've gone to a grammar school, but my mother didn't want to move me. I stayed at that school until I was sixteen and did my O Level and CSE exams, but it wasn't a great school. I knew this because we were encouraged to go into secretarial work and no one advised us to broaden our horizons, although there were some great young teachers. They said if I really wanted to do well academically, I needed to leave and do my A Levels at another institution as my school didn't offer the subject choices or the environment to do well.

At sixteen, I attended what was then called Tottenham Technical College and did my A Levels there. It was a good experience and I met great people, many of whom I am still in touch with today. My A Level results could've been better but still, I secured a place at Middlesex Polytechnic at the time, studying geography and geology. However, my mother wasn't keen on me studying, even doing my A Levels; it was a real struggle to study in the house and I eventually moved out. I spent a lot of time in the library, and she resented that. She was a church pastor who wanted me to be a good Christian and thought education would take us away from the church. I struggled to get her support. She *wouldn't even allow for her income to be assessed for me to receive state funding. Eventually, I was independently assessed and received support from welfare services.*

*I initially wanted to become an environmental planner and secured a studentship (an academic scholarship) for a course at the University of Reading, but I got cold feet. I didn't know of any Black environmental planners, and I would have had to leave London – where was I going to live? In the end, I decided to apply to do a PGCE (Postgraduate Course in Education) at Goldsmiths, University of London so I didn't have to move, and I'd be able to stay in touch with friends. Whilst I was doing my teacher training at this school in Peckham, they offered me a job, so I worked there for two years.*

**What was your motivation to get into academia and how did you secure your first opportunity within this space?** *When I was doing my teachers training, I took an evening class at Birkbeck University on African women's writing, which was run by a South African exile called Lauretta Ngcobo who was a novelist herself. She introduced me to African culture and texts that I hadn't been exposed to before. That course sparked my interest in Africa, and I decided that I wanted to study Africa more, so I took a year out of teaching and enrolled in a master's at SOAS which I was fortunate to receive government funding for. I spent a lot of time really immersing myself in African issues and many of the Africans who I engaged with were refugees and exiles, and were struggling, especially mentally, being away from home. I knew then that I wanted to further my studies around African refugees on a PhD level. I heard of a programme at Oxford that a group of people had created called The Refugees Studies*

*Programme and they were holding seminars, so I started to come to Oxford to attend and become more involved. The head of the programme at the time said that I should apply to do my PhD at Oxford because that was where things were happening with regards to research around refugees. So, I did, and secured a government scholarship to do it. Whilst I was doing the research for my PhD, that was when I knew I wanted to have a career in academia. I love research, I love being in the field and talking to people. I get really excited about trying to understand the social context that we see around us and unpacking that. It's a bit like being a detective, finding these little nuggets and trying to discover the links between them. Talking to people, hearing their stories and trying to weave that into a narrative and analytical framework that combines theories and empirical data in order to understand fully the things we see, that was why I wanted to be an academic. But I also liked teaching and knew from my experience in the classroom that I was good at it.*

*After I completed my doctorate, my first teaching job was in the US at Dartmouth College, one of the schools in the Ivy League. I knew I wanted to teach on Africa, preferably within a geography department, but I didn't know of any Black professors in the UK in my research discipline of geography. I remember going to conferences and feeling so isolated. I would be one of only two or three Black students out of hundreds. There weren't many Black British geographers before and there still aren't that many now, although numbers have improved slightly. I knew some African American and Caribbean scholars based in the US and they told me to come to the big conferences there, so I went to the African Studies Association conference and met a lot of academics. During those times, they used to do preliminary job interviews at the conferences. I was called by Dartmouth College for a follow up interview and I got the job there.*

**According to research by the Higher Education Statistics Agency, less than 1% of UK university professors are Black. What do you feel are the barriers to entry for Black aspiring students?** *Funding can be a barrier. I was lucky because there used to be quite a bit of funding available, especially if you had a good academic record, but I know there isn't as much now. Also, you need people to have faith in you, to tell you that you can do a PhD, mentors who can support you. I was fortunate to have this. Many white students have a network of undergraduate tutors who support, encourage, and nurture them. It is not the same for Black students. Once you secure funding, you have to get admitted into your chosen university to do the PhD. Many universities have studentships, so if you're admitted, your name will have to go forward for a studentship which means you will need to have really good referees from your previous institutions. I always say it's super important for students, especially Black students to think strategically. Cultivate supporters as you go through your academic journey so they can write good references for you. I also think it's hard to envision doing a PhD if you're not around people who are thinking similarly. Being at SOAS and around others, especially African students, who had studied at African universities and knew Black professors, made me realise pursuing academia as a career was possible.*

**Conversations about race have been more prevalent over the last year, how has it been navigating those conversations especially in such a white institution?** *It has been difficult. In 1991, I was the* *first Black person to be appointed as an academic at the University of Oxford. The next person, Dr Raufu Mustapha, came in 1998, and interestingly, he and I were PhD students together in the 1980s. It was great having him at Oxford as we were able to discuss with each other what we were experiencing or saw happening. Another thing which has helped is having a network of other Black scholars, predominantly in North America, where I can explain what I've experienced in my institution and ask for advice – do I let this situation lie or do I confront it? Because the reality is, you can't fight every battle. Again, you have to think strategically – which battles can potentially help or hinder you? Having friends in other workplaces, outside of the context of where you work, who can share how they have dealt with racism in their institutions is also helpful. It's really these support networks which have kept me going.*

**What challenges have you experienced in your career and how have you overcome them?** *One of the challenges I've faced is being accepted as a legitimate researcher and purveyor of knowledge. Within my space and department, it took a long time for them to recognise that my work was valuable, especially as my research is Africa-focused. Some of the scientists within the department work on Africa, but amongst the social scientists and the political scientists, until quite recently I was the only one.*

*Learning to navigate who amongst my colleagues was likely to be an ally and who would view me as a threat was also another challenge. At Oxford, my first article was on race. It was titled 'Geography of Race or the Racism of Geography' and I sent it to an academic journal, which immediately rejected it. Initially, I thought it was provocative and they might want to publish it. It was supposed to be a left-wing journal, but the editor sent it back and said they didn't have space for it. I then understood the politics of race and how to deal with colleagues. It was easier for me to deal with right-wing colleagues than liberal and left-wing colleagues who hide their racism.*

*Dealing with the perception of being a professor at Oxford was also difficult, especially amongst other Black academics, as people assume that you are an elitist, which isn't the case. For many years when I was amongst other Black academics, I would just say that I taught at a university without making a reference to it being Oxford, otherwise I would be treated differently and potentially excluded.*

*Many people say to me that I have accomplished quite a lot and I reply that my white colleagues achieved much of these fifteen years earlier than myself, because they never have to deal with people who didn't see them as legitimate academics, they were recognised earlier. I supervise many white students who focus on Africa and when they graduate, if other scholars or policymakers want an expert opinion in the area that I have supervised them on, they will approach my students, they won't come to me. My white students are seen as the experts and not me. Unfortunately, that's how racism works, they'd rather have our output than us because that's seen as easier than having to engage with us. Many of my students are attuned to this and do let me know when they have been approached. That's been a challenge and continues to be a challenge – if I was a white academic researching Africa, I would've got my professorship fifteen years earlier, and all the other accolades would've come earlier too; I see it happening for young white academics now.*

*Throughout my career, I have just continued to remind myself that I'm a great teacher and I know my research area very well. If there are negative comments, I do my best to ignore them, because I know my capabilities and my strengths.*

**What have been some of your career highs and lows?** *Winning the Undergraduate Teaching Award and the Supervisor of the Year Award from the graduate students at Oxford were high points, because it reflected the positive feedback and reviews I received all the time for my teaching. My PhD students recognised me, even if I didn't feel the institution always did.*

*Another high point was having my portrait painted in 2017 by the artist Binny Mathews. I was nominated by students to have my portrait painted as part of the university's Diversifying Portraiture project. The painting now hangs in the Examination Schools' building.*

*A low point in my career occurred in the early to mid-2000s. I was struggling to bring up my son on my own, carrying a high teaching load (my module was very popular) and my publication record was stalling. I wanted support from my department and recognition that caring responsibilities – and even the daily grind of racial microaggression – can affect performance, but I felt there was hostility. I had to see a therapist to restore my confidence. I ended up taking sabbatical leave and producing a book a year later. Nowadays, there is greater consideration and adjustments made for people with caring responsibilities.*

**What has been the best career advice given to you?** *The best career advice was given to me a few years ago when some other senior academic women and I were talking to young people and one woman advised us to not turn down offers so quickly. It's* *easy to be presented with certain opportunities and think no, that's not for me. She said that actually it was best to look into them, to investigate and explore them, and then decide if that thing is for you or not. As I've moved forward in my career, I have found that to be really helpful advice.*

**What advice would you give to Black students and professionals starting out and advancing in their careers?** *Make sure you know yourself and by that, I mean know what your strengths and weaknesses are and work to your strengths. Throughout your career there will be criticism, naysayers, people that try to undermine you, but always remember the value of your contribution and that it's unique to you. It doesn't mean these things won't hurt or harm you, but you have to find ways of protecting yourself psychologically. I prioritise my mental health and well-being in a few different ways, which include daily exercise and talking to friends. I find that when I talk to other Black people, their experiences aren't too dissimilar to mine, even if we work in totally different professions. Don't bottle things up and hide them. Even now if I encounter racism in some space within my college or university, I tell someone who can potentially act on it. Also, build networks as soon as you can and keep genuine allies close. If it wasn't for my white allies writing references for me, I wouldn't be where I am today. You need sponsors who will support and advocate for you.*

# DR NIRA CHAMBERLAIN OBE PHD HONDSC

*Mathematician*

Dr Nira Chamberlain PhD HonDSc is one of the UK's leading professional mathematicians and was the President of the Institute of Mathematics and its Application (2020-21) making him the first Black President of the IMA and of a major mathematical learned society in Europe.

Nira has two mathematical doctorates and is also listed in the Powerlist Top 100 Most Influential Black people in the UK for five years running (2018-2022). In 2018, Nira was the winner of the Big Internet Math Off title – World's Most Interesting Mathematician, which was an invited international mathematical communication tournament and voted for by the general public.

Nira has over twenty-five years of experience at writing mathematical models/simulation algorithms that solve complex industrial problems. Nira Chamberlain developed mathematical solutions within industries such as the defence, aerospace, automotive and energy sectors. This has included periods in France, the Netherlands, Germany and Israel. During his career, Nira has been invited to speak at several prestigious events such as the New Scientist Live, The Royal Society- Destination STEMM, Oxford University – The Reddick Lecture, and at King's College London – Maxwell Lecture to name a few.

Popular talks include: 'Saving Aston Villa', 'The Black Heroes of Mathematics' and finally, 'The Mathematics that can stop an Artificial Intelligence apocalypse!'.

## Tell us about yourself?

*My name is Dr Nira Chamberlain, I was born and raised in Birmingham, United Kingdom. I am of Jamaican heritage with my mother and father coming from the Jamaican parishes of Hanover and St Elizabeth respectively. I have a PhD, MSc, and a BSc in Mathematics as well as this I am a Chartered Mathematician and a Chartered Scientist. I have an Honorary DSc from Greenwich University. I am also a Fellow of the Institute of Mathematics and its Applications, a Fellow of the Operational Research Society, as well as an honorary member of The Mathematics Association.*

*Listed by the Science Council as one of the UK's top practising scientists, my name was also added to the elite Who's Who in 2015, making me one of only 30 mathematicians currently to be fêted in this way. The first Black mathematician to gain this achievement since the Who's Who establishment in 1849.*

*In 2020, I became President of the Institute of Mathematics and its Applications (IMA). The IMA exists to support the advancement of mathematical knowledge and its applications and to promote and enhance mathematical culture in the United Kingdom and elsewhere for the public good. It is the professional and learned society for qualified and practising mathematicians, with a membership of around 5,000 comprising of mathematicians from all sectors, as well as those with an interest in mathematics.*

**What was your motivation to pursue Mathematics and how did you secure your first opportunity within this space?**

*When I was at secondary school, mathematics was my strongest subject, but I was not the best at it. However, my career teacher attempted to discourage me from the area by saying I should become a boxer. I believe the teacher suggested this because of my colour. This made me feel very discouraged and despondent. Upon learning this, my parents told me 'You don't need anybody's permission to be a great mathematician.' This started a process where I started to live, breath, sleep and eat mathematics. My first job was part of my mathematics degree. I worked on a RAF base writing simulations about Kitchens! Sounds strange but the problem is quite complex – When is the best time to refurbish a whole RAF Kitchen to minimize cost over 50 years?*

**As a mathematician, you write algorithms to solve complex issues. What do you think are some of the misconceptions about a career in mathematics which might hold people back from pursuing it?**

*People believe that a mathematician is someone who finds mathematics easy. This is not the case. A mathematician is someone who sees a mathematics problem and never quits until they have solved it. That's a mathematician. Also, mathematics is very creative, and people don't realise this.*

**Black representation within STEM careers is low. Why do you think that is? Do you feel that things are changing?**

*For me it was lack of role models and diversity in advertisement of STEM subjects. Even when I watched TV in Jamaica in the*

1990s, all the scientists working in the Jamaican science labs were white.

It took a while for me to land my first graduate job. However I persevered and after nine months, I decided that at the next interview the job was going to be mine! I went in and blew the interviewer away by writing a live mathematical proof of an engineering application! The rest is history.

However, there came a time when I wanted to pursue a PhD, but I was told by a university professor that I was technically weak and naïve. Several years later I found an academic that judged me on my mathematical ability rather than my race.

Do I feel things are changing? There is more awareness and discussion about Black representation in STEM, but challenges remain.

**You created the Black Heroes of Mathematics online campaign to highlight Black mathematicians in history. What inspired you to do this and which Black mathematicians (past and present) do you think more people should know about and why?**

The Black Heroes of Mathematics started out as a poster social media campaign, and then it became a presentation, a music video and now it's an annual two-day mathematical conference!

The vision of the conference is "To celebrate the inspirational contributions of Black role models to the field of mathematics". Why do I do this? I was inspired by the film "Hidden Figures" which is about three African American female mathematicians who helped NASA in the space race. I wondered if there were other "hidden figures" both in the past and the present. When I went to various Black History Month events, mathematicians were not well represented. So, I decided to do some research to find the Black Heroes of Mathematics!

A past Black mathematician we should know about is Euphemia Lofton Haynes. Euphemia was the first Black female to get a PhD in mathematics in the world. She's Black, she was in her 50's and of course she is a woman. She proved to the world that mathematics is indeed for everybody.

A current Black mathematician we should know about is Professor Edray Goins. He used to write a blog that inspired me called – 'The Diaries of a Black Mathematician'. He is now working on a history project for African Americans in the mathematical sciences. I am the lead for updating the Mathematicians of African Diaspora webpages www.mathad.com.

**What challenges have you experienced in your career and how have you overcome them?**
*In my formative years, I was ignored and marginalized too many times.*

*I had many ideas, and the leadership never fully trusted my mathematical ideas. One day I had an idea of calculating the peak gas pressure in a car engine. I gave the leaders my papers. It was dismissed and my paper was used as scrap to write their notes on. One year later I went to work in France, and the French engineers had come up with a similar idea to mine. This was vindication to show that I was not wrong, and my ideas were not weak.*

*However, I realised that mathematics is the poetry of logical ideas. I had to think like a mathematician but talk like a lawyer. From now on my mathematical ideas had to be so watertight that they were unchallengeable. As a result of this, I became a better* and stronger mathematician, and my reputation grew as the person who could do the mathematics that nobody else could do!

**What have been some of your career highs and lows?**
*Starting with career highs, the creation of a mathematical cost capability trade-off model for the Royal Navy Aircraft Carrier, the HMS Queen Elizabeth. This was at a time when the £6.2 billion project was still at the computer design stage and the first sheet of steel had yet to be cut. My mathematical model convinced the client that this prestigious aircraft carrier should indeed be built and saw me cited in the Encyclopaedia of Mathematics & Society – making me one of only a handful of British mathematicians to receive such an accolade.*

*Other highlights include:*
1. *Wrote a computer virus that helped a Formula One car drive faster.*
2. *Invented a new method for doing long multiplication.*
3. *Gave a lecture on the 'Mathematics that can stop an Artificial Intelligence Apocalypse' at Maxwell Lecture – King's College*
4. *Gave a lecture on 'Modelling the Competition' at Oxford University*
5. *Gave a lecture on 'The Black Heroes of Mathematics' at the Royal Society.*
6. *Chairing the Black Heroes of Mathematics Conference 2020*
7. *Winning the title World's Most Interesting Mathematician -2018*

*My lowest point was my PhD viva. A viva is an intensive inter-view by external and internal examiners. I was working on my PhD part time while working full time, so I had been at it for six* years. I wrote a simulation that had predicted a fascinating pattern. However, when I discussed a major PhD result at my viva, the examiners were not convinced. They said how do we know this is a universal law and not just a computer blip! I left the room with no PhD award but a challenge to prove that my results was a universal law.

I was potentially going to fail my PhD after working on it for six years. Then I was reminded of the scripture from my Christian Faith:

Philippians 4:13 "I can do all things through Christ who strengthens me."

Totally inspired, I worked on my PhD over the next two years. During this time, I worked outside my applied mathematical comfort zone. I had to learn and use pure mathematics to prove that my results were not a computer blip, but indeed was a universal law. I went back to the external examiner with an improved thesis and a pure mathematical proof of my results. I was then awarded the PhD and became Dr Nira Chamberlain.

**What has been the best career advice given to you?**
You don't need anybody's permission to be a great mathematician. My parents told me this and it reminds me that if I had listened and believed the career teacher and the university professor, I would never have become the mathematician that I am today.

**What advice would you give to Black students and professionals starting out and advancing in their careers?**
My advice to Black professionals is:
1. Don't limit yourself.
2. Don't sell yourself short.

3. *Don't hold anything back.*

4. *Keep on moving forward.*

*Live your God-given dreams, live your God-given passion, be excellent and always try to give something back.*

# BELL RIBEIRO-ADDY MP

*Labour MP for Streatham*

Bell Ribeiro-Addy has represented her home constituency of Streatham as a Labour MP since the 2019 General Election. Born and raised in Brixton Hill, Bell is a dedicated feminist, anti-racist and trade unionist who currently sits on the Women & Equalities Committee in Parliament. She also chairs the APPG on Black Maternal Health and the APPG on African Reparations.

Bell cut her teeth in student politics, serving as the National Black Students' Officer. She later worked as a campaigns officer for the Palestine Solidarity Campaign before joining Diane Abbott's office as a political adviser and later Chief of Staff.

After Chuka Umunna defected to the Liberal Democrats in 2019, Bell was selected by local party members as his replacement. Following her election, she served as a Shadow Immigration Minister under Jeremy Corbyn.

During her time in Parliament, Bell has been a strong voice for equalities, calling on the UK to make reparations to the Global South in her maiden speech, consistently raising health inequalities and fighting for a fair and humane immigration system.

**Tell us about yourself?**
*My name is Bell and I have been a member of parliament for Streatham since 2019. Streatham is the constituency I have lived and*

grown up in my entire life. Streatham includes Brixton Hill, Tulse Hill, Clapham Common and a little bit of Balham. I'm not like the typical millennial who may have moved around quite a bit, I've only ever lived in two places within a mile radius of each other, except for those three years at Braford University in West Yorkshire where I studied Biomedical Sciences with Ethics and Philosophy of Science.

**Where did your motivation to pursue Politics come from and how did you secure your first opportunity within the space?**
*During my time at university, I didn't expect to become involved in any form of politics at all, and in fact I didn't realise I was involved in politics, I thought I was just campaigning as we had a massive issue with the British National Party (BNP) there. They were putting leaflets through our doors calling for an all-white Britain. I complained a lot about that and eventually I was asked to get involved and that's how I learnt about the work of the Labour party who were campaigning to get the BNP out. I also had a very close friend of mine called Victor, an international student who was helping me to re-establish the African Caribbean Society. He had changed over from an undergraduate to a post graduate degree and as far as Victor and the rest of us were aware, you're allowed to work twenty hours a week as an international student, and you're allowed to work extra during the holidays. He had a friend that would go to London during the holidays but didn't want to lose their university job, so Victor took on his friend's extra hours during the holidays. However, it turned out that as part of his international student visa, he wasn't allowed to work those extra hours and as a result he was detained, locked up and wasn't allowed to wash for three days. When he didn't get on the plane, he was beaten up and taken to an immigration*

*detention centre where he was held for quite a long time and that's when I started to get in contact with several campaigns and tried to get the university to take more action. Unfortunately, he was removed from the country quite quickly and the university didn't return him his fees because they said he could successfully complete his masters from abroad.*

*I was then massively involved in the NUS Black students' campaign and became a full-time officer once I finished my degree. Campaigning to me came second nature because it didn't feel like I was doing a job but my parents, especially my dad, very much emphasised that I needed to pursue a career. Through the Black students' campaign, I became involved with the Society of Black Lawyers and thought about how I could combine my campaigning experience with a recognised career path and decided I would become a lawyer. I started my Law studies but it's extremely expensive and halfway through my course, I ran out of money. At the time, through my campaigning, I had come to know the MP Diane Abbott. I had worked on her leadership campaign and other things she had done in the past on Black education, and I started to work for her part time covering for someone. That was in January 2012 and from there, I held about five different positions in her office, which was probably the best experience for the job I have now. At this point, I still didn't believe that working in politics would be my career path, I just saw myself as a campaigner, supporting someone that I admired greatly.*

**What impact did working for Diane Abbott have on you, in terms of seeing a really accomplished Black woman in the political space, when thinking about your own career?**
*To me, Diane Abbott is a national treasure. She is the first Black*

woman elected to parliament and she's not someone that has gone quietly. There are more Black and Asian politicians in parliament today but not all of them have spoken so openly and consistently on matters of race, immigration and all those social justice campaigns which don't really make you many friends. She's been vilified which is enough to put you off wanting to get into politics, but to me, regardless of what career I would pursue, working with Diane was important because I got to see someone who was really standing up for the community. Also, if the most senior Black woman politician in the country can't be taken seriously, then what Black woman in any other sphere of society would? Having watched the abuse she faced, I didn't think becoming an MP is something I would do, but I also had the best role model to follow.

**Black female politicians face large amounts of racism and sexism. We see it publicly in the media and there are probably things that also happen privately which we don't see. What have those experiences been like and how do you navigate them?**
I'll be honest, it's quite difficult. I remember Diane never spoke out about it for a long time but there was one week where we were just bombarded with hate mail towards her, and a lot of it is brought on by the media sensationalising stories attempting to make Diane look bad. This particular week where things were bad, Diane had spoken at an anti-racism event in which there were many people who voted for Brexit and she literally said at the beginning of her speech something along the lines of, 'I know there are many people in this room who voted for Brexit, but the police have reported an increase in racist abuse so it's clear that some people are using the vote to carry out acts of racism.' Several

of the British tabloids decided to report that Diane called every-one that voted for Brexit racist, and it sparked a wave of abuse. People were ringing the office screaming the N-word, sending death threats and as a team we were exhausted. Another female colleague and I went into Diane's office and said to her that she needed to speak out publicly about the treatment she was receiv-ing, and she finally did.

I have often been asked what's the most surprising thing about working in the House of Commons and for me, it's the number of times I've heard or read the N-word. You don't expect in what is considered this prestigious and professional place that you'd be subjected to that so much and it takes its toll. I've realised that with abuse, even if it's not directed towards you but it's directed at someone that looks like you, you still feel it. I remember the first tweet I made to announce I was standing for my post and Diane retweeted it immediately which was great, but then under-neath it was the first piece of racist abuse directed at me and my heart sank. It had only been a couple of minutes.

We experience so many microaggressions. One of the things that is constantly said to us, and it's been directed at me a few times as I assert my view is, 'if the honourable member had read . . .'. I don't go around speaking about my intelligence, but I can read quite well. In not so many words, it's being implied that I am stupid, and I don't understand what is being asked. Another one is being constantly asked for your pass. I remem-ber when I first started working for Diane, she had been an MP for nearly twenty-five years and when we walked into the House of Commons together, a police officer came out of nowhere and asked to see her pass. I remember thinking, 'Who does he think he is talking to? This is Diane Abbott.' She very calmy

*took her pass out and showed him and when they enquired
about me, she explained we were together. Once we got into the
lift, I asked her if that happened a lot and she said more often
than I might think. It doesn't really happen to her anymore, but
it does still happen to me occasionally despite having worked
there for ten years, although I know they are currently trying to
work on this.*

**Many Black people are disenfranchised with politics, and to
some extent also a career in politics. What would you say are
some of the misconceptions that our community have about
politics and working as an MP?**
*I think it's difficult to understand what an MP can do especially
when your party is not in government and that's something that
I feel sad about; that I can't deliver on many of the things we
said we would do if we were in power.*

*Our communities don't suffer from a lack of talent or lack
intelligence in the way that we are portrayed, but often we lack
the information. The education and information that would
help us to understand democracy and democratic processes
typically isn't directed towards us. Knowing who can vote, the
difference it makes and even knowing that the Black vote in this
country could swing any election. That's not asking Black
people to act as one homogenous group to vote for a particular
party but to understand the voting power we have as citizens.
However, that's not communicated to us and here's where we
see the impact of racism because if it was, people would have
to listen to us in the way they listen to other large sections of
society.*

**What impact do you think there would be with more Black representation in parliament?**

*We've seen that with more Black representation in parliament, certain issues are discussed which usually wouldn't. However, we shouldn't be fooled into thinking that Black representation automatically translates into better outcomes for Black people. I'm from a working-class background and I've made it into parliament but that is very rare. If we look at where ethnic minorities have been given higher positions, for example the current Home Secretary, the Home Secretary prior and the past two Chancellors are all from ethnic minority backgrounds, however that hasn't led to more money in the pockets of Black people or the end to the hostile environment for Black people. It's just meant representation. Whilst it's important that we see more of us in parliament, this needs to translate into tangible policies, for example more women and LGBT people in parliament has meant overall we've got to a position where in the Labour party we have a women shortlist and same-sex marriage is now legal in the UK. We need to get to a place where Black representation means something. When Diane Abbott took Doreen and Neville Lawrence (parents of Stephen Lawrence) to meet Jack Straw, Shadow Home Secretary at the time, he committed to launching the Macpherson Inquiry when he became Home Secretary. The Macpherson Inquiry translated into legislation such as the Race Relations Act and although the recommendations weren't fully followed through, it meant something. Representation without that is just a face and unfortunately, it's a face that some people point to and say there isn't an issue because there are Black and Brown people in parliament.*

**For those that want to get into politics but don't know how, what would be a good starting point?**

*One of the things we did in Diane's office was provide young people with work experience opportunities because a lot of people get into politics through connections and that's just another way of keeping young people of Black and ethnic minority backgrounds out. Check to see if your local MP is offering work experience.*

*There's been a few times I've spoken to people who have said they want to get into politics and when I ask why, what do you believe, they don't have an answer. If you don't have an agenda, a set of views, something that you want to change, then there's many other things you can do that would be less stressful and where you'd earn more money. A career in politics may not be for you. Also, there are 650 MPs exactly and there are several different ways to be involved in the political sphere. You can be an MP, you can be a councillor or if you're in London, you can be part of the Greater London Authority. You can also work as part of a campaign. There's a website called Working for an MP that has information around when MPs jobs go up and the details for organisations that work in and around parliament with campaigning jobs to do with changing legislation.*

**What challenges have you experienced in your career and how have you overcome them?**

*Racism. Imposter syndrome and a lack of self-confidence and belief in myself which I think many women struggle with. We're more modest and we generally don't sell ourselves in the way men do. I know from the many applications that have passed my desk that men are more likely to apply for jobs, even if they don't meet all the criteria. When I speak with other Black people, many of us relate to working twice as hard to be considered as good as our colleagues. Our colleagues have the time to go to the pub after work to network, whilst we stay behind in the office working a little later to be considered on the same level as them and that's not healthy. Work-life balance is important. Progressing in your career comes with more pressure, responsibilities and often as Black people our abilities and competencies are questioned more. When I worked in Diane's office, I was really lucky because within that space, she was always there to affirm and validate me. I eventually ended up running her office which I don't think everyone thought was a great idea. To put a young Black woman in charge of your office in quite a white environment can cause issues. I was given the title Chief of Staff not because it changed the nature of my work (I was still doing the same things the day after I got the title), but so people understood that I had the authority to make decisions and give my opinion on certain matters. That title was for those around me, not for myself or Diane who knew my abilities.*

*I experienced financial challenges, coming from a working-class background and being stuck in debt, just to further my education and increase my access to opportunities. Most internships and work experience that get you through the door are unpaid, but how can you afford to work for free after leaving university? Many of us are unable to take up those roles because we're less likely within the Black community to have other means of financial support, which removes us from many opportunities which are available to others.*

*The lack of access to information at times was also a challenge. I acknowledge that being able to meet Diane Abbott quite young through my own interests in campaigning, attending conferences and the political education I gained from that provided me with a great privilege. But there were many things I didn't know and sometimes I wonder if my journey might've been different somehow if I had known about certain scholarships or grants, other things that were available.*

*As I've progressed within my career, I've found it important to say what I mean and do my best to shrug off feeling like an imposter, no matter how often people speak down to me in the chamber or elsewhere. I remind myself daily to have self-belief and know that if I am acting on behalf of my constituents, on behalf of people that are being discriminated against, then no matter what anybody says, I must be doing the right thing.*

### What have been some of your career highs and lows?

*Winning my election was a big high. I was a Shadow Immigration Minister for only a few months, but during that time, I was able to speak up for the Windrush generation and make enough noise to the extent that now our party doesn't appear to be leaning towards the government's immigration plans which is important. Working for Diane was amazing and being involved in a lot of the work that she did, for example having the first reparations meeting in Parliament in 2013. You wouldn't think a meeting like that would be possible in a room of statues and paintings of men that probably owned slaves.*

*My maiden speech was also a career high for me because I was so nervous and stressed over it for such a long time and then it ended up going viral. It was great to see how well received it was by Ghanaians but also other parts of the African diaspora. More recently, being able to launch the All-Party Parliamentary group for Black Maternal Health and opening up about my own experiences, as it's not something I thought I could do. The topic of Black maternal health is important but it's also very sensitive. I saw that the organisation Five X More weren't getting the debate in parliament despite all the signatures they were getting, and I realised that I'd need to do something to make it happen. Once I spoke about my own experiences, a week later I was given the date for the debate. It was hard and painful to do, but it was worth it.*

*In terms of lows, the Labour party losing the general election in 2017 and 2019 because so much hard work went into campaigning. Also, I remember in 2017 when Diane was receiving a lot of abuse, there was a young Black woman that worked in Diane's office who was absolutely brilliant. I have the privilege of meeting a lot of young people and she was the type of person who really wanted to get into politics which was funny because I was her manager, and I didn't want to be an MP at that point. There was this day where the abuse towards Diane was really high, the press was chasing her and I remember at the end of the day in the car going home, the young lady sighed and said to me, 'It's not worth it'. To see a bright-eyed young woman brought down by what was happening with the abuse and the toll it was taking on our team was a such a low point and she has since moved into the private sector. It's probably one of many reasons why Diane for a long time didn't speak openly about the abuse she received because she never wanted her experiences to deter young people, especially young Black women from considering a career as an MP.*

**What has been the best career advice given to you?**

*I was given this advice during my time as a student, but it was that you need to do things outside of your studies to show you are a well-rounded individual. A degree won't be enough to stand out when you're competing against thousands of graduates. This advice was based on the fact that often in the Black community, there is so much emphasis on going to university, facing our books and getting the highest grades. The problem is that there will be someone else who has the highest mark and has accomplished several other things.*

*Another great piece of advice given to me was to try to find a job that doesn't always feel like work. There will always be parts of your job that aren't as fun, but if you really hate it, you should think about pursuing something else. Unfortunately, in our community we're not exposed to a variety of career paths, we're often encouraged to become doctors, lawyers, accountants, careers which are viewed as being safe and stable and there is nothing wrong with that, but there is so much choice out there.*

*It's also OK to pivot. I was going to work in bioethics and then I went to study Law and now I'm a MP.*

**What advice would you give to Black students and professionals starting out and advancing in their careers?**

*Be informed and get as much advice as possible. Find people like you in the industries you aspire to be in and ask them a lot of questions. You often find that people are willing to help if you reach out and if you don't ask, you don't get.*

# CRAFTING YOUR PERSONAL BRAND

I studied international business at university and one of the modules I took was on branding. I remember the lecturer showing us a bunch of company logos and asking us what were the first things that came to our mind. For example, when I think of Apple, high quality products and sleek experiences come to mind. When I think of Ben & Jerry's, beyond their ice cream, I think of a brand that is socially conscious. A company's brand is how it's perceived by those who experience it. How we perceive a company or organisation will impact how we behave towards it as consumers – Do we buy their products? Do we recommend their products? – which is why companies spend millions on carefully crafting their brand.

When I first started working, I never thought about how this could be applied to myself. The penny dropped for me when I would overhear conversations about people when they had left the room. Some colleagues were discussed favourably, and others were not. It made me wonder, *damn what do they say about me when I'm not around?*

Amazon founder Jeff Bezos said, 'Your personal brand is what people say about you when you're not in the room' and he told no lies. Not one. As time progressed, I would hear these types of conversations more often and what I realised was that it wasn't by chance that some individuals were viewed more favourably, given more opportunities, and were advancing quicker in their career. Those individuals acted with intention and strategically carved out their personal brands. It was something that to some extent I could control and something I *wanted* to control.

## Personal Branding when Black

An observation I made upon starting work is that many of my non-Black colleagues already had preconceptions about me, just because I was Black. Most of them had never grown up around Black people or had Black friends so everything they knew about Black people was based on what they read or watched (and let's face it, the media do a great job of portraying the Black community in a negative and one-dimensional way). These colleagues were quick to engage with me on conversations around pop culture (which, on a whole, is massively influenced by African Black culture), for example, anything to do with Kanye, Beyoncé or Cardi B, but not so much with regards to anything else. 'Did you see Beyoncé's performance at the Grammys?', 'Have you seen Kanye's latest tweets? What do you think is wrong with him?' *Erm, am I Kanye West's mate? WTF?* They would even switch up the way they spoke to me, because they thought I would speak like that, for example, greeting me with 'sisssss', or 'girllllll', when I had never ever addressed them in that way before.

Crafting a personal brand is a way for us to create and control our own narratives. Some non-Black colleagues still hold colonial ideas of Black people as being lazy, incompetent and needing to be controlled and kept in our place. They don't always view us as leaders, hence why the number of us at management level is significantly smaller than the concentration of us in entry level and more junior positions.[*] Black women in particular are tasked with overcoming the 'Angry Black Woman' stereotype. When we show assertiveness and difference of opinion, often we are then labelled as 'hostile' or 'aggressive'. Our ability to create a personal brand where we tell our story is essential when navigating these institutions (the workplace and beyond) which are determined to attach negative labels to us. Creating a personal brand is about us being able to exert influence over how we are perceived and ensuring that the best parts of us are visible. So many decisions around our career are made when we are not in the room, for example our compensation, promotion opportunities, and other chances for progression and development. How we are perceived will impact whether those outcomes favour us or not.

## The Benefits of Creating a Personal Brand

Creating a unique, authentic, and meaningful personal brand will differentiate you from your peers and increase your visibility and create transparency. This in turn fosters trust, a sense of familiarity and as a result should improve our chances when trying to advance within our organisations, secure external career opportunities, and even negotiate our salaries, all aspects of our career which can be difficult to navigate as Black employees.

---

[*] Mckinsey & Company. 'Race in the Workplace: The experience in the US Private Sector.' (21 February 2021). Retrieved from: https://www.mckinsey.com/featured-insights/diversity-and-inclusion/race-in-the-workplace-the-black-experience-in-the-us-private-sector

## Crafting your Personal Brand

Three things you should ask yourself are:

**1. How do my colleagues and peers currently perceive me and why?**
This question is a great way to understand if your personal brand in the present reflects what you want it to and, if it doesn't, this highlights what you need to work on. Carla Harris, Vice Chairman of Wealth Management and Senior Client Advisor at Morgan Stanley, author and gospel artist, said it best: 'If you would like to manage a large group of people, but you are not perceived as being motivational, inspirational, organised, it doesn't matter that you can do it, it doesn't matter if you did do it, you won't get the opportunity to do that, because in that environment you are not perceived as such.' A useful exercise would be to jot down three words you would use to describe your personal brand and then ask one or two colleagues, friends or other individuals outside of your workplace that you collaborate with on side projects to describe you in three words. This should reveal things that are crystal clear about your personal brand and maybe some gaps in how you are perceived that you can then act on. This could be a great exercise to do a few times a year as your personal brand evolves.

**2. How do I want to be perceived by my colleagues and peers?**
Your personal brand should be unique and authentic to you. It shouldn't feel forced but a natural culmination of all the things you already are and aspire to be. Crafting a personal brand is a strategic exercise, the key questions being: how do people perceive me and how can I influence that? A personal brand is not creating a new identity or pretending to be someone you are not.

**Creating your Personal Brand**

Your personal brand should be a combination of:

- **Your greatest skills and strengths:** We all have a range of skills and strengths, but which ones would you say are your greatest? The ones that you are known for, the ones which would differentiate you from the next person? Are there skills and strengths that are unique to you? Are these the ones you want to amplify?

- **Your passions:** What are the things that really drive and motivate you?

- **Your values:** What do you stand for? What are you not willing to compromise on?

- **Your purpose:** What is your 'why'? What keeps you going on the days when you just want to give up? How do you plan to positively impact the local community or wider world?

- These things together form your personal unique selling proposition, what differentiates you from others

## 3. What do I need to do to get there?

To bring your personal brand to life in your career, you need to do the things you want to be known for, a more importantly you need to be seen doing them consistently, otherwise you will lose credibility. If we take the footballer Marcus Rashford MBE as an example, activism is now cemented as part of his personal brand. He consistently speaks about child food poverty across his social media and on wider media platforms and has made the government do a complete U-turn (on two occasions) to extend free school meals to kids from low-income families during the school holidays. He documents his visits to various food banks, showing us that he's actively involved and not just a figurehead; he shares with us the letters he writes to the government. He lives his personal brand and shares that with us, garnering our respect and our trust.

In your workplace and as part of your broader career, there are a variety of things you can do consistently to build and bring your personal brand to life:

**Say yes more (strategically):** When you're in the early stages of building your personal brand, saying yes to relevant opportunities is important. Whether it's agreeing to speak at an event, running a workshop for your team members, agreeing to create content and more. By getting more involved in a wide spectrum of things, you enable people to see another side to you, and you do the hard work for them by filling in the gaps in their mind about who you really are. They can now vouch for you. Over the last two years, I've said yes to more public speaking opportunities and yes to delivering workshops on topics I'm interested in because I want to be known for those skills and interests of mine. The key here is to say yes strategically to tasks that not only bring value to your employer, but also help you accomplish your career goals. Black employees are sometimes guilty of taking on non-impactful tasks, just so we can be seen to be doing something, but then we don't derive the positive career outcomes we hoped for. I have cried many times over the years having stretched myself thinly at work to then realise it amounted to nothing. Unfortunately, no one will tell you that those tasks are meaningless; your colleagues and manager are just happy they're completed

As your career evolves, so will your priorities. It may not be possible to say yes to most things after a while, but that's OK – if you craft your brand well (and say yes more) in the beginning, you won't need to because you would've created this solid foundation.

**Create original content:** Whether it's a blog, video, podcast, infographic etc., content is a great way to communicate your personal brand to a wider audience and foster interaction. For example, within your workplace, volunteer to write for your company's internal blog or even do this for an industry publication. Outside of your workplace, use platforms such as Medium and LinkedIn to write and share articles aligned with your brand. Share your achievements and keep people up to date with cool things you might be working on. Use tools such as Canva and Adobe to create visually engaging infographics that can be shared across multiple platforms. You might want to use platforms such Revue and Substack to launch a newsletter if you want to routinely communicate certain messages to your audience.

Three things to note about content creation are:

1) **Have an objective**: What is the objective of the content you are creating? Is it to secure new employment opportunities, establish yourself as a thought leader in your industry, secure a powerful sponsor or something else? This will help dictate the type of content you create and even which social media platforms you decide to utilise.

2) **Quality over quantity**: Focus on putting out quality, meaningful content which connects with people instead of 'content bombing' and putting out loads of middle-of-the-road content just to be seen.

3) **Use the platform(s) that makes sense for your brand:** Don't feel like you must be creating on all platforms. For example, for those on the design side of the creative industry, Instagram makes sense as you can make your page a visual portfolio. For individuals that want to be seen as thought leaders in their industry, LinkedIn, Medium and Twitter are great as they are platforms centred around sharing thoughts and opinions in long and short form. I've been blogging career advice for students and early-stage professionals on Medium for over three years now. My following is small but because I did this consistently and I would share it on other social media platforms, it led to me writing for student career blogs with thousands of readers and then being invited to speak on panels at corporate organisations. Most recently, I've written articles for news aggregator HuffPost and Fortune.com, one of the world's leading business publications, and when pitching, I was able to use my blogs as examples of my writing experience. This started from me understanding the platforms and the types of content that made sense for my personal brand and the audience I was trying to reach.

**Network:** Attending in person and virtual networking events, joining online communities, and contributing to the wider conversations happening within your workplace and wider industry are great ways to build your brand as they provide the opportunity to interact with others and amplify the things you want people to know you for.

On a basic level, people are more likely to advocate and promote people whose brand they are familiar with. Advancing in the workplace can be difficult for us and it's not because we aren't great at our job, it's often because no one (besides our immediate team members) knows us and can vouch for what we represent. It's also difficult because many opportunities depend on decision makers being familiar with you. They tend to value similarity, and we don't look or sound like the majority of those in power – white men.

We spend so much time working hard to mitigate the impact of the inequalities we face in the workplace and in the process, we neglect things like networking because we see it as a distraction. But it's important to find a balance. When decisions are being made in rooms you're not in, several people that can say 'yes I know him / her' and provide several reasons why are better than none, or just your manager. Early on, I used to consistently receive the same feedback; I was doing a fantastic job, but I wasn't known to some of the key decision makers and therefore making the case for my progression was difficult.

**Help others:** Sharing your expertise, coaching, and training others could be an effective way to reinforce your personal brand. You can host workshops within or outside of your workplace for a group of people or if you have a particular expertise, you can consult on an individual basis in your free time. The best thing about doing this is that you can get people to provide reviews and testimonials which provide your personal brand with legitimacy.

**Please also remember: Your personal brand is not static**
Your personal brand will require proactive management. As you grow and evolve in your career and as a person, this may also require your personal brand to change, reflecting your newfound interests, skills and a new purpose. That's OK and to be expected but be sure to review the messages you communicate as part of your brand and make changes where necessary.

### Social Media and Personal Branding: Be Careful

Social media platforms such as LinkedIn, Twitter, Instagram, YouTube and others can be great for building and amplifying your personal brand. Depending on how you leverage them, they can act as a virtual storefront into the variety of things you have to offer, and this can lead to numerous opportunities. I've seen people secure new jobs, grow their side hustles, and become respected voices on certain topics through their use of social media. However, there is a dark side.

Social media creates this false sense of comfort which I think is due to how accessible it is. Once you open the apps on your phone, within seconds you can share with the world. You'll be debating with someone online, tweeting your thoughts on a trending topic, taking undercover pictures in your meeting, and posting them to Instagram stories with a caption about how bored you are. It's all fun and games until one of your more controversial tweets goes viral and you receive backlash, or someone tags your employer under one of your posts or someone finds an old post of yours from ten years ago which would be deemed offensive and reshares it. In the last few years, so many people have lost their jobs or had opportunities rescinded because of their activities on social media. The iPhone notes apologies have become a staple. Your social media gives the world a lot of insight into who you are – make sure it's reflective of your personal brand today. A few tips:

1. **Do a social media cleanse:** Go through your social media accounts and review the things you've posted, shared,

liked etc. Anything that seems inappropriate or not aligned with your brand, delete. For some social media platforms this might be easier e.g., for Twitter, there are a few online 'Tweet Delete' platforms which allow you to review and delete hundreds of tweets at once.

2. **Make use of privacy settings**: Use your privacy settings to take greater control of who can see your posts, share your posts, and tag you.

3. **Create separate accounts**: Think about creating separate social media accounts – one for friends and family that you keep private and another for professional purposes.

## Create a Strong Narrative

Your personal brand doesn't have to be centred on one thing. For example, you can be a data driven marketer with an interest in sustainability and passionate about working with social mobility organisations. We can create a seamless personal brand through effective storytelling. Going back to my Marcus Rashford example, the activism elements of his brand are rooted in his personal experiences of growing up and experiencing food poverty, a story he has communicated with us and it now makes sense why this is a topic he is so passionate about. Where possible, share insights and connections which root your brand in your own personal experiences, hobbies, and more which will make it more authentic.

**Be yourself – who you are is non-negotiable.** I recently came across this talk on YouTube given by Caroline Wonga, the CEO of the Black media brand Essence, where she said this, and I felt it. So much of our experiences as Black people can feel like we are constantly minimising/altering ourselves for white acceptance within and outside of the workplace but there is a real power in being ourselves as much as we can. I say 'as much as we can' because I think it's difficult and a little unrealistic to advise that we bring 100% of ourselves into spaces that aren't always safe for us. But this doesn't mean when building your personal brand you can't stay true to yourself. Embrace all the things that make you YOU. There is no one like us. Jay Z said it best: 'We are the culture. Nothing moves without us.'

# RESOURCE: PERSONAL BRANDING

There is no time like the present to get started on crafting or improving your personal brand. Here is a table made up of the four key aspects I mentioned earlier to get started.

| Your greatest skills and strengths | Your passions |
|---|---|
| Your values | Your purpose |

If social media is part of your personal branding strategy, it might be worth creating some form of content table to help organise yourself like the one I've created below as an example.

| Week Beginning | Create | Post + Share | Connect |
|---|---|---|---|
| 11/ 05 / 2021 | 5 Instagram posts Draft 2 articles for personal blog | 2 x posts on Instagram 2 x posts on LinkedIn (topics of networking and personal branding) | Reach out to (insert names) via LinkedIn) |

# TREVOR NELSON MBE

*Radio Broadcaster, DJ, and Presenter*

As a pioneer in the Black music scene, Trevor started his broadcasting career at then pirate station Kiss FM. He went on to A&R artists such as D'Angelo and signed Lynden David Hall at Cooltempo / EMI records.

In 1996, Trevor moved to BBC Radio 1 to present the first ever national R&B show 'The Rhythm Nation'. Trevor continued to present the Saturday slot 7-9pm for a further 17 years.

Trevor joined MTV in 1998 to host their flagship R&B show 'The Lick', the show aired for 11 years on MTV base making it the longest running show on the channel. He hosted the first ever MTV Africa Awards from Abuja, Nigeria.

He has released 12 incredibly successful compilation albums over the last 20 years, the most recent being *Trevor Nelson Soul Selection* and *Trevor Nelson Slow Jams*.

Trevor has won numerous honours including 4 MOBOS and an MBE for his work with the Millennium Volunteers. In 2010, he was awarded the Sony Radio Academy special gold lifetime achievement award for his services to broadcasting.

Trevor currently broadcasts across two radio networks: BBC Radio 1Xtra Sunday 11am-1pm and on BBC Radio 2 Trevor Nelson's Rhyth m Nation, Monday-Thursday 10pm-midnight.

**Tell us about yourself?** *I grew up in Stoke Newington, Hackney. My parents are from St Lucia, my dad came here first, and he was a bus conductor and he sent for my mum to come here, and she was a childminder. When I was around the age of seven or eight, my dad changed his job and became an insurance salesman, improving his life and even the way he spoke. He even used to correct us when we spoke slang. My dad used to speak to potential customers on the phone who weren't Black and go to their houses, and they were definitely not expecting to see a Black man, so my dad had a lot of balls and seeing this as a child probably subconsciously had an impact on my career.*

*As a child, I was rather bright and could read at the age of three and write my name. Me and two of my classmates got the highest grades in our eleven plus and our headteacher recommended we go to a grammar school, although I really wanted to attend one of the local schools. I went to the interview for the grammar school and got in, I was the only one out of the three of us to do so.*

*It was the first time I was around majority white kids as Hackney back then and even now was a very multicultural part of London. I never felt like a minority growing up in Stoke Newington, I felt this great sense of community. However, at school I was one of three Black kids in my class and there were over twenty white kids and a few Asian kids. It was a real snapshot into what my future environments would be like.*

*I finished school with eight GCSE equivalents, I didn't do A Levels or go to university even though it was free back then. I wasn't sure what I wanted to do career-wise, and I knew that in my dad's eyes I was a failure because he always thought I was the brightest child. My two younger sisters went to university. We all* ended up doing well with our careers, despite the different paths we took. Sure, we were all intelligent, but I have to credit my parents for their strict parenting.

**What was your motivation to work in music and how did you secure your first opportunity within this space?** *Music was always my favourite thing, I loved listening to it, I was hooked on records at the age of thirteen, but I didn't have any money to buy it because the pocket money I did get wasn't enough to buy records and my grocery job paid me £1 an hour.*

*When I finished school, I had no real idea of what to do. The only experience I had was working in retail and I just wanted to earn money to fund my hobby of collecting records. At around twenty-one years old, I was managing a shoe shop in Bethnal Green and outside of this, I lived in the record shops. Then this opportunity came along. During the 1980s, there was this obsession with 'Rare Groove', grooves that were obscure and rare. I knew a lot about older music even though I was quite young. There was this guy that ran a record shop in Hackney that I used to go to, and he had a catalogue from America with rare albums that he had never heard of and back then Soundsystem culture was the biggest thing. People weren't playing music in clubs, but on sound systems at house parties and everyone wanted to hear Rare Groove. The shop manager approached me and said that he could get me a job if I could help him identify the best songs to get from the US catalogue.*

*At that time, I started DJing, and I didn't want everyone in Hackney to have the same music as me, but I decided to take the job anyway. He would import the records I selected and then sell them for like £20 to £50 in the shop, which was a lot* of money back then, and then the Soundsystem DJs would buy them. This led to my next job at a warehouse, importing new records over the phone and that was how I got into the music business.

**When did you realise that you wanted to be a DJ full-time and how did you go about building your name and brand? How difficult or easy was this?** *Around the time I had my warehouse job, I started a Soundsystem in Hackney with a few other guys called Madhatters. We threw parties; we tried to do a party a month, sometimes every two months, in derelict flats or community spaces and charged £5 on the door, drinks were free all night and everyone enjoyed the music. I never made any money throwing these parties, but people were listening to the music and, in a way, I was starting a brand without even realising.*

*There was this one party I did in a block of flats in Leyton and at the time I had a new job working in a record shop. This new pirate radio station had started called Kiss FM and it had some of my favourite DJs on there. There was a guy called Tosca who was at the party, I didn't know he had a lot to do with Kiss FM (it turns out he was one of the original founders). The next day, he came to the record shop where I worked and told me he enjoyed the party, liked the music I played and asked if I wanted to join Kiss FM. I had never DJ'd on radio in my life or spoken a lot on the microphone or anything, but I was super excited and that was it, I was on Kiss FM. I had the graveyard shift, starting at 1 a.m. and finishing up at 4 a.m. Sunday morning.*

*With regards to branding, I used to promote my parties on Sunday, Monday, and Tuesday, notoriously the least profitable nights. It was a struggle. We were never given the more popular* nights like Friday and Saturday, so I never made money for years, but I knew that I had to put myself out there, I couldn't just wait for the phone to ring. The first gig I had was in this reggae club in Clapton, I was given a Thursday night and only thirty people turned up in a club that could hold five hundred people and only three people paid. I had the club for one night only and the manager looked at me and said never again. My mindset was the thirty people that came really enjoyed it and the next gig we have, more people will pay. By putting my name and Soundsystem on flyers, I was gradually building a name for myself.

One day, I bumped into Jazzie B from Soul II Soul and his Soundsystem was becoming well known, they were beginning to make some money doing some big parties at pretty big venues. One time, we were both booked at this venue, and he came up to me and said he had heard of me, heard I had tunes, and we both shared our respect for each other. He invited me to come to his office (which was the back of a shop on Camden High Street) but he called it his office. Jazzie was someone that honestly believed a desk was an office, a Soundsystem is a business, and a business is an industry. I wasn't thinking that way, but he was, and he really opened my eyes to a lot. For most of us DJs, we didn't realise that DJing and promoting ourselves was building a brand as such. Jazzie oversaw all areas of his brand and he made realise that's what I needed to do, and although I already had that drive in me, I stepped it up a bit. My whole thing was every radio show I did had to be the best radio show ever, every gig I did had to be my best ever gig, because in my head, if I always gave my best, one more person would buy a ticket to my party, one more person would listen to my show. I took this gradual approach and things started to happen for me, first on radio and then TV.

**How did you find the transition from DJing at parties to being live on radio? What have been some of your main learnings being a radio broadcaster?** *It was pretty difficult. I remember a few weeks into my show at Kiss FM I bumped into a guy I knew from Hackney, and he said that I sounded like a 'white man' on air and I'll never forget. I've always spoken the same my whole life. I went home that night and had a mini-identity crisis. I questioned myself and wondered if I sounded like a 'sell-out'. It was a big moment for me and made me realise the importance of being myself. I spoke how I spoke, and I wasn't going to change that because of one person's opinion.*

*The transition was also difficult because suddenly, I wasn't speaking to the audience I was used to talking to. We were London-wide; we were legal. It wasn't just the nightclub crowd; it was your everyday person who was now listening to us. It was difficult for all of us at Kiss FM to make that transition, the realisation that we were now commercial. I wasn't great at first, but I did get better.*

*Another thing I realised was that many of my peers were obsessed with nightclub gigs, they loved the glory of standing there front and centre, everyone cheering them etc. I felt differently, to me the biggest gig you'll do is your radio show, so more time needs to go into making that right. You're going to reach more people and make an impact on them; a lot of people don't even go to nightclubs and they're the ones who will listen to the radio more. Gigs are great and they pay, but they are a fraction of your real audience. I used to look at my fellow DJs and think, why are you fighting over who will go up next on the line up? That to me wasn't important.*

When I got the opportunity to join Radio 1, I made an important decision to stop using the 'Madhatters' tag and go by my actual name. Everyone knew me as 'Trevor Madhatter', or 'Madhatter Trevor' because my Soundsystem was called Madhatters. As boring as Trevor Nelson might sound, I thought that if I wanted to make a mark, I needed to do it with my actual name.

**Over the years, the role of the DJ has evolved, no longer just behind the decks but also being presented with other business opportunities. What advice would you give with regards to balancing both?** *I probably would've retired by now if I had let business motivate me ahead of the creative process. When you've established your brand, you become picky because naturally you want to protect it, so that means not saying yes to every opportunity, especially ones that don't fit in with your brand. For example, when I put compilation albums out, they have to be big, otherwise I won't put them out. It's easy to say yes when lots of things are coming your way, but I always ask people are you brave enough to say no? This can be difficult at the beginning of your career because you start to think 'but what if this opportunity doesn't come around again?'. I totally get that some opportunities that may not seem like an obvious fit for your brand are a good way to keep your profile out there, and for example to increase your social media following which is important nowadays to ensure people remember who you are.*

*During my time on MTV, the BBC reached out and offered me a few projects. I was contacted by the team who worked on the lucrative Saturday night segments and they asked me if I wanted to present anything on Saturday night TV and I said no, it just* didn't appeal to me. *If it's not right for you, then don't do it. Through the opportunities you take and don't take, you need to make it clear what you represent. Not everything that comes your way will be good for you. This idea that all publicity is good publicity is nonsense.*

**What challenges have you experienced in your career and how have you overcome them?** *I'm often asked if I've been subjected to racism in the industry and I always say if I have, it's happening in meetings I'm not privy to. For example, I wouldn't know if I wasn't considered for an opportunity because I wouldn't know if I was up for it if I wasn't in the room at the time. I've never experienced anything blatant to my face.*

*I would say a key challenge has been the preconception of what Black people are like, the perception of the Black man as the aggressor, that you dare not say the wrong thing to, especially if you're a darker-skinned Black man. I just continue to focus on music, which is my passion.*

**What have been some of your career highs and lows?** *Kiss FM getting a license, a London-wide license. Choice FM had a license to broadcast in South London and parts of North London, but Kiss FM was the first dance music, London-wide legal station. That was a massive high point because it was the day, I became a legal DJ and broadcaster, the first time I got paid as a proper broadcaster.*

*When I joined Radio 1 in 1996, that was a career and life-changing moment for me. In 1998, when I got the opportunity to present* The Lick on MTV, *the channel's first dedicated R&B show, that changed my life. I remember getting the call and thinking: 1. I have never been on TV before, and 2. they didn't play much Black music on the channel at the time, and my speciality is R&B, so how will that work? I didn't take the call too seriously, so I was shocked when I got the job. I remember on my first day walking in and I had a list of small requests and thankfully my director was also a Black guy, similar to me in many ways, we were both bald-headed and we got on like brothers. That show became the longest-running music show in MTV Europe history, running for twelve years. I came up with the name* The Lick *and I remember thinking I have to name this show, because if I let MTV do it, they'll call it something like 'The Bomb', something that wasn't authentic. 'The Lick' was something we'd say back in the day to describe something that was cool e.g. I went to this party and it was 'the lick'. We expanded with The Lick parties, hosting them in large venues that typically never had a large number of Black people before. The queue would regularly go around the whole block. I'd never seen our community queue so early for an event in my life. It took off, and I threw a party every month for five years all over Europe. I was basically applying all the graft I had put into my early house parties, but this time I had a budget and a big brand backing it.*

*I haven't had many low points in my career and that comes from being selective about the opportunities I've taken on. I think the lowest point for me was being yards away from someone being shot at the MTV party that I had. We weren't running the party at the time, if we had been able to oversee it, that wouldn't have happened. It was during a time when stuff like that happened at the occasional event and it was unfortunate because a lot of work had gone into organising those parties to elevate the Black music scene. One of the most frustrating things was that I didn't see my white peers struggle in that way. When they organised events, their only focus was on how big the event could be, what sponsorships they could secure.*

**What has been the best career advice given to you?** *The best advice came from a man called Mark Goodier; his company put me forward for the Radio 1 role. He was already presenting the Radio 1 chart show, he'd been on Radio 1 for years and what he said gave me confidence. It was simply 'everything's going to be all right'. What he was saying to me was that things were going to work out, and I gave this exact same advice to Radio 1 DJ Clara Amfo. It was my way of saying that despite all the nerves you might feel, once you're on that show, you'll be fine, you've got a future beyond what you think, because it's so easy to doubt yourself and think you might not be good enough.*

**What advice would you give to Black students and professionals starting out and advancing in their careers?** *Dedicate yourself to becoming better in whatever you do. I've mentored loads of DJs over the years and one of the things I ask is 'do you listen back to your shows after you do them? Really listen?'. I recorded every show I did on pirate radio, every show I did on MTV, so I could listen and watch them back to see how I could improve.*

*Try and leave your mark, so it helps the next person coming through. When I was at Radio 1, due to the success my show and other Black specialist music shows had, 1Xtra was then created. Whilst at MTV, The Lick's success inspired them to create MTV Base. We showed them the greatness of our music, its popularity and they gave it its own platform.*

*Try not to lose your personality when you go into the workplace and be yourself. Be selective about the things you chose to discuss openly in the workplace too. For example, if you have ambitions to progress and move on to another company, sure that's fine but don't broadcast that in your current workplace, because people pick up on that. Don't talk about what you're doing next, appear passionate about what you are doing now, in your current role. My parents used to say to me 'you have to work twice as hard as the rest' and there is definitely still an element of that which exists today, but I also think you have to give the indication that you are prepared to and at all times you are ready.*

# JAMELIA DONALDSON

*Founder of TreasureTress*

Jamelia Donaldson is the founder and CEO of @TreasureTress — Europe's largest monthly product discovery subscription service for girls and women with kinky-curly hair and also the co-creator of The Teen Experience, a monthly workshop series which offers Black and mixed-race teen girls personal development skills and more.

Since launching in 2015, with a huge online community, and an active and thriving offline presence, TreasureTress has proven that natural hair and Black sisterhood can truly go hand in hand.

While delivering monthly haircare packages to over 26 countries monthly, TreasureTress has grown to become much more than 'just a subscription box', now building digital campaigns for brands, consulting the largest ethnic beauty brands and hosting the most spoken about offline activations for and by Black women in the UK's major cities including their annual pop up shop.

Jamelia has been featured in Forbes, Buzzfeed, Gal-Dem, Good Housekeeping and Pride Magazine just to name a few. Jamelia has recently launched #ShesObsessedThePodcast to highlight the experiences of successful and game-changing Black British Women and in 2021 received AdWeek Europe's Future Is Female Award.

**Tell us about yourself?** *I'm Jamelia Donaldson and by profession, I am the founder and CEO of TreasureTress, but more generally as a person, I would say that I am hugely passionate about travel, learning, my friendships, my family, and I'm just curious about life in general and how big life can get. Both my parents are Jamaican, and I grew up in a single parent household, but I have a good relationship with my dad. Growing up, education was really important, as my maternal grandmother, who passed away when I was two, was a teacher and my mum was a headteacher (she's now retired). Travel was always an opportunity for us to learn something new. My mum was definitely not buying me the latest trainers, but she was absolutely taking us on holiday. Reading books was a big part of my growing up as again, my mum being a teacher, everything surrounded literacy, history, anything academic. I used to be into dance when I was younger (I used to be hardcore!), but then I got to an age where I found it difficult to balance both, so I decided to focus on my studies. To some extent I regret that a little because I don't feel I should've had to sacrifice my creative side, but I did do really well in school. Instead of doing A Levels, I did the International Baccalaureate which is seven subjects instead of four and is internationally recognised. I decided to do that because, as I said, travel was a huge part of my upbringing and in my mind, whatever my career was going to be, I was going to do it all over the world, I wouldn't be tied to one place. This meant that I wanted my qualifications to be transferable wherever I went in the world.*

*I actually applied to study Law at university, but I missed the required mark by one mark and I was absolutely gutted. I thought it was truly the end of the world, because in my mind I had convinced myself that I was going to be a lawyer, so to not be able to do the degree I wanted was frustrating. I studied Business and International Relations which is quite funny now because business was not top of mind when I selected it, but I thought how hard can it really be and international relations sounded like you to get to travel and that was my thought process pretty much.*

*In my second year, I went to Uganda with a university society I was part of, and we helped to build a school. For me, it was my first time in Africa which was really important to me and secondly, it was the first time I saw how much of a bubble we live in within the western world. Africa as a continent is portrayed in a certain way, especially the children who live there, but what I saw was that wealth doesn't equate to happiness as the children that I saw in Uganda were much happier than the children I saw in London. That was an important life lesson for me.*

*Year three was my workplace placement year, so I went to Beijing for one month to do PR and marketing. I came back and then went to New York for roughly eight months to do entertainment and fashion PR which was fun and then I came back to London. I hadn't earned any money throughout my placement year as I wasn't paid for the internships I had done, and I remember thinking I needed to earn some money before I went back to university. I had some savings from working in my first two years of university and I received grants, but by my final year, I had nothing left and I came from a single parent household so there were no handouts going. I went on the student recruitment site Milkround looking for an internship and came across this Business Operations role at the financial services firm BlackRock. I studied for the interview like it was an exam because no one from my family came from that background and I knew I would really have to apply myself in the interview to secure the internship. I ended up securing the internship and managed to get a graduate job offer which was great. I graduated from university with a first class and went back to BlackRock to start my graduate role. I was one of three Black graduates out of the 300 graduates globally.*

**What was your motivation to pursue entrepreneurship? How did the idea for TreasureTress emerge?** *I was at BlackRock for just under three years and I enjoyed it. I was on a rotational programme, which meant I got to work in a few different teams in the company which was really beneficial for my learning. My graduate scheme was coming to an end, and it was time for me to decide which team I wanted to stick with, however if I'm being honest, by year two of the scheme I was already getting this itch that I wanted to do something else, something more creative. When I was in New York, subscription boxes were on the rise and I remember at the time thinking it would be really cool to have something like this in the UK. I said to myself, 'if this doesn't exist in the UK by the time I come back, I'm going to create it myself.' However, when I returned, I got caught up with my graduate job but it was still in the back of my mind. In year two, I started TreasureTress as just an Instagram page for a few months and then eventually I launched, and there was roughly an eight-month period where I was working full-time and running TreasureTress at the same time. I was waking up at five every morning, working on TreasureTress for two hours then getting ready as quickly as possible to go to work, finishing work at 7 p.m., getting home and then working on TreasureTress until 1* *a.m. and it wasn't sustainable. I eventually decided to hand in my notice and take TreasureTress full time, which was really daunting, but essential.*

Prior to launching TreasureTress, you studied Business and International Relations at University, interned in New York and worked in financial services after graduating. What did you learn across those experiences which you were able to take into starting your business? *I'll work backwards:*

*When I was worked at BlackRock, it was definitely business etiquette for example, writing emails, pitching to clients, hosting client meetings, process management and improvement, how to conduct yourself in a professional environment, finding ways to use your voice when you're the youngest person in the room and the only Black woman in the room. It also gave me an appreciation for creativity because finance is not the most creative industry.*

*From the PR world, I learnt the importance of building and maintaining strong relationships. Pitching to clients, organising events and building a community were things I learnt from working in PR.*

*The two experiences are polar opposites, but they gave me a really good tool kit to use when starting my own business.*

What were those first few weeks and months like transitioning from your full-time job to running your business? What should Black professionals think about and plan for before making that decision? *It was tough as I had never done anything like that before and, at that point, I didn't have a network of people to lean on. I would say don't rush the process. As much as entrepreneurship is glamourised, we ultimately need to remember that the goal is to have multiple streams of income. A job keeps you anchored, keeps you connected to different people and it provides you with that consistency, as it's really hard to be creative when you're worried about money. You can't be creative, innovative and forward-thinking in your business if you're worried about how you are going to eat. As much as entrepreneurship is seen as attractive, we really need to question the foundation we are trying to build for ourselves. For me, quitting my job right away wasn't an option because I needed to save enough money so I could launch TreasureTress. I didn't have the financial safety net that people from other communities typically have, so I would say keep your individual circumstances in mind when making these types of choices. Social media can give the impression that we're all starting on the same level and those that are ahead just worked much harder than everyone else, but the reality is, we don't have an equal starting point and we have to respect the position that we are starting from. Not that it can limit us but we need to be realistic about what we can and can't do, based on our starting point. This means not rushing into decisions like quitting your job.*

**Entrepreneurship and side hustle culture has boomed in recent years. What do you think are some of the misconceptions about running a business? What should Black founders focus on when launching a business?** *A big misconception about running a business is that it's better than having a job. You see on social media all the time people posting things like 'why work to build someone else's dream when you can build your own', but the reality is, even though you own your business, you're actually working for* *the people on your team. Don't get it twisted! You have to work hard to make sure you can pay them every month. You are always working for someone. The people on your team, your clients, if you have investment, then you're working for your investors. Your ego needs to be stripped, because if your ego is involved in your decision to start a business, then you're going to fail. This is because you are more concerned with the press features, highlights and the glamour of it all than the actual day to day reality if it.*

*I would advise Black founders to really focus on building a community. Listen to your customers. I received my first PR feature on the back of quitting BlackRock, the headline was something like 'Black Founder Quits Finance Job to Help Girls Fall in Love with Their Curls', which was just luck really, as I didn't go out there seeking it. This came after two years of working in complete silence on TreasureTress in the background. Customers and community should be your focus because it's your customers that are paying you. Just because a business is getting a significant amount of press, it doesn't mean they are making any money. The number of followers you have and the number of press features you get don't dictate how successful your business is, because there are many businesswomen who are forward-thinking and innovative but the revenue their businesses are actually generating doesn't match what you think it would be. Focus on your own numbers, but your numbers are only going to be as good as your community and your customer base.*

The various obstacles Black founders face when launching and scaling a business, including lack of funding and access to key networks, is well documented. For any budding Black entrepreneurs who might be feeling discouraged, what advice would you give? *Start building a network as soon as you can. I've bootstrapped TreasureTress completely; I haven't taken any investment funds to this day. Initially, I didn't realise that I could, I couldn't comprehend asking a stranger for money for an idea that isn't really anything yet. In my mind I always thought you had to build a business before getting investment but now I know that wasn't always the case. As it's something I have thought about a lot more, I've started building relationships with angel investors and there are a growing number of Black angel investors in the UK that are willing to help and have a keen interest in making sure we have the same access to capital. Building out your network is key – both Andy Ayim MBE (founder of The Angel Investing School) and Andy Davis (angel investor and co-founder of 10x10) are two of many great people to know in the start-up and investing space. Google them and if you can't directly contact them, they have created loads of resources online which are useful.*

What challenges have you experienced in your career and how have you overcome them? *Getting caught up in the corporate politics of bigger brands and being reminded that although I've done well, I'm still a Black girl and should maybe pace myself. TreasureTress has been really successful, we're market leaders, you can't discredit the work we've done in our market, and yet it's still really hard to get through certain doors. A few times, I've been reminded indirectly that I'm a Black girl and will need to go through a certain process – how dare I try to go directly to the source. That's a challenge because I've done the work, I've got the* receipts and still this is how I'm treated. As the decision maker in my company, I should be able to speak directly to the decision maker(s) in another company. I think I should've stood up for myself more in the past, but I was trying to be respectful and manage relationships. I've been able to overcome these challenges by learning from experience, talking things through with mentors and ensuring I don't repeat the same mistake twice. Imposter syndrome is real – having a solid support network of people who are rooting for you and believe in you is extremely important.

**What have been some of your career highs and lows?** *Securing the first TreasureTress office was a huge accomplishment because up until that point, I had been working from my room and different coffee shops for ages. Getting the second office was an even bigger accomplishment because it was at the peak of Covid-19 and it allowed us to bring our warehouse and our office space together. It also allowed us to hire a steadier warehouse team and it gave the full TreasureTress team the environment they deserved to work in. Also, the Forbes feature was a big deal as it was something that had been on my vision board for a while, so for it to happen was really exciting. All our events have been high points, but in particular our first and second pop-up shop, which completely exceeded our expectations in terms of the number of attendees. For me, that was proof that this idea that randomly came to me and I acted upon had positively impacted loads of people.*

*Career lows can come thick and fast. Building a team is one of my proudest moments but it's also one of the most difficult things because managing people is not easy. When you are so connected to who you service, your team ultimately reflects who you serve so you really care about them and it's hard to switch between professionals and personal sometimes. Other career lows include when things just didn't go to plan like logistical issues – products are meant to arrive but the brand informs you they are still in the US and won't be arriving for another two months, although you planned to build the boxes the following day.*

**What has been the best career advice given to you?** *The best career advice came from Andy Ayim, who said that I needed to be very intentional about the life I'm creating and not just the business I'm building, because after all, I'm the thing that matters most.*

**What advice would you give to Black students and professionals starting out and advancing in their careers?** *Build a reputation of excellence. I love Black Twitter, it's jokes but there is this narrative of 'I'm not working a nine to five', 'I'm demanding more salary or I'm quitting' etc., and it's like have you even done the work? Are you even good at what you do? Have you built a reputation for what you do? A portfolio of excellence, regardless of what career path you take or industry you're in is important. You want to be known as someone who doesn't produce mediocrity.*

# NENE PARSOTAM

*Founder of Vine Creatives and
Co-founder of We Are Stripes*

Nene is an executive creative director and art director having worked in the creative advertising industry for the past seventeen years. She has worked with some of the largest brands in the world including Wall Street Journal, Disney, L'Oréal, HP, Warner Bros, Jaguar, Pepsi, Pizza Hut, Visa, Samsung and Vodafone amongst many others. For these mega-brands, Nene created and crafted digital and online advertising campaigns, traditional and digital billboard designs, branded and rebranded these brand's subsidies, designed websites for product launches in various international countries, and designed user interfaces as well as art directed creative teams on photoshoots.

Nene co-founded and currently runs VINE Creatives, a branding and investment agency with a focus on businesses which are run by and for the African-Caribbean diaspora. Nene also co-founded the ethnic diversity creative career initiative *We Are Stripes*, which aims to get more underrepresented talent into various creative industries.

**Tell us about yourself?** *I was born and raised in Hackney, more specially Stoke Newington to what I call hardcore, super-strict Nigerian parents making me a first generation British-born Nigerian. I've seen myself as creative from a very young age; my* *way of expressing myself and my ideas was through drawing, painting and arts and crafts. My parents, however, were very academic with my father being a nuclear (that's right, nuclear) physicist and my mother an accountant for most of her career. They both loved physics, so they 'encouraged' me to study it as part of my further education. I knew I wanted to pursue a more creative career, but it was very difficult to convince my parents of its value, so I opted to go with what they recommended. At college I studied 4 A Levels: maths, further maths, physics and computing and then at university, Multimedia Computing and Computer Science. That didn't go down well with them at all. I did however manage to get into university where my degree, while still very technical, did have a creative component.*

**What was your motivation to get into advertising and design and how did you secure your first opportunity within this space?** *I wanted to be an animator and work specifically for Disney, so getting into advertising wasn't the trajectory I was on at the time. I've always loved the quality of their storytelling and their character design. Unfortunately, I didn't get the grades I needed to go to the only university at the time that was offering an animation course. This was down to the A Levels I was 'encouraged' to take; out of the four of them, I failed three. Ironically, I was offered a place with a university that had a specialist animation course on the strength of my portfolio which I had to prepare for the entrance interview. Through clearing I got a place at the university I attended, finished my degree and put together a second online portfolio with my own self-initiated work. I applied to be a junior interactive designer with the Lloyds TSB Bank's in-house creative team and successfully got the job. I think* *this was based on my interview answers as opposed to solely on my work.*

**Throughout your career, you've been a freelancer as well as working in-house. What would you say are the main differences between both and what advice would you give to those who are planning to transition into freelancing?** *The main difference I would say when it comes to freelancing within agencies and working in-house would be speed. With in-house, it is usually on one client, so you have more time to focus on the task assigned to you as you only have that client's project to work on. With agencies you have multiple clients, all with different projects and timelines (some of them very short) so you have to work very quickly. If transitioning into freelancing, aim to have a very strong creative process and be very organised. You have to hit the ground running in a freelance role because the time you would normally have to understand how the business works, what the company or agency culture and process is like, is a lot less than when you are hired for an in-house company. Your process would be regarding how you come up with ideas, how you flesh them out and get them ready to present to your management team or leaders. How do you absorb a brief in order to ensure you under-stand what is being asked of you? Do you work better in a team brainstorming or do you need a few hours on your own to come up with ideas? How do you do quick research and then group your ideas into concepts? All of that is part of your creative process and will need to be concrete as well as flexible, as every freelance assignment will be different. You can also speed up if need be. However, if timelines are too short for you to be comfortable enough to produce good work, then say so to the* *management. As creatives, the more time you have on a project the better the work will be.*

**Many Black creatives, especially Black women, are asked to work for free or accept little compensation for their work. Why do you think this happens so often and how can they ensure that not only are they paid their worth, but also that they know their worth?** *The lines of 'we will give you exposure' or 'we don't have any budget' are well used lines. Companies, brands and individuals use them because they work. And many creatives still fall for those lines and do amazing work for exposure (what does that even mean?!) or because a company claims to have 'no money'.*

*I have seen many young Black female creatives, blindsided by a large brand with those lines and because the brand is large, they take it. It comes from a combination of not understanding how a company or brand works and wanting validation of their work from that large brand.*

*This is especially if you have little experience in the creative industry; that ignorance is certainly used against you. Let me say this: brands and companies that approach creatives for work have money. They wouldn't do the campaign or project without it. Even if it is charity work. If a company can get away with using you without paying, they will. It's human nature. So, arm yourself with a bit of knowledge. Find out what you would be paid for in regard to what they are asking and how much they would spend on the project they want you involved in. Find out your market value and rates so you are armed with numbers so you can make a counteroffer. You have to find out and decide what your worth is. If, with that knowledge they still won't pay, then you can and should say no. That would be a lack of* integrity on the company's part, and you don't want to work with a company that doesn't have that. It's another form of exploitation.

This is something that unfortunately is an issue within the Black community. I have seen people only pay attention to a Black-owned brand or company after they have made in-roads with a large brand or corporate. It's a shame because it means we don't often see our own potential and seek validation from a brand as opposed to the work and impact we do as a community. This, I feel, translates to not seeing our own values and worth in the creative work we do, which then leads to doing more work for free to get a sense of that value. It's a bit of a vicious cycle.

Having said all that, I will bring a bit of balance. I will say be open to working for free but do it at your own discretion, not because someone has asked you to. If you want to give your time and expertise to a cause or pro bono project, that should be your choice. Also, consider negotiating with the person or company that you are working with and asking for other compensation. In-kind payments such as expertise exchanges, contacts or mentions in press and PR. If they can't or won't pay you, then be clear on what you would like in return for the work you do for them if the project seems too good to pass up. This can sometimes be more valuable than just getting money. Regardless, get everything in writing. I can't stress this enough. Treat the project as if you were getting monetary compensation and have contracts drawn up and signed. Believe me, it will save a lot of stress and heartache should the project go south.

**What was the motivation to co-found your own creative agency VINE Creatives, servicing businesses run by and with a focus on**

the African-Caribbean diaspora? Having worked across both agency and client side – how important do you think it is to have Black ownership (as the co-founder of your own agency) within this space and why? *I co-founded VINE Creatives with my husband, as early in our careers we were often approached by African-Caribbean entrepreneurs who wanted us to give them the same quality of work that we were at the time producing for clients at agencies and corporations. There are many talented and driven entrepreneurs in the community with great businesses. Unfortunately, we found that many were not presented correctly, and this often impacted the growth and perception of their businesses. As much as we may claim to 'not judge a book by its cover' when it comes to businesses, if we are honest, perception is everything and companies that are presented with strong visuals and clear messaging often do better than ones that don't. We especially found this to be true once a Black-owned business looked to fundraise. Also, I have found that there is an unspoken but very real expectation of Black businesses to have poor branding, brand visuals, poor messaging, and poor service. I truly hate this, and VINE Creatives strives with its clients to position Black-owned businesses in the best possible light and showcase what they can do.*

*I think it is very important that there are companies who are Black-owned in this space such as ours. Being ethnically diverse, both myself and my teams understand the cultural nuisances of the communities we work with, beyond just dropping terms like 'African prints' into Google. We once came across a company that had used Adinkra symbols (which are Ghanaian) for the branding of a company that wanted to be positioned in Nigeria. To the design studio that did the branding, Africa was Africa and therefore all fifty-four countries were interchangeable. They are not, and this lack of understanding is what has led to many tone-deaf and offensive campaigns and creative work over the past years. This is from agencies or brands who clearly didn't get any insight from the community in order to fully understand who they were speaking to. Ownership is important as it allows us to build and expand the economy within the community. Something that will go far to establishing our value among ourselves, greater trust and legacy for future generations.*

Social media has provided a great platform for creatives, especially Black creatives to showcase their work from music to designs and more. But unfortunately, this has led to numerous big brands and influential individuals copying the work of Black creatives without giving credit or any prior discussions being had. How can Black creatives best protect themselves? *Social media has indeed been an amazing way to showcase creative work and I have found many outstanding creative individuals that way. However social media is its own behemoth and a very big place so it would be almost impossible to stop someone somewhere from ripping off your work. Again, knowledge is key here. Research and find out what your rights are as a creative in general and then about how those rights extend to social media. This is so that you understand what power you have if you see someone has used your work without your permission. I have met many creatives who know nothing of licensing or intellectual property rights.*

*As unsexy as that part of your trade is, it's vital that you learn about it. The Design Council, British Library and other bodies such as the Association of Photographers, provide valuable* information on this topic. For names and logos, invest in getting them trademarked. For physical designs, consider having them patented. For music, imagery, and photography I would say be very selective in what you post. Don't post all your best stuff to socials. Leave some for your clients, work with other individuals or influencers on collaborations or exclusive content for your followers on platforms like Patreon. That way you can put contracts and paywalls in place that will help to protect your work should you see where it is not supposed to be.

**What challenges have you experienced in your career and how have you overcome them?** *This is a tough one. And it's unfortunate that I will have to say this (as it was said to me and turned out to be very true) but you will have to be exceptional at what you do to really be taken seriously, especially in the creative industries which are very subjective and very competitive. I have been to agency after agency and at first, the people I worked with were not fully convinced that I could do what I said I could do. This could be down to the fact that I'm both Black and female and was in a creative role, something which when I first started out was quite rare. I was often underestimated, as some would tell me to my face, they didn't think I was good enough (I kid you not). Others it was subtler, by giving me work which was way below my level of expertise. Instead of getting angry and bitter about it, I would use that underestimation to my advantage. It's very easy to blow people out of the water with your work and really impress them when their expectations of you are lower than they should be. So, I would say be really, really good at what you do. People will notice and after a while it becomes not about you and your race* or gender but the strength of your work, which is what you want anyway, right?

**What have been some of your career highs and lows?** *I think a few standout ones would be the working with LooksLikeMe on the Black Panther inspired shoot which went viral in 2018 and got the attention of the director Ryan Coogler and Lupita Nyong'o, which was amazing. Also, designing the site for Samsung mobile phones when it launched back in 2007, app design for Dior, campaign work and a website for Cadbury. Judging the Industry Craft category at the Cannes Lions Festival of Creativity in 2019 was a fantastic experience and a major career highlight. Not only was it a lot of fun, but my fellow jurors were also amazing professionals and the fact that I had a chance to decide the top 3% of creative work in the world was an honour. I have been in this industry for a long time and when I have moments of doubt that I've passed my prime, I look back on these achievements and remind myself that I still have a lot to give, and I can still produce good work.*

*With regards to career lows, I will never forget my first design role, I was tasked to find some images for a brochure we were doing for a bank. I didn't yet know the difference between royalty-free (pay once for the image and use as much as you want to) and rights managed images (where you pay depending on how often and where you would use the image). I chose rights managed images and because the brochure was for a bank, tens of thousands would have to be printed and be distributed to their branches across the nation. The image ended up being just over a quarter of a million for usage costs which, of course, the client hadn't budgeted for. When my manager found out,* obviously he and the account handler at the time were not happy at all about the mistake as they now had to go and explain it to the client. I was mortified and cried at work (something I vowed afterwards never to do ever again). It taught me to check and recheck everything, but also to ensure that I knew as much as the people I was working with, so I would never make that sort of mistake again.

**What has been the best career advice given to you?** *Learn how to be creative and inspired without copying or ripping off another creative's work. Learn the process of HOW to be creative then apply it to the medium you are working with. You need to draw from your own experiences and worldview. Tell your story. Infuse it with things that you like and are important to you. Don't just go to Pinterest or Instagram for your ideas. It took me ages to wrap my head around that advice, but it's very, very good. It's how you come up with original ideas or original ways to execute an idea that makes your creative work richer and more memorable.*

**What advice would you give to Black students and professionals starting out and advancing in their careers?** *If you are a creative, produce the work and you will be amazed at the opportunities that will come your way when you do. Do not sit and wait for the 'right time' or the 'right equipment' etc. Use what you have. Collaborate with your associates and create a short piece on something you care about deeply. Try not to follow trends or copy someone else. But most importantly, seek and find help. There is a tendency within our community to try and do every-thing on our own. Social media does at times perpetuate this* *notion that individuals succeed on their own. Nothing could be further from the truth and you will be very surprised at the many team members an artist or influencers will have around them to get them to where they are. So try not to do everything yourself as no one succeeds alone. Any gaps in your knowledge, do your research, sign up for courses, listen to podcasts. There are infinite resources out there. Also, I strongly recommend getting a mentor. A mentor will help you with things that are often not taught outright and are learned by hard experience. This can range from how to deal with rejection to navigating company politics to how to conduct yourself in a professional environment without losing or suppressing your true self. Seek out mentorship schemes and/or reach out to an individual you admire in your chosen field through your network or colleagues. They may well say no, but then they might say yes. Take a chance as the insight gained from that relationship is invaluable.*

## AKAMA DAVIES

*Director of Global Solutions, Xaxis and*
*Co-Founder, We Are Stripes*

Akama co-founded DEI consultancy organisation *We Are Stripes* and is Director, Global Solutions at Xaxis, part of GroupM, the world's largest media investment group. Prior to that, he was Head of Brand Performance at Verizon Media and Global Lead for Verizon Media's Multicultural employee resource group.

Akama has been awarded multiple industry accolades in his career to date. Recently, Akama won MediaWeek's Rising Star Media Owner, was listed in Campaign Magazine's 30 under 30, and won Future Leader of the Year in the Tech Leader Awards, alongside judging for several media industry recognition bodies including M&M Global, Festival of Media, DMA, Performance Marketing and MediaWeek Awards, among others.

Regarding diversity and inclusion, Akama has also been listed in the Dots 100 Black Creatives Inspiring Change, Campaign Magazine's 50 Trailblazers, The IPA's iList, and a finalist for the UK Social Mobility Awards Rising Star category. He was also instrumental in creating the Black Is The New Black exhibition at the National Portrait Gallery. He's been a public champion of neurodiversity with articles published in *City AM*, *Data and Marketing Association – Dyslexia Employer Guide* and *AdWeek Europe*.

**Tell us about yourself?** *I am incredibly proud of my Nigerian heritage, and I am the first member of my family to be born in the UK. I am a Southeast Londoner born and raised. I studied History at Queen Mary, University of London. Initially, I was supposed to study Law, but I missed my grades by two marks which was arguably the moment that set me to explore amazing new avenues and, ultimately, my career today.*

*In 2015, I co-founded We Are Stripes, an organisation whose mission is to create opportunities for people from BAME backgrounds across the media industry. We offer consultancy and diverse talent recruitment support for companies and career development workshops and placements to ethnically diverse creative talent. Time outside of work nowadays is spent with friends, family, and my daughter.*

**What was your motivation to get into advertising and how did you secure your first opportunity within this space?** *I have a fantastic partner – Emma. I owe her a lot, both personally and professionally. She was the one who encouraged me to go for an interview for my first advertising role at AOL. I'm a firm believer that having purpose and balance outside of work helps your career inside of work, and I have been fortunate enough to have amazingly supportive friends, family and, of course, her. What I love about advertising is that it allows you to use your talent to create. Nothing gives me more satisfaction than seeing an idea formed in your mind take shape in real work and collaborate with colleagues to realise it. Knowing that the work we do today creates what's next for tomorrow. Revolutionising the way consumers love brands through innovation and iteration. This year we have been* fortunate enough to have our continual innovation formally recognised and awarded across the industry.

**What are some of the key skills that you believe are necessary to thrive and advance your career within advertising and why?** *I always say no matter the companies' size, no one deals with companies; you deal with people at companies. The ability to work with and understand people in advertising both from an industry perspective and the audiences you are trying to reach is critical.*

*The other point to note is that advertising is a broad and varied industry with many different disciplines and departments, from finance to data science to creative production. No matter your interest and skill sets, you have a role and opportunity in the advertising industry.*

**We've seen a series of advertising and branding blunders over the last few years, which were racially insensitive and highlighted the lack of Black people in key decision-making areas. What changes are happening in the industry to ensure we see less of these instances going forward?** *A specific development we've seen in our industry as a product of the global Black Lives Matter activity in 2020 is many high-profile public promises. This makes it easier to hold organisations to account. There is movement in the right directions – arguably not enough – but still movement, nonetheless.*

*More than 200 leaders signed Creative Equals' letter in* Campaign *magazine to address the industry's implications following George Floyd's murder. The letter outlined ten pillars to act and hold the industry to account, ranging from leadership KPIs to preferred supplier lists.*

*In January of 2021, the* Drum *published an update on how the ad agencies had followed through on their promises. The good news is that we have seen some commitment, for example, WPP pledged $30m over the next three years to fund inclusion programs within WPP and to support external organisations, but certainly, there is more to do.*

*You need to fundamentally ensure you have more ethnic diversity and diversity overall at every stage and production. But crucially, you need to ensure that talent has a voice and platform to speak up and prevent some of these missteps as soon they see a brand is going down that path.*

**You co-founded We Are Stripes to help drive more BAME talent into the creative industry. What have you learned about the obstacles that are unique to Black talent trying to get into and progress within the industry?** *Some of the consistent barriers we see preventing Black talent from progressing and entering the industry are:*

- *Awareness: companies often allege not knowing where to find diverse talent in the creative industries. Meanwhile, a lot of Black talent aren't aware of the industries' career opportunities and pathways, especially as these careers are non-traditional for the generations above us. This is compounded by the fact nearly 40% of creative roles are never advertised, according to The Creative Mentoring Network.*

- *Microaggressions: Microaggression produces the same neurological response as a physical assault, even triggering the same parts of the brain. It's often the death by a thousand cuts that drive talent away from the industry.*

- *The pressure: Often you don't just represent yourself. You're seen as representing all Black people in professional scenarios often because you are the only one in the room (and sometimes even the only Black person who has ever been in the room). In many of the senior meetings I've been in, I am the first or the only one and acutely aware of that fact – I'm also aware that others are aware.*

**What challenges have you experienced in your career and how have you overcome them?** *Perception can be seen as reality. Just be aware of the bias existing in your work, either consciously or unconsciously. Understand that there is a game on some level, and you need to play your part in it and play to win. I take pride in exceeding people's expectations of me and using this as fuel. It may seem like a common adage from my parent's generation, but Black employees and applicants need to be twice as good to get half as much as their white counterparts – live that principle and you will be in a strong place. This will mean you leave nothing to chance.*

**What have been some of your career highs and lows?** *Winning* Campaign *magazine's MediaWeek Rising Star Award. It was a single moment that represented all the hard work that had been put in before it. It's often the work you do in the dark that makes you shine in the light. To be recognised in front of the entire media industry as their top talent was such a great honour and accolade. It has opened several doors for me and has set me on a path to even greater opportunities to come.*

*A low point was when I struggled to get a career break after I finished uni. I faced months on the shelf, and as I graduated in the heart of the recession in 2011, it made things even harder for recruiting young people. I applied for literally hundreds of jobs until I got my opportunity. Don't take it personally. Keep pushing for what you want, and always consider you may have to take a different route to get to where you want to go.*

**What has been the best career advice given to you?** *The best career advice I've received is to build your personal brand. The important decisions in your career are made when you are not in the room. What do you stand for? Think of the three adjectives that describe your authentic self, e.g., open, confident, generous. Then think of the three adjectives your organisation values, e.g., fun, hard-working, knowledgeable. Identify which of those words intersect. If you exhibit those behaviours for ninety plus days, you will have built up your personal brand and stake in your company.*

**What advice would you give to Black students and professionals starting out and advancing in their careers?** *A saying I always revert to is to never be a king in the area of your comfort zone and only want to do things you know how to do well. Among the things that prevent people from acting is the fear of failure. Don't wait for things to be just right. Don't wait for things to be ideal – they may never be ideal. Always strive for greater personal development. Also, ensure that you have professional or senior advocates for you in your company outside of your direct manager – cheerleaders who state your case for promotion, development, and opportunities.*

# BUILDING A NETWORK

You've probably heard the cliched phrases:

*It's not what you know, it's who you know.*

*It's not who you know, it's who knows you.*

While it is debatable that what you know isn't important, the emphasis on being known and knowing others is key here. Way before joining the corporate workplace I observed that when people engage with one another and share parts of themselves with others, it breeds a certain familiarity and comfortability. If that person was someone 'alien' to you before, now that you know a bit more about them, you start to trust them and as your relationship develops, you might see them as someone you can rely upon and lean on. I saw how this translated early in my career, when some of my peers would go to all the after-work drinks and the new joiner networking events, while I would go home. My mindset at the time was that I had done my job well and contractually worked my hours (sometimes more), my job was done. However, the following day would be unbearable. Some of my colleagues would talk about all the contacts they secured and start scheduling catchups. Managers would banter with them all day about the antics of the night before, while I sat there, with a meek smile on my face not being able to partake in the inside jokes. Over time, these individuals would be put forward for opportunities I never heard of, and their names would slowly creep into catchups with managers as people I should 'think about' emulating. I noticed they did other bits of work for people outside of their immediate team and then boom! They'd be nominated for internal awards and all over the company intranet. I remember thinking, *who the hell nominated them?* Long story short, I followed suit. I started to attend the networking events, put in catchups, offered to help others, join all the various networks and slowly but surely, I started to see similar results, but *wheeeeew*! It wasn't without its challenges.

## The Importance of Networking

Networking and building a network exposes us to information and individuals that can be massively beneficial to our careers. Many of us don't have access to and are often excluded from the informal networks our white peers are part of, so we need to be proactive and initiate many of these relationships and connections ourselves. A further disadvantage comes from the fact that many of our white counterparts, particularly those of middle and upper classes have been building their networks since college and university or have connections through their family. For example, our current Prime Minister Boris Johnson, former Prime Minister David Cameron and the former Chancellor of the Exchequer all attended Oxford University and were members of the elite infamous dining club, the Bullingdon club.* Boris and

* Theguardian.com. 'Cameron desperately embarrassed over Bullingdon Club days.' (4 October 2009). Retrieved from: https://www.theguardian.com/politics/2009/oct/04/david-cameron-bullingdon-club

David were members of the same social circles before Oxford, having both attended Eton. It's not surprising that they all ended up at the top of British politics given this history. Through networking within your workplace and outside, you may be exposed to information regarding key developments in your industry or new opportunities that aren't widely being advertised. It will also provide you with a great opportunity to amplify your personal brand, increasing your visibility among your work colleagues or those in your industry and beyond. Engaging with others may provide you with new ideas and a fresh perspective which you can apply to your own career. Networking, being part of diverse networks and building your own network may also put you in a position to help others by sharing information and opportunities that come your way. I used to be part of this network for women in technology which had predominantly white members. They would share lucrative opportunities that weren't be circulated in the predominately Black online networks I was part of and I always forwarded them on.

## Unfamiliar Territory

I want to shout out the numerous Black professional network communities that have been created over the last few years and have provided safe online and offline spaces for Black students and professionals to network with each other. Despite what some people think, Black people aren't a monolith, so when we come together, we're coming from a range of different countries, socioeconomic backgrounds, religions and much more – all of which shape our perspectives. This means networking among each other isn't necessarily always the easiest and doesn't come without disagreement, but, despite this, I still feel like there is this common thread that binds us together.

But what I learnt early on was that trying to form relationships in spaces where I was a minority was very different. Two experiences come to mind: the first was when I was around the age of ten. My white friend was a member of her local Brownies club (a section of the Girl Guides or Girl Scouts as known in the US) and she invited me to come along to a fundraiser where her and her mum would be selling cakes. Upon entering the hall, I noticed I was the only Black kid and didn't know anyone else apart from my friend, but I was pretty unphased because I thought I'd make friends. I stood with my friend and her mum at their cake stall, and no one bought any of their cupcakes, but were purchasing from all the other stalls. I then left their cake stall and decided to try and make friends with the other kids, but as I would approach them, they would run off like I had a disease or something. They were gathering together pointing and laughing at me. I was trying to be their friend and they didn't want me anywhere near them. Their parents and the other Brownie staff didn't take any action. My friend's mum started to put two and two together: no one was buying from their cake stall and the kids didn't want to engage with me; it was clear what was at play here.

The second example is when I was around nineteen at a formal networking dinner for students interested in financial services careers. I was on a table with several other students, there were around eight of us, including one senior lady and the point was that we could ask her questions to learn about her career and the industry she worked in, and she would rotate with another senior person after a certain period of time. Funnily enough, she was sat next to me and just as I finished eating and placed my knife and fork on the plate, she scolded me in front of our table for how I positioned it, just before the waiter came to collect it. The table went completely silent, no one knew how to react. I didn't know there was a right way or wrong way to position my cutlery and it was just humiliating.

I mention these examples because they serve as a reminder to me that often the environments in which we are expected to network and initiate relationships are not always welcoming of us.

## Networking Whilst Black

### The pub. We are tired!!

When it comes to in-person networking, whether it's your workplace or wider industry, so much of it takes place within pubs, bars or hired venues where drinking is involved. Without sounding dry and like a Debbie Downer because I do like the occasional drink, but honestly, is it every day? I get why picking a pub or bar as a location may seem like a good idea; it's a way to wind down after a long day and takes the edge of something super formal, but the reality is it's pretty alienating for those who don't drink or are just not familiar with or into this 'getting lashed' pub culture. Growing up, sure I saw my family have drinks, but not frequently going to the pub to get 'wasted'. And if you think microaggressions when your colleagues are sober are bad, alcohol-fuelled microaggressions are even worse.

Major relationships and connections are formed at these after work drinks that materialise into far greater things and so we go, even when we don't really feel comfortable, because we know we need to for our careers. It provides us with an opportunity to get to know a wider subset of our colleagues, increase our visibility and get on the radar of those who are more senior. However, we must exercise caution – we can't fully let loose like our non-Black peers because we risk being judged and condemned in a way they wouldn't.

## Code-switching and conforming

Something that many of us do, whether consciously or subconsciously, is code-switch. This can be broadly defined as 'adjusting one's style of speech, appearance, behaviour, and expressions in way that will optimise the comfort of others in exchange for fair treatment'.[*] We aim to present a version of ourselves that is not reminiscent of the harmful racialised stereotypes that many hold about Black people so we can fit in. Code-switching is a survival mechanism for us. Many of us wouldn't be able to navigate the workplace and other institutions without it.

When we're networking, code-switching is something I feel becomes even more prevalent, because we have this very short window of time to make a good impression and establish a connection that we can then build upon. Research in the US shows that when Black employees code-switch, it increases the perception of us as professional and also enables us to be seen as leaders.[†]

[*] Harvard Business Review. 'The Costs of Code-switching.' (15 November 2019). Retrieved from: https://hbr.org/2019/11/the-costs-of -codeswitching
[†] Harvard Business Review. 'The Costs of Code-switching.' (15 November 2019). Retrieved from: https://hbr.org/2019/11/the-costs-of -codeswitching

However, this constant behaviour-switching is exhausting and studies have found it can lead to burnout.[*] It feels like we are doing two jobs: the one we are hired to do and also the job of showing our white colleagues that we aren't like the Black people they perceive us to be. Furthermore, in the eyes of some of our Black peers who have made the decision not to switch, we're seen as 'sell-outs', which causes some friction and I get it. I must admit, when I was an intern and I saw Black men and women code-switch, particularly Black men, who adopted this 'geezer' East End dialect out of nowhere, I was slyly giving them the side-eye. 'Why are you trying to be like THEM?', were my thoughts, and then once I started working full time, it all made sense because I became that person. I changed the way I spoke and even my hair; it was either relaxed or I wore a weave, but never braids or in its 4C state. (Confession: I wore my hair in braids at work for the first time two years ago).

Even outside of work, I remember when I was a teenager, some of the other Black girls where I lived called me a 'coconut' and an 'oreo' because I changed the way I spoke when engaging with white adults. Whilst we seem to think code-switching will bring us closer to our white peers, 1. it doesn't and 2. it can also alienate us from members of our own community who don't quite understand the 'tight rope' we walk between two worlds every day.

Professionalism in the workplace is very much defined by white-ness because we live in a world where white ideologies dominate

* Hewlin, F., Patricia. 'Wearing the Cloak: antecedents and consequences of creating facades of conformity.' (2009). Retrieved from: https://pubmed.ncbi.nlm.nih.gov/19450009/

and so we conform in many ways to demonstrate to our colleagues that despite our visible difference, we are 'just like them'.

## Black and Introverted

Because of popular culture, I think there is the expectation of Black people to be loud and extroverted. Your colleagues expect you to be the 'office jester', participate in all their conversations (even when they are topics you can't relate or add to), turn up to all the social events and generally entertain everyone. However, when you don't play the role, it can have an adverse impact on your career. Whilst white employees with introverted personalities are shown kindness and understanding, Black employees are often punished for those same traits. It's viewed through the lens of being 'rude', 'disrespectful', 'unfriendly'. In a Twitter thread that went viral, one Black woman explained that her introverted personality was consistently used against her during performance review discussions, despite being a high performer. In another Twitter conversation on the matter, a Black person tweeted: 'We don't get to be genuine to our personality traits without consequence. It's so frustrating.'

This expectation to always be smiley, happy, talkative, and bursting with energy can make networking an anxiety-inducing and exhausting experience. It's also unfair given some of the wider societal issues that disproportionately affect our community. For example, why would we want to smile and crack jokes when we consistently wake up to videos of unarmed Black people being killed by the police? No one expects this of white employees, but Black people at work are expected to take this 'grin and bear it' approach to everything no matter what.

Although I generally wouldn't call myself an introvert, I'm much more of an introverted person in the workplace. This is going to sound *soooo* ghetto (lord forgive me) but I used to go to networking events, stick to a corner of the room and eat the food (well the food that actually tasted good) before going home. This was not because I didn't have food at home, I just found it all too much. I didn't want to engage in small talk, I didn't want to laugh at jokes that aren't funny, and I didn't want to pretend to be someone I wasn't to make everyone but myself feel comfortable. Some of the things that helped me that you may find useful if you are an introvert are:

- **Being selective about the networking activities you partake in**: As important as networking is, it can also be draining, especially when you feel the expectation to perform. Only pick the events (in person or virtually) that you believe will bring true value to you.
- **Taking advantage of virtual networking**: So much of the anxiety and pressure that can come from networking is based on the sometimes-awkward nature of in-person interactions and the way that people can force their presence on you. With virtual networking, you are in the comfort of your own space, it feels so much easier to be yourself. Make more use of virtual forms of networking.
- **Going to events with someone you know**: Something that I found massively helpful was initially going to networking events with colleagues or friends who knew I was more introverted. They would introduce me to others, as for me, starting the conversation was always the hardest part.

## Opening Up

Establishing mutually beneficial networking relationships requires us to offer up some information about ourselves to others. Relationships, especially ones we hope to last within the working context, are dependent on our colleagues feeling a level of familiarity and closeness with us but for this to happen, there must be a level of trust which we often don't feel for a few reasons:

- **We fear information we share about ourselves being used against us later down the line.** This is something that happens more often than we think. In the #Blackintheoffice twitter hashtag where Black British employees shared their experiences of workplace racism, a Black employee anonymously submitted a story where she had opened up to her colleague about her past struggle with depression as he had also opened up to her about some personal things. However, he later used this information against her when she was trying to get promoted. Several people submitted similar experiences.

- **The information we do share might further reinforce widely held stereotypes which may alienate us further and could hinder our progression opportunities.**\* This could be our musical preference, our hobbies or what we do on the weekends as examples.

\* Harvard Business Review. 'Minorities hesitate to share information about themselves at work. That's a problem for everyone.' (March – April 2018). Retrieved from: https://hbr.org/2018/03/diversity-and -authenticity

**Networking up AND across**

In a NewsOne television interview, actress, writer, director and producer Issa Rae (best known for the HBO series *Insecure*) famously said: 'We have a tendency to network up, but it's really about networking across. Who's next to you? Who's struggling? Who's in the trenches with you? Who's just as hungry as you are? And those are the people that you need to build with.' Issa was speaking the truth. If I think about my own career to date, my peers, those at the same stage as me, have played a massive role in my development. It's my peers who fought on my behalf to negotiate my salary, my peers who recommended me for numerous speaking engagements, my peers who I brainstorm ideas with for potential new projects. It's so important to not conflate roles and titles with influence and power, because sometimes it's the people right next to you who might have the most significant impact on your career. Don't sleep on them or underestimate how you can help each other. There is value to be gained in networking both up and across.

## Tips for Successful Networking and Building a Network

**Set goals**: It's easy to neglect networking when we have our heads down focusing on our work all the time. Set yourself a target to attend a certain amount of online and/or offline networking events and reach out to a certain number of people over a time period. For example, attend two events a month and reach out to one person in your industry or desired industry every week.

**Network to network:** This might slightly contradict my next point but it's good to network to just network and meet people. The constant pressure to network for job referrals, career exposure and more can be intense and can take the joy out of it and you'll end up super disappointed if things don't materialise.

**Be strategic:** If there is something specific you're trying to accomplish from networking, be strategic and do some planning and preparation. Before engaging with others, be clear about what it is you want to communicate about yourself, e.g., talents, skills, things you're passionate about and what you hope to find out.

Make a list of the key people you want to interact with (or it could be just one person), and do your research on them, specifically trying to understand what is important and of value to them, where you have similarities between you that you can leverage and maybe how you can help them. This will help you craft how you approach them. When I was gathering contributors for this book, before approaching any of them in person or online, I watched and listened to hours of interviews some of them had done via YouTube and podcasts. Even having a look at their social media pages gave me a good indicator as to what was front of mind for them. I created some notes and highlighted it if we shared similarities, e.g., attended the same university or had similar family heritage. I used all this information to craft a unique introduction to each person which paid off.

**Be proactive:** Successful networking shouldn't be one-directional, and by this, I mean you reaching out and initiating every connection. It should also be about people equally wanting to be part of your network and seeing the value in that. One of the ways to make this happen is to share with your network things that you are working on, your areas of interests and expertise and update them on your career. When I initially had the idea for the book, I shared this with my network, who shared it with their network and, again, loads of people started to initiate contact with me, many who just believed in what I was doing and offered to help in any way.

**Mix it up:** There is no one way to network and I think it's more effective if you try a few ways because then you can tap into different types of people. Whilst we often associate networking with in-person events, you can also network online which has become more evident during the pandemic when that was the only way to network. Attend virtual events, utilise social media to reach out to people and engage with their content and show your interest. Join online communities whether that's a Facebook, LinkedIn, or WhatsApp group. I'm part of three to four and they're great as people share all types of opportunities and many are willing to make introductions. They often provide a safe space to ask for help, with many helping others in the group with their CVs, job applications and much more. At work, whilst it's good to email individuals of interest to arrange coffee, try something different like getting involved in community outreach projects or other side-of-desk work which will allow you to interact with people outside of your immediate team. I'm part of a programme at work where I mentor a student from our partner university and the three days of training we had enabled me to engage with people in my organisation outside of my team, many who I am still in touch with and seek advice from.

**Diversify your network:** When building your network, make sure you have a range of people with different skills, expertise, at different levels etc. For example, having a core network of solely senior professionals may not be very helpful as they might all be far too busy to help you in any way or having a network of just people in your current industry when you are hoping to pivot into another industry. The types of people are also important, such as people in your network that will be your cheerleader, people that are naturally connectors, those that are 'realists'. You need a mixture of them all.

---

**Different Types of People to Have in Your Network**

**The Connector:** They are a super networker and as a result, they know everyone, and everyone knows them. If you share your interests with them and what you are working on, they will introduce you to others who can help and may have more expertise. Even if they can't connect you with someone directly, they will still assist you in finding the right person.

**The plug:** Whilst the connector introduces you to a range of people, the plug introduces you to new opportunities, information and resources. They will do things like sending you the links to relevant articles and events, tag your name under posts where someone is requesting expertise.

**The Hype Man:** Also known as the cheerleader, this person will champion and celebrate your successes publicly and privately like it is their own. Even when things aren't going so well, they will still speak life into you and remind you that things will get better. Regardless of whether you are in the room or not, the hype man will always have your back.

**The Striver:** They share similar goals to you and as you both work towards achieving them, you can be there to support and motivate one another.

**The realist:** The realist keeps it real with you. They will let you know if you're doing too much or you're not doing enough in order to get to where you need to. This isn't someone that shoots down your goals, but they give you that tough love if they see that you're straying off course.

This isn't an exhaustive list and you can have several of each type of person or one person could embody many of these, but hopefully this gives you insight into the roles different people can play in your network and also the type of person you can be in someone else's network.

## Maintaining Your Network

Another perceived cliché, but your network truly is your net worth, so look after those relationships. Following that initial conversation and connection, continue to nurture and grow those relationships.

**Offer help:** When you're developing long-lasting relationships, it should be mutually beneficial and not just one-sided. Make sure you're offering your expertise, making introductions and finding ways to also help those in your network.

**Be genuine:** Don't just reach out to those in your network when you need something. Show a genuine interest in what they do. Congratulate them when they share their successes, check in on them if you haven't been in contact for a while.

**Follow up and follow through:** Closely linked to the above, make sure you follow up with those in your network and if you say you are going to do something for someone, be a person of your word and do it.

## RESOURCE: NETWORKING

As discussed, there are numerous different ways to network and engage with people, whether in person or online. Below I have provided a few email templates that I created which have helped me when reaching out to people. This worked for me but feel free to adapt to your own personal context.

**Scenario 1: You're reaching out to someone you admire in your industry for the first time as you're keen to learn more about what they do and hopefully schedule a meeting**

*Hi* [insert name],
*I hope all is well and you're having a good week!*
   *My name is* [insert name] *and I am a* [insert your occupation and company].
   *I'm reaching out because* [insert the reason you are reaching out]

This should be made up of:
- How you became aware of them, e.g., you saw something they posted online.
- A little flattery. Express your admiration of them and why, e.g., a particular skill and expertise they are known for, their achievements.

- Personal context. What is the connection between them and you for, e.g., are you looking to pivot into the industry this person is in?

*If possible, I'd love to meet for a coffee or connect online to learn more about* [insert subject matter area, skill, experience etc] *if this would be okay?*

*I look forward to hearing from you.*
*Kind Regards*
*[insert name]*

**Scenario 2: You're reaching out to someone for the first time as you would like them to participate or contribute to a project or initiative you're working on (could be work or non-work related)**

*Hi* [insert name]
  *I hope all is well and you're having a good week!*
  *My name is* [insert name] *and I am a* [insert your occupation and company].
  *I'm reaching out because I'm currently working on* [explain your product/project/initiative. Refer to other individuals or organisations involved and the overall goal and vision] *and I'd love for you to be part of it.*
  *The reason I'm reaching out to you specifically is because* [insert the reason].

Like the above, this should be made up of:

- How you became aware of them, e.g., you saw something they posted online.

- A little flattery. Why do you want them specifically to be part of what you are working on?
- The requirement. What will their involvement entail, e.g., a contribution for your book, a thirty-minute interview for your podcast/YouTube video, speak at an event you're hosting or more. If they reply to your email and agree, you can provide more specific details.

*By* [refer to their potential involvement], *you will* [insert what they can also gain such as financial payment, access to well-known organisations or more]. *The aim is to show that this will be mutually beneficial.*

*I have attached* [insert something which gives further information, e.g., a link to your website, podcast, YouTube, informational document etc.] *which hopefully provides more insight, but feel free to ask any questions.*

*I can't express how much I would love for you to be involved and I'm more than willing to be flexible around your schedule. I look forward to hearing from you.*

*Kind Regards*
[insert name]

**Scenario 3: You're reaching out to someone you engaged with at a networking event (this can be adapted if the event was virtual)**

*Hi* [insert name]
*I hope all is well and you're having a good week!*
*My name is* [insert name] *and we recently swapped details at* [insert name of event].

*It was great meeting you, and funnily enough I came across this* [insert resource e.g., podcast, article, book] *which reminded me of the conversation we had on* [insert topic] *which I really enjoyed.*

*It would be great to keep in touch! I'm going to be attending* [provide details for another networking event] *which might be of interest to you, and I look forward to speaking again soon.*

*Kind Regards*

[insert name]

# DIONNE CONDOR-FARRELL

*Senior Developer, Transport for London*

Dionne is an award-winning leader, senior developer, tech coach, mentor and public speaker, who is passionate about improving diversity in tech. As a senior developer, she specialises in Android app development and Java and open-source technologies and has been working in the technology industry for twenty years. She has experience of developing a variety of bespoke Java web applications, Java API services and mobile apps for the public transport, education, and employment services industries.

Dionne is passionate about improving diversity in tech, and especially encouraging more women and people from Black Asian Minority Ethnic backgrounds into tech (as well as retaining them) in an industry commonly viewed as very mature white male dominated. She helps women in established non-tech careers with a desire to transition into hands on tech roles through mentoring and coaching. She also helps employers to build relationships with underrepresented communities to attract diverse tech talent.

*Dear reader,*

*If you are reading this you are probably at an important time in your life, making decisions on which direction to go in your career. Know that the decisions you make now will not be set in stone.*

*As a senior developer, I believe my university education (a BSc Business Information Technology degree) set a good foundation for my career. It introduced me to the importance of information technology in supporting business growth, as well as introducing the wonders of the World Wide Web. However, I don't believe it made me job ready. I learned far more to prepare me for a real career in tech from the internet than anything I ever gained from my degree course. However, there are many things that your university degree and the internet cannot prepare you for, and there are a lot of lessons I have learned from experience, that I wish I knew at the start of my career, such as:*

***It's okay not to know what direction you want to go.*** *In the first few years of my career, tech innovations and updates weren't very speedy, so my employer expected us to learn everything and anything about a particular version of a tech product and be the Subject Matter Expert (SME) of that product. Not anymore. Tech now changes quicker than the weather, so you will constantly be researching and experimenting with different tech, and therefore your interests and ambitions will change rapidly too, opening up a wealth of opportunities to change direction numerous times during your career, and fall into an area of tech you truly enjoy working with. Even if you are not interested in pursuing a whole tech career, sorry to break it to you, but tech will influence many parts of your chosen career, so learning tech skills is a must.*

*Don't sweat it if you don't know for sure what you want to get into from the get-go. Consider doing something like a graduate scheme or apprenticeship that will give you the opportunity to try different areas of a business (e.g., during my two-year graduate scheme, I moved teams every six months and tried system testing, business analysis, requirements, and programming teams before deciding to specialise in programming at the end of the scheme). The key is to keep trying things until you find an area you enjoy and become passionate about. Also consider getting yourself a mentor who can support you during your career.*

*__I am a unicorn.__ It is likely that you will be the only Black person, or one of a handful, in the company you choose to work for or in the department you end up in. For me there has rarely been anyone that looks like me doing hands-on tech roles in any of the four companies I have worked for in the last twenty years. It's always been the same landscape and vibe, so I naturally ended up being forced to become 'one of the lads' or feel isolated. In recent years, I've had the pleasure of working with just four Black male developers, but I think I must have worked with only one other Black female developer in the last twenty years, and that was a contractor on a six-month gig back in 2008.*

*Also, I've had to get used to shocked looks and disbelief when I tell people I am a developer. A regular comment I get is 'Noooo way! But you look . . . normal' or 'why don't you consider people management instead?'. I kid you not, I have been mistaken for a PA, manager, secretary, tea lady, cleaner and, not that there's anything wrong with any of those jobs, but couldn't it be possible that I can be Black, female and a developer all at the same time?*

*After all these years, I've finally learned to accept that I am indeed a unicorn, and I have learned to embrace it. Being your authentic self is important in these types of situations, as many* who are 'the only one' find themselves conflicted with conforming versus bringing your true self to work. My advice to you is if you want to keep your sanity, being authentic is the key. If you work for an employer who does not value diverse cultures and you do not feel comfortable bringing your true self to work, then that is not the company for you, and you should consider somewhere else that does welcome, support and truly embrace diversity.

**You must believe in yourself first.** Imposter syndrome is a killer of dreams. You must believe in yourself, before expecting your employer or anyone else to believe in you. Speak up in meetings, share your ideas and concerns and be a voice to be heard. Usually there are no right or wrong answers and there's probably about ten different ways to solve a problem, so if you have an idea share it amongst your team and get the recognition you deserve.

**Learn the art of networking.** I've always been on the shy side when I initially meet people, and I have learned the hard way by losing out on many opportunities because of this. Whether it's face to face or via an online community it is important to build up your experience of networking and get comfortable with it FAST! Even if you hate it, push yourself to find an informal group to break your networking fears to start with. There are many free events each week around the UK and virtually, and many communities to join through community sites like meetup. com. Many job opportunities have been identified, collaborations started, and tech problems solved through a quick chat with someone new at a networking event. It also definitely pays to tell an authentic story of yourself when networking.

*Make work-life balance a habit from the start.* Your health and well-being are the most important assets you have. Without it you will not fulfil your potential in any career you choose. Working late hours to impress your boss is a waste of your life and rarely helps you to climb the career ladder quicker. Adopting a work-life balance habit early on in your career will help you to stay focused and help you survive the years to come. Find activities and hobbies that you enjoy that can raise your heart rate a little every day and build it into your schedule. Remember, your health and well-being are your most important assets.

*You need to take responsibility for your own career development.* I will say that a little bit louder: YOU need to take responsibility for your own career development. Don't rely on your employer to map out your career development plan, organise courses and constantly pay for it all. Some employers are great and will flash the cash every year or two, but a lot of them will choose the paths or courses relative to their agenda only, and not necessarily the ones that meet your career desires. You need to be the author of your career journey and you MUST invest time and, in some cases, some of your own money into your continuous development and education, or your skills will eventually go downhill. Climbing up that hill once you realise you're near the bottom is a bittersweet pill to swallow; when you realise your skills are five years behind due to the ageing tech or methodologies your company is still using or your skills are no longer marketable, so just don't do it to yourself. Invest in yourself, both in tech and soft skills, and keep the opportunities knocking at your door until you're ready to answer them. REMEMBER, your career development is your responsibility.

*I hope by sharing some of the lessons I have learnt during my career, it will help you to navigate your career without making many of the mistakes I made early on. I wish you the very best of luck on your career journey.*

Dionne Condor-Farrell

# AKIMA PAUL LAMBERT

*Partner, Hogan Lovells*

A Grenadian national by birth, Akima Paul Lambert is a high stakes dispute resolution practitioner. Her specialism is large, multijurisdictional disputes on behalf of high-net-worth individuals and large corporates. She is a specialist High Court litigator and also has experience in commercial and investment treaty arbitration. She is also dual-qualified in the UK and in the U.S.

Akima is ranked in the UK's leading legal directories as being 'professional', 'brilliant' and 'dedicated'.

She has a strong commitment to diversity, equity and inclusion and was listed as an EMpower Ethnic Minority Future Leader Role Model 2020, recognising her significant contribution to ethnic minority inclusion at work. She was also named in 2021 as Senior Leader of the Year in the Professional Services Category by the Black British Business Awards, the UK's premier awards for Black British talent. She also speaks frequently on climate change and the importance of pro bono, and was nominated as one of Hogan Lovells' Pro Bono Fellows.

Akima is also a serving diplomat and serves as a Grenada's Ambassador to the Holy See.

**Tell us about yourself?** *I am Akima Paul Lambert, a Partner at Hogan Lovells International LLP. I was born and raised in*

Grenada, in the Caribbean. I am a complex commercial disputes specialist, conducting litigation and arbitration for large multi-national companies in England and other jurisdictions.

I moved to the UK in 2001, to Cambridge, at the age of 18 having never lived outside my town of 10,000 people, let alone the perimeters of the 133 square foot island. I missed my family terribly. It was a tremendous culture shock. Everything was new and everything and everyone seemed cold. I essentially went from the warmth and jocularity of island life into a completely new tempo with no preparation. I couldn't get used to the food and I was freezing all the time. I remember researching whether I could transfer to the University of the West Indies.

I was extremely lucky as I soon made some very good friends at my college (Clare College) and the other Caribbean students in the Caribbean society took me under their collective wings. We are still friends today. Crucially, I soon discovered London and its Grenadian/Caribbean diaspora, so I found my village, so to speak. I later threw myself into Cambridge life writing for the Cambridge Student and running in the local student elections. I was then a glutton for punishment, choosing to move to Paris as part of my degree a mere two years later, to begin the cycle of adaptation and orientation once more.

**What was your motivation to get into the Legal sector and how did you secure your first opportunity within this space?** *In 1998, I won the regional award for the best results in the Caribbean, and I later won one of Grenada's island scholarships for the best results at A level. Winning an island scholarship meant that I was allowed to pursue whatever avenue of study I desired.*

*I chose to be a lawyer because it combined my passion for*

advocacy with my desire to connect with others. To be honest, in my ultra-Caribbean family there were only two options- to be a lawyer or a doctor as they were regarded as the most stable professions. Being a lawyer was a good fit to my personality.

My route into law is rather boring. I secured my first job as a trainee in the usual way. I had excellent grades when I left university, so I applied to quite a few firms. I completed a few vacation schemes and was lucky to receive offers from all of them. In the end I chose Hogan Lovells because the people there seemed to like their job. That was important to me, even at that stage. I grew up in a home where my mother liked her job very much and I wanted the same for myself.

**Did your time at Cambridge prepare you in any way for joining the working world and if so, how?** *Attending Cambridge prepared me somewhat for the working world in that I can navigate new environments easily and comfortably, especially when I am the 'only one' in the room.*

*I do, however, feel that I was not fully prepared for the world of work. At Cambridge, my competence was a given. There is no place to hide in one-to-one supervisions. I was treated as I was: like a highly intelligent student. I did really well and was receiving high firsts and 2:1s in most subjects.*

*I found that in the world of work my competence was not a given and I had to prove myself at every opportunity. There was no presumption of competence even with a Cambridge degree. So, in that sense, I was not prepared.*

**There has been a lot of research which shows that Black women who wear their natural hair in the workplace are perceived to be**

less professional than their white counterparts. **As someone who wears their natural hair at work, what advice would you give to Black women who don't feel empowered to do so or worry about the impact it may have on their career?** *I decided to wear my hair as it grows at work when my niece started saying that she wanted 'down hair' like her friends (meaning straight hair). I wanted her to feel a sense of pride in the way her hair grew naturally and see that this was possible for women in the professions. I love showing up every day to work wearing my hair the way it is naturally.*

*I did, however, have to battle internalised fears. The fact that I decided to wear my hair in locs meant that I had to face up to the fact that some people may have negative assumptions and additional biases. I had to decide what was more important to me. I chose showing up as my authentic self. To date, I only know one other partner at a law firm who wears her hair in locs: there is a stereotype of what 'partner hair' looks like.*

*I do, however, strongly feel that it is a choice and that Black women have enough on their plates to worry about without adding guilt for not showing up with their natural hair at work. To those who want to, I would say, give it a try. It is not as big a deal as you think it is.*

*I focus on making a positive and memorable first impression with my intellect, diligence and wit; my hair becomes the least of my worries in pitches and with new clients.*

**You are the co-founder of Creating Pathways, a cross mentoring programme for mid-level BAME associates at City firms. What inspired the creation of this programme?** *A few years ago, Pamela Dusu (a Senior Project Development Lawyer) and I were in* *conversation: we observed that fewer young Black lawyers seemed to be coming through the ranks. We saw what the studies now say: Black lawyers were leaving private practice earlier and at much higher rates than their peers. We had both been contacted by bright minority trainees and associates who had similar concerns. Some had failed to qualify, others had qualified but did not feel included, many more had become disillusioned because their sense of otherness had heightened. We wanted to help but we knew there was no easy solution.*

*We put our heads together to research what was needed. We came up with the idea of a cross-firm mentoring programme that would allow for structured career intervention at an early stage. We put the idea to Paulette Mastin (Chair of the Black Solicitors Network) who offered support. Dozens of senior lawyers in private practice and in-house followed.*

**Research from the Law Society showed that Black Lawyers make up less than 1% of partners. As a Partner at your firm, what do you see as the main factors throughout your career that led to your promotion to this position?** *I have been very lucky to have done good work over the years which has allowed me to develop the competencies needed to distinguish myself in this field. A lot of hard work is a given. During the pandemic year, I conducted a twelve-week trial completely remotely, with a very small team. The importance of resilience cannot be understated.*

*However, I do think that having good mentors, allies, advocates and sponsors assisted me tremendously.*

**What challenges have you experienced in your career and how have you overcome them?** *As a Black woman, I know that I am* *hyper visible. There is a sense of being under the microscope a lot more. I have tended to manage this by always doing my best and seeking to do better at each stage. I always ask for feedback that I can take on board. My advice would be to profit from the hyper visibility. Be remembered for the right reasons- your diligence, your competence and your ability to build relationships.*

**What have been some of your career highs and lows?** *Getting through the rigorous Hogan Lovells promotions round to be appointed Partner was a definite highlight. The fact that I managed to do this at a time when my daughter was only a few weeks old fills me with pride.*

*As a litigator I get a thrill from arguing and winning cases. There is nothing quite like being in court, and I have been lucky to have managed several cases that have made it before the Court of Appeal. My recent win at the Black British Business Awards as Senior Leader of the Year was also a definite highlight.*

*I have been fortunate to have had few low points in my career. Leaving Lovells was a low point at the time. I really loved the firm and the people I worked with but unfortunately, the work I was doing at the time was not a great fit for me. Fast forward to today and I'm back, working with great people and work better aligned to me.*

**What has been the best career advice given to you?** *The best career advice given to me was to seek out a sponsor. Sponsorship makes all the difference: having someone who can advocate in a room when you are not present is invaluable in building a career in the legal sector and other professions.*

**What advice would you give to Black students and professionals starting out and advancing in their careers?** *I would advise Black students and professionals to be resilient. It is very easy when you see the statistics to become disheartened and frustrated before you even embark on your journey. It is, however, a journey. It is a marathon and not a sprint. And along the way, be willing to learn.*

# CHRISTINE OHURUOGU MBE

*British Track and Field Athlete*

Christine Ohuruogu is Britain's most successful female athlete ever. She competed internationally in athletics from 2003 to her retirement in 2017, winning seventeen major athletics medals. Between 2006 and 2008, she held the Olympic, World and Commonwealth 400m Champion titles at the same time. She captained the British athletics team on many occasions and continues to act as a mentor to the top British athletes.

Christine was the Olympic 400m Champion in 2008, silver medallist in 2012 and took bronze in the 4x400m relay in 2008 and 2016. She won the individual 400m title at the World Championships in 2007 and 2013 and took a further six World Championships medals in the 4x400m. She was the 2006 Commonwealth Games 400m Champion and won 4x400m golds at the World and European Indoor Championships.

In 2013, she was awarded the Sky Sports and Sunday Times British Sportswoman of the Year, Cosmopolitan magazine Ultimate Sportsperson of the Year and was shortlisted for the BBC Sports Personality of the Year.

Christine has a degree in Linguistics from University College London and recently completed her law degree at Queen Mary, University of London. She played netball for England at under-seventeen and under-nineteen levels before taking up athletics at the age of sixteen. In 2009, she was appointed Member of the Order of the British Empire (MBE) in the New Year Honours.

**Tell us about yourself?** *My parents were born in Nigeria and came to the UK in the early eighties. My siblings and I were subsequently born in London.*

*Academics were very important growing up; we were expected to do well at school. I always loved active play when I was young and, in my teens, played every school sport I could manage. I started playing club netball at fourteen. I was able to combine my sports and education, which I think stopped my parents from being too dismissive about me playing sport.*

**What was your motivation to get into sports and how did you get your start in this space?** *I didn't have a real motivation to get into sports per se. I was an active child growing up. I loved running around and playing out with my friends. At primary school I relished PE lessons and couldn't wait for after school sports clubs to start. I started netball at primary school and then my love for playing netball followed me to secondary school. I just loved being active and sports was where I could channel my love of movement.*

**Since retiring from athletics, you've completed a second degree in law (following your first one in linguistics). What made you decide to go back and study and how important do you think it is to plan ahead for when you retire or if your sports career unexpectedly ends?** *I had decided on a career in law and to begin the journey towards becoming a barrister I had to go back to school and get a degree in law.*

*It's not necessarily important to have a plan, but it's important to have an idea of where your strengths lie and then the areas that you might need to work on alongside your athletics career. For example, if you enjoy talking and presenting ideas, you think you might like to pursue a career in presenting, and in preparation for that you will need to seek out opportunities where you can speak in front of people. If you might like to be a blogger, are you creating blogs in your spare time? Draw on ideas, see what you would like to do, know what your skillset looks like, what things can you improve upon while you are an athlete. I don't always think you should plan ahead, but it helps to think about what is ahead.*

**You've spent a large part of your life successfully committing yourself to be the best possible athlete, which must've taken a lot of discipline and motivation. How did you stay motivated and not allow yourself to stray from routine when you're for example injured and things aren't going so well?** *I always put myself in a position of control and that is, ultimately that I can do what ever it is I would like to do. So, if I want to get a job done, I can choose to go ahead and do it or I can choose that I won't do it. The fact that you acknowledge you have a choice is powerful. It is helpful to surround yourself with people who can support you and keep encouraging you. You need people who will recognise when you are flagging a little bit and will gently remind you of what your goals are and where you're planning to go. You can get too stuck in your own way which stops you from clearly seeing your goals.*

*You have to be mature enough when you undertake any kind of task that it's going to be multi-faceted, there are going to be times when it goes really well and there are going to be times when it doesn't go well at all. With that understanding you have to keep going. I always gave myself two options. If you don't want to do it then quit. If you don't want to keep training, then quit. But the thing is I'm too stubborn and so I'm not going to quit. I keep going.*

*In times of injury, I always had a good team around me. So even if I was injured, my therapist would be working above and beyond to get me fit. When they were working 100% to get me fit, I needed to get on with the job. It was encouraging for me to know that my team was working hard to get me back on my feet.*

**You show a lot of support to up-and-coming athletes, how important do you think it is for sports people who have had a successful career like yourself to offer guidance and support to those coming up?** *It's important because as I look back on my career I see that I was able to learn my craft through the eyes of other athletes. It was not necessarily the case that I did things exactly how they did it, but they provided a template which are important in providing a guide as to how things can be done. It's also a way to show you how things shouldn't be done too! I hope that I am able to provide reference points for the athletes, and not necessarily tell them to do things the way I did. I think I am a unique athlete with a unique way of doing things and all other athletes are the same with their different approaches and talents. With a template an athlete can see a variety of options.*

*However, if you do think they are going off-kilter in a way that may not be beneficial to them, then because of our experiences, we can guide them in the right way and tell them 'I don't think that is a good option for you' or 'I don't think that is going to work out well' and try to suggest another path. At the same time, you can say: 'I haven't really seen that before but I see something in you that you could carry that off, so you go and we'll support you and if I can find any more information to help you on your journey then I can pitch in.'*

*In summary, we can provide them with options and give them guidance when things are not going so well. We've all been there. We've all seen and experienced a load of things. We can help.*

**Outside of the performance aspect of being an athlete, what else do you think is important for athletes to focus and be mindful of and why?** *I think it always helpful to be mindful of the bigger picture. I know sport is a world in itself and I've noticed that more than ever since I have retired. I miss the crazy word of sport and nothing can even come close to it from what I've seen. It's a different world. But you always have to be mindful of a bigger picture. Sport is just one aspect, and you have to be careful how you define sport in the grand scheme of things and also how you allow sport to define you as person. I say be mindful of that because that's where usually people can find themselves straying into trouble and creating unnecessary pressure and stress for themselves. The big picture is that we have a great opportunity. We get to do something that we love every day and not many people have that chance to go and compete for their country or to run as fast as we do or jump as high as we do, so I think it's always good to have that in perspective, especially when things go wrong.*

*I think it's important to remember that what we have is a beautiful opportunity to really push our bodies in a way that's just not done and that's awesome. Whether you fail or whether you succeed it's still a pretty awesome feat to recognise anyway. I think it's important to focus on wellbeing, focus on being honest athletes, honest to yourself and honest to others, maintaining integrity in your work. Wellbeing is focusing on how you're doing and to be self-aware of how you come across to other athletes. Be self-aware of how you are as a person, not just as an athlete, and don't allow the pressures of the sport to turn you into something or someone you wouldn't want to be friends with. See the bigger picture; don't allow sport to cloud your judgement.*

*Use sport as something that can make you better and not something that can overwhelm you or consume you. Use sport to encourage you to be better not worse as a human being.*

**What have been some of your career highs and lows?** *I have had many great high points. Being able to compete in my hometown of Stratford in 2012 and winning an Olympic medal there was a particularly memorable moment for me as my whole family – my seven siblings and my parents were in the stadium cheering me on. In terms of low points, I have faced many challenges. Bouncing back requires a good support team. Surround yourself with people that will provide you with a safe place to decamp and rebuild.*

**What has been the best career advice given to you?** *The one that comes to mind is, 'it is never as bad as you think it is'.*

**What advice would you give to Black students and professionals starting out and advancing their careers?** *Always set out with hope in your step. Hope and passion will get you through anything.*

# ALICE DEARING

*British Swimmer and Co-founder of The Black Swimming Association*

Born and raised in Birmingham, Alice Dearing started swimming when she was eight years old after her mum saw an advert in the local newspaper for swimming lessons.

In 2016, Alice announced herself globally, winning the World Junior Open Water Championships, to compliment her Gold medal at European level a few years prior.

Now 24, Alice is one of the top marathon swimmers in the world, and in summer of 2021 achieved a historic moment in British Olympic history as she became the first Black woman to represent Team GB at the Olympic Games.

Her commitment to driving diversity in swimming has been recognised around the world, and as Co-Founder of the Black Swimming Association she has raised awareness of the importance of swimming as a life skill within the Black community, inspiring generations young and old. Away from her philanthropic work Alice recently completed her Masters in Social Media & Political Communications, is an avid gamer, and an afro hair advocate.

*Dear Reader,*

*Our stories all have different beginnings, lessons and experiences. We may often find ourselves at an impasse with different paths available or feeling like there are no options from which you can win from. However, it is these moments of fear, doubt and uncertainty which shape our knowledge giving us the power to make opportunities for our future selves.*

*My name is Alice Dearing, and I am currently twenty-four at the time of writing this. In 2021, I became the first Black woman to swim for Team GB at the Olympic games, competing in the marathon swimming (10KM open water) event. Also, at the time of writing this I am concluding my MA in social media and political communication at Loughborough University with my dissertation due in less than 14 days! I hope this letter can serve as a light to people spanning all generations on a story of resilience and stubbornness. My career is not over yet and I have full aspirations to compete at Paris 2024, but for now I do have some lessons and learnings which I hope can inspire people to be proud of themselves and own what they want to own.*

*Swimming has been a part of my life for over sixteen years now – two thirds of my life thus far and that percentage only grows with each day – and through it I have experienced the lows and highs which every elite athlete contends with.*

*I first learnt to swim aged five in the local council lessons at a pool less than two miles from the home I grew up in in Birmingham. I vividly remember having two of my six armbands taken off me in the 'deep end' of the learning pool and looking at mum with a shocked, fearful smile. After progression through these lessons, my mum got in touch with the swimming club who trained at that pool asking if myself and my thirteen-year-old brother could join. We began with three sessions a week, he in the upper squad and I in the junior one. We both fell in love and were eager to go each week. My first competition was the club* championships, and I just loved the feeling of competing. Eventually we moved on to another club where I first qualified for counties and then regional championships aged nine and ten respectively. The first crossroads I reached with swimming was when I was twelve and was offered a scholarship to an independent school to be able to swim alongside my education. My mum and I jumped at the opportunity, being able to have a good education was key to myself and her as I have always been very career driven and didn't see much potential of getting this from swimming.

Through my teenage years my dedication to swimming ebbed in and out of love and hate. The life of an elite swimmer involves wake ups at 4am, the shock of diving into a cold pool at 5am and mixing a full-time education and social life into it all. There were times that I wanted to back out of it all and just not have to deal with the pressures of training, school and life. My mum was my guardian during this time, she gave me the space I needed but also the confidence to keep going. Knowing that I would be lost and bored without swimming.

We began to see the results of this resilience when I qualified for my first GB team aged fifteen in the 400m Freestyle for the European Junior Championships. That summer when I had turned sixteen, I became European Junior champion in the 5km open water event, this was my second ever open water race and was the beginning of my open water/marathon swimming career. Since then, I have swam at three European championships, three world championships, an Olympic games, numerous world cups and became World Junior Champion in the 10km event in 2016.

Another life change came when I moved to university, seeking to take both swimming and education to the next level to give myself the best chance in the future. I began at Loughborough University in 2015 studying Politics with a minor in English. I graduated with a 2:1 in 2019 and will be finishing my MA in the autumn of 2021.

As mentioned, every athlete goes through difficult times in their career. For myself, this was in 2017 when I lost the two things which I had hinged my self-worth in the sport on: my funding and the squad which I trained in. My heart was broken, and I was unsure of what to do next. I began looking at my CV and getting a part-time job in retail hoping to finish my studies and move out of Loughborough in the next year. Neither of those things happened, I got in and began to swim again as I wasn't ready to move on but didn't know what to do. After a month in limbo, I moved squads to the Loughborough University swimming program and began to love swimming again. Both of the two aspects I had lost brought me pride but also pressure. In my mind I had dropped as low as I could, what else did I have to lose? I could only gain from here. This mindset took me a while to reach but when I did, I began to swim faster, feel happier and step into the person who I wanted to be. Whilst this experience caused me to have some of the worst weeks of my life, it has shaped my way of viewing swimming and life and allowed me to relax and learn to enjoy all it has to offer.

Another large part of my life and experience is the barriers which I hope to help break. In 2019 I helped co-found the Black Swimming Association (BSA) which is advocating to improve inclusion in swimming from grassroots to boardroom level. Racism has no place within life and society and the issues within swimming are decades old and whilst change is happening it is not happening quick enough. That is why the BSA was founded;

to make sure people from all backgrounds and races have access to learn to swim and racist tropes and stereotypes are not being repeated. These barriers range from the stereotypical idea that Black people cannot float effectively due to their bone density – the BSA are conducting research with the RLNI to disprove this notion – to the historical lack of swim caps available which cater to Afro-Caribbean hair. Barriers such as these have prevented Black communities from feeling like swimming is a place for them. However, I want to stress that this is not something which will continue for long. Firstly, there are amazing brands such as SOULCAP who have created larger swimming hats to give room for afro hair to be protected. And secondly, the BSA has made it is mission to encourage and advocate for Black communities, something which the governing bodies of aquatic organisations in the UK are excited to be a part of, working with the BSA to make swimming available to all. This work and changes will not happen overnight, but we endeavour to change the landscape for swimming for Black people, making the barriers an issue of the past.

Through my experience of founding the BSA and using my voice to encourage more to swim it has deepened my understanding of what swimming is and can mean to an individual. It has caused me to realise swimming is more than a sport, it is a life skill and an activity which can just be loved for what it is, not what success or glory it may bring. Encouraging someone to learn to swim 25m is as important as encouraging someone to win Olympic gold as they are both personal achievements.

One aspect of my life which sometimes causes a conflict in my mind is becoming the first Black woman to compete for GB in a swimming event at an Olympic Game. I am hugely proud of this *achievement and wear it as a badge of honour which I hope will inspire people to realise it is do-able! However, there is a part of me – the competitive side – which wants to ensure I am also remembered for my swimming achievements as well as the cultural change I hope I can affect. Also, there is another part of me that is hurt it took so long to get to this stage of a Black woman competing for GB in a swimming event. But it has happened now and that's all that matters! Getting to swim at the prestigious sporting stage in the world is something I'll always be proud of and honestly, shocked I managed to achieve. My aim is to compete again at Paris, stand shoulder to shoulder with the best women in the world and prove that I am one of them. This is already so exciting.*

*I have given a brief summary of my story so far as I hope to display what stubbornness can bring you. There will be people who don't think you can or should, at times one of those people may be yourself – it definitely has been for me! – and those who want you to fail and stay in the space you're expected to be in. But trust in your passion, dedication, and talents. Occupying a space in which there aren't many who look like you, talk like you or identify the same way can be difficult but it is also incredibly empowering both for yourself and others who watch and support that journey. I also want to highlight what teamwork can bring you, my perseverance through swimming came massively from my mum, dad, brothers, and friends who helped me become a better athlete. Find the people in your life who want to support you. And finally, I want to stress the importance of giving yourself downtime and looking after your mind. Managing swimming, education and some form of social life has taught me the importance of time management and allows me to find time where and when I need to relax! Life can be so busy and hectic and often we neglect our mind and own safekeeping for other issues. Find what you need to do to keep healthy and happy.*

*To everyone reading this from across all industries and all walks of life, I wish you the best on your journeys and I hope the issues which you may face do not deter you from why you set out in the first place. Let your lessons and experiences guide you, find those who want to see you succeed and love yourself.*

*Alice*

# NEGOTIATING YOUR SALARY

*(Because money affi mek!!!)*

After nearly two years in my graduate job, I decided I wanted a change. While I was earning great money, promotional prospects were looking good and I really liked the team I was part of, I longed to work on projects that were innovative and tech focused and to get a taste of what it's like to work with external clients.

When I made the move to another company, something which I don't think I told anyone is that I took a significant pay cut in my new role. SIGNIFICANT! In my new role, I was earning less than my graduate scheme salary. Looking back now, what's mad is that I didn't even think about negotiating. I thought that making a career pivot meant by default taking a lower salary (which does not have to be the case). I had spent two years working at one of the world's most prestigious investment banks, completed internships at several other 'big name' corporations, graduated with a 2.1 from a top university and did numerous other activities showcasing my diverse skill set, yet in my head, none of this seemed like enough leverage to negotiate.

## Why Don't We Negotiate?

Thinking about my own reasons, to be honest, I didn't think about negotiating because I didn't think I could; I truly didn't understand my worth, the amount I had already achieved and the value I could bring so early into my career. This was coupled with the fact that I didn't know how to negotiate, it wasn't something I researched or was even aware of at the time. Also, I think as a Black employee, especially when you work for a well-known and established company, you fall into the trap of feeling 'grateful'. I know I definitely did. We know how competitive the application process is and feel like one of the 'chosen ones' when we are selected from thousands of candidates. When we look around and realise that we are the only Black person or one of a few that 'made it' in, we don't want to rock the boat or seem 'ungrateful' by asking for more money, even if it's what we deserve. I think so much of this mindset stems from our families, especially our parents and grandparents. Many of our grandparents came to the UK and were generally happy to get a job and be paid, it didn't matter if their white peers earned more, it was about survival, building a life here and being able to send money back home to help their family. I remember telling my granny about my plans to negotiate for more money and her immediate reaction was '*Oh lardddd, be careful you don't want to upset the people dem and lose your job*'.

As a woman, especially a Black woman, I'm very much aware of the double-barrelled biases we face and how this emerges through tired tropes and negative stereotypes that come with being seen as seeking to challenge and disrupt the status quo. The fear of a negotiation backlash is real. If I was to come across as passionate or expressive during negotiations, I would likely be labelled 'greedy' or 'too pushy'. This could then impact my workplace reputation and hinder future promotional opportunities. The margin for error in salary negotiation is so small, especially when you're Black. According to research, Black professionals in Britain are twice as likely to be turned down for a pay rise after negotiation than white professionals.[*]

## The Impact?

Companies are knowingly underpaying Black employees and they are banking on the fact that for some of the reasons I have mentioned above, we won't ask for more.

According to the *Ethnicity Pay Gaps: 2018* report from the ONS (Office for National Statistics), white British workers earn on an average 3.8% more than all other ethnicities and this increases to 20% for some ethnic groups.[†] UK-born African employees earned 7.7% less than white British employees with similar education and job characteristics. Following the release of these figures, Kathleen Henehan, a policy analyst at the think tank Resolution Foundation, explained: 'BAME groups continue to face significant pay gaps, compared to white workers. What's more, these pay penalties hold even

---

[*] Robertwalters.co.uk. 'Driving Diversity and Inclusion in the Workplace.' (March 2021). Retrieved from: https://www.robertwalters.co.uk/hiring/campaigns/diversity-and-inclusion.html?utm_source=PR
[†] Office for National Statistics. 'Ethnicity Pay Gaps in Great Britain: 2018.' (9 July 2019). Retrieved from: https://www.ons.gov.uk/employmentandlabourmarket/peopleinwork/earningsandworkinghours/articles/ethnicitypaygapsingreatbritain/2018.

after accounting for workers' qualifications, experience and the types of jobs they do."

The disparities also exist in the US, where there is far more data, especially when you account for the intersection of race and gender. According to research from PayScale, for every dollar a white man earns, a Black man earns 87 cents, which is less than male workers of other races.[†] The gap increases for Black women, who earn 62 cents for every dollar a white man earns, trailing behind white women who earn 79 cents, and everyone else.[‡]

Looking at the research in the US, a report commissioned by Lean In to understand more about the pay gap for Black women discovered:

- The most educated Black women, Black women with bachelors and advanced degrees, experience the widest gap, earning 35% less than white men on average.[§]
- Black women are paid less than white men even when doing the same job.

* Resolutionfoundation.org. 'Black and ethnic minority workers continue to face significant pay penalties.' (9 July 2019). Retrieved from https://www.resolutionfoundation.org/press-releases/Black-and-ethnic -minority-workers-continue-to-face-significant-pay-penalties/
† Payscale.com. 'Racial Wage Gap for Men.' (7 May 2019). Retrieved from: https://www.payscale.com/data/racial-wage-gap-for-men
‡ Nationalpartnership.org. 'Black Women and the Wage Gap.' (March 2021). Retrieved from: https://www.nationalpartnership.org/our-work/ resources/economic-justice/fair-pay/african-american-women-wage- gap.pdf
§ Leanin.org. 'Black women aren't paid fairly and that hits harder in an economic crisis'. (August 2018). Retrieved from: https://leanin.org/ data-about-the-gender-pay-gap-for-black-women

- Despite Black women asking for pay rises and promotion at the same rate as white women, they are still less likely to be successful. For every 100 white men promoted to manager, only fifty-eight Black women are promoted.

**Black Women and the Pay Gap**

Both race and gender mean Black women are the victims of dual discrimination when it comes to being fairly paid. The London School of Economics (LSE) Inclusion Initiative [?] undertook analysis of pay over the last seventeen years to discover who was in the top percentage of earners, and they found that regardless of whether they are born in the UK, Black women have the lowest probabilities of being in top earners.* 1.3% of white men born in the UK are in the top 1%. This drops to 0.2% for UK-born white women and to less than 0.1% for Black women born in the UK. When you take into consideration other factors such as age, marital status, education and occupation, UK-born Black women are still disproportionately affected by pay disparity and when looking only at the Black and ethnic minority population, research found that UK-born Black women are still less likely to be in the top 1% of earners.

The reason these disparities exist are simple. Employers don't value the work of Black employees; we are not seen as equals. Companies pay us what they believe we are worth and not surprisingly, Black employees are always deemed to be worth less

* Lse.ac.uk. 'Black women are lease likely to be among UK's top earners'. (3 March 2021). Retrieved from: https://www.lse.ac.uk/News/Latest-news-from-LSE/2021/c-March-21/Black-women-are-least-likely-to-be-among-UKs-top-earners

than everyone else. It's not because we lack motivation or will-power – research conducted by the Policy Institute at King's College London revealed that 13% of Brits believe that is the reason why Black people earn less.[*] The truth is the opposite. Black employees are highly ambitious; research from the *Business in the Community: Black Voices* report highlighted that 74% of Black employees want to progress in their careers, compared to 42% of white employees.[†]

The data is further compounded by the fact that Black employees are more likely to be in lower paid, insecure jobs[‡] and that we aren't being promoted at the same rate as our peers, especially into senior roles, which means we therefore aren't seeing those significant salary increases and bonuses.

While many companies are required by law to publish their gender pay gap every year, this is not currently the case for ethnicity pay gap reporting, which tells us everything we need to know regarding how much of a priority this is to the government; it's not. We can't afford to wait for initiatives that may never come, instead we must take a proactive role in trying to influence what we are paid.

[*] King's College London. 'Unequal Britain. Attitudes to inequalities are Covid-19.' (February 2021). Retrieved from: https://www.kcl.ac.uk/policy-institute/assets/unequal-britain.pdf

[†] Business in the Community. 'The Race at Work: Black Voices report.' (23 August 2020). Retrieved: https://www.bitc.org.uk/report/race-at-work-black-voices-report/

[‡] TUC.org.uk. 'Insecure Work and ethnicity.' (2 June 2017). Retrieved: https://www.tuc.org.uk/research-analysis/reports/insecure-work-and-ethnicity

## The Turning Point

When I decided to change jobs again, this time you better believe that I had my negotiation hat on. I had a very clear salary expectation in my mind. This number was a combination of a few things:

- A calculation of my living expenses and what I needed to not only survive, but thrive.
- Research I had done around the average salaries in the role and industry, at the level I wanted to move into and for my location.
- My experience and skill level at that point which I could bring to a new employer.

I told myself that if I wasn't being offered a particular number or anything near, I would negotiate and I did! For two years, I earned substantially less than when I graduated from university, and sure, sometimes when making career changes you have to take a few steps back to take several steps forward. But I didn't even fight for myself, even when I had the grounds to do so. The impact on my life as a twenty-three-year-old at the time still living at home, with few bills to pay was minimal but as we go through life, that pay gap increases, in parallel with the growing number of responsibilities (many with financial implications) that we take on.

We really play ourselves when we don't negotiate to be paid our worth. It's so much more than just that monthly pay cheque we receive, but it's the impact of the income we lose out on and how that affects the quality of our lives today and in the future. For those of us that came of age and haven't been able to tap into the bank of mum and dad or are the first people in our families to 'make it' and so we use a significant portion of our salaries to support our household (the 'Black Tax'), we understand how the pay inequalities our parents faced, in addition to other aspects of systemic racism, have to some extent disadvantaged us. According to research gathered by Lean In, Black women in the US lose out on almost one million dollars of lost income over their lifetime, when compared to white men.[*] That's a large sum of money that could've been saved, invested, used to create businesses, to access better health care options and much more. That monthly pay cheque which many of us don't even question, our means of living, how we survive – we need to ask ourselves if we are truly being paid our worth.

Asking for and receiving a fair pay which is reflective of our skills and experience and is the same as our peers in the same roles and levels as us can provide us with an enhanced quality of life and security which our community has been denied for so long. We need to negotiate because when we don't, we enable these pay disparities to manifest in the form of other inequalities in our lives, as we can see in the data. Research shows that for every £1 a white British family has; Black Caribbean households have about 20p and Black African households have 10p.[†] Black African households have the second-lowest rate of home ownership[‡] and Black pensioner

* Leanin.org. 'Black women aren't paid fairly and that hits harder in an economic crisis'. (August 2018). Retrieved from: https://leanin.org/data-about-the-gender-pay-gap-for-black-women
† Runnymedetrust.org. 'The Colour of Money.' (April 2020). Retrieved from: https://www.runnymedetrust.org/projects-and-publications/employment-3/the-colour-of-money.html
‡ Gov.uk. 'Home Ownership'. (4 February 2020). Retrieved from: https://www.ethnicity-facts-figures.service.gov.uk/housing/owning-and-renting/home-ownership/latest

families receive almost £200 less than white British pensioner families.[*]

While these disparities aren't solely the result of being underpaid, it's easy to see how it could contribute. When we negotiate our salary, we are negotiating for better present and future outcomes for ourselves.

## Myths About Salary Negotiation

There are so many myths about salary negotiation and talking about money in the workplace more generally:

- **You need tonnes of experience to be able to negotiate:** This isn't true. What you need is the ability to take the experience you do have and craft a great pitch and narrative around it, centering it on your USP (Unique Selling Point) and achievements within your current role, or how your skill set and experience can bring value to a role in another organisation.

- **It's all about the money:** Although I have spent most of this chapter talking about negotiating from a financial standpoint, it's worth looking at your overall benefits package to see what else is of value to you and can be negotiated, e.g. vacation days, learning and development allowance, health insurance and, especially since this pandemic started, flexible and remote-working arrangements.

[*] The Guardian. 'Financial inequality: The ethnicity gap in pay, wealth and property'. (June 2020). Retrieved from: https://www.theguardian.com/money/2020/jun/20/financial-inequality-the-ethnicity-gap-in-pay-wealth-and-property

- **We shouldn't talk about money with our peers**: This is probably the most harmful because it's us not talking about salary that makes it's easier for these companies to get away with not paying us fairly. We need to be talking with each other and our non-Black colleagues, male and female to see how we fare in comparison. Knowing that your white colleague Susan who does the same job as you is paid £10,000 more than you every year, despite having the same amount of experience (maybe you have slightly more) and similar qualifications is massively important when navigating the salary negotiation conversation because it gives you leverage to question these disparities. This level of openness in many ways goes against what many of us were told growing up within African and Caribbean households, in respect to not 'chatting our business', and the topic of money in itself is still very taboo in our society, although the rise in podcasts, books and financial literacy platforms are helping (@blackgirlfinanceuk on Instagram is a personal favourite of mine). However, staying silent is not helping us and is feeding the issue. We need to speak up.

- **If you earn a lot of money already, you shouldn't negotiate**: You might be thinking that since you earn enough money to pay your bills, save, and live a good life, why would you need to negotiate a pay rise. Isn't that greedy? I'm here to tell you that it's not. Just because you're not struggling financially, it doesn't mean that you are being paid your worth. I came across a twitter thread where this woman explained that she was earning a salary of $100,000 which she thought was great and later found out that many of her peers in the same role as her where she worked were making $125,000. She didn't need that extra $25,000 but the most important point is that she wasn't being paid fairly. It's so easy to blindly accept a certain salary because it might be more money than we've earnt before, it might be more than what your friends and family are making so it seems like a lot, but that doesn't mean it's a reflection of what you bring to your organization and role. Never settle.

**Actress Jessica Chastain Helped Octavia Spencer Make Five Times Her Salary**

During a panel discussion at the 2018 Sundance Film Festival, Oscar-winning actress Octavia Spencer shared how fellow actress Jessica Chastain helped her negotiate a salary five times what she was initially offered for a film they were starring in together. Spencer explained that during a conversation between the two actresses on pay equity between men and women in Hollywood, she highlighted that women of colour earn substantially less than white women. When they spoke to the specifics of their salaries, Chastain expressed that she was unaware of the pay disparity between them and she promised Spencer a favoured nations agreement which meant Chastain's deal was tied to Spencer's, meaning they would earn the same. A week later, Spencer was making five times her asking salary. After the panel discussion went viral on social media, Spencer tweeted: I am making 5x my salary bc Jessica stood with me. I don't know what or if it cost her anything as far as her rate, I just know she stood with me, and am eternally grateful. (sic)

## Tips for Negotiating Your Salary

### Pre-negotiation
### 1. Do your research

If you don't go into a salary negotiation meeting knowing what your market value is, you allow for your manager or recruiter to control the conversation, so make sure you do your research.

If you're applying for a new job externally, find out what the average salary is for the role you're applying to, at your desired company, industry, the level you're applying for and location. Websites like Glassdoor, PayScale and LinkedIn Premium can be useful. These will give you a pretty good idea as to what salary you should be expecting. Talking to others in your desired field might provide even more accuracy and similarly when negotiating internally, asking your peers what they earn will be massively beneficial.

When negotiating for that pay rise, your research should include looking at your existing benefits package to see if there is anything else you'd be happy to negotiate.

Understanding who the key decision-makers are with regards to getting that pay rise is also key. Something I've learnt is that very often, the person you have that conversation with is not the person who is responsible for the budget where your pay would come from. While the conversation may happen with your manager, do they make the final decision or is it someone else or a committee? If you know who these people are, try to get on their radar beforehand so they know of you and the great work you've done.

Assess the current environment in your organisation and use your better judgement to decide if you've picked the right time to have this conversation. For example, if your company just announced a massive cost-cutting exercise due to poor company performance, you might reconsider whether now is the best time to have that conversation.

## 2. Come up with your number

As I mentioned earlier, I did my own calculation of what I needed to earn to live comfortably (not only being able to pay my bills but save and enjoy life) and I paired that with insights I gained from researching the average salary for the role I was applying to (considering the industry, experience, location etc). I came up with a range and here I would say make sure your range is higher than your desired figure. I say this because if your desired salary is £45,000 and you give a range in your negotiation of £40,000 to £50,000, they are likely to price you at the lower end. Whereas if you say £50,000 to £60,000, if they offer you £50,000, then you have secured more than what you wanted which is a win! Also to note, if possible, try not to disclose your past salary if you're going for a new job because recruiters tend to use that as a base-line for how much they offer you and it's usually never in your favour. I remember for one role, the recruiter said, 'but we are already offering you £5000 more than what you're earning.' So what?? Having learnt my lesson, when I've been asked to disclose my current salary since, I reply with something along the line of, 'Based on my experience and skills, along with the research I have done on salaries within this industry and for my role, my salary expectation is between (I provide my range).' I centre my answer on what I expect to earn and why, instead of what I currently earn.

### 3. Prepare your pitch

Whether you're negotiating for a pay rise or a salary at a new job, you need to be able explain and quantify why you are worthy of said amount. Create a one-pager, documenting all your wins and where possible (and depending on the context of your job), quantify them and link them to the wider department or organisation goals. Show how the success you've achieved in your role has contributed to better department or organisation outcomes. When negotiating your salary for a new job, similarly you want to show that you can replicate the success you've achieved previously in this new organisation, and you want to reference any unique skills and expertise that highlight additional value you can bring.

This is also applicable if you don't have years of experience too. Talk to the experience you do have and remember – how you tell it is how it will be received, so even the most basic experience can sound mad impactful if you season it up with some punchy language.

Make sure all your points are snappy and easy to remember and practice saying them, like a pitch! If your negotiation isn't in person or over the phone but via email, still make sure your points are concise but full of the key details. I have an excel tracker which I regularly update with workplace achievements, because beyond salary, it's super useful to have this information to hand for performance conversations.

### 4. Plan for different outcomes

Be strategic and think in advance about the different ways the conversations could go and how you'd like to respond. Whilst you can't prepare for everything, it's good to try and pre-empt these things so you aren't totally blind-sided in the meeting.

If your potential new company isn't willing to offer the salary you've asked for, you may want to find out what else is negotiable. Your remuneration package is made up of a whole host of other benefits including health and fitness, childcare and sometimes training and development – you might be about to negotiate these things. I remember one company offered me an increased training budget so I could do a bunch of certifications.

If you face resistance for that internal pay rise, you could ask for clarity on what else you need to do in your role to qualify for it and, again, what else can be negotiated.

If you are offered an increase in pay that isn't the number you hoped for, how do you plan to respond?

## 5. Gather your allies

Make sure you're cultivating relationships with other people in your department and organisations and making them aware of the great work you're doing, so they too can advocate for you, which should enhance your chances of getting that pay rise. When negotiating with a new organisation, if you know people in the organisation already that can speak to your work, great, but if not, try to establish relationships with people who can give you advice on how to navigate those conversations based on their internal knowledge.

When I applied for a role at a company a few years ago, I reached out to this guy (let's call him S) who worked there via LinkedIn to seek advice with the application process. I reached out to this person because we had a few mutual LinkedIn connections and he was in the role I was applying for, with roughly the same amount of experience as me, based on his profile. With his help, I successfully went through the process and received a job offer, however the recruiter very abruptly rejected the salary range I requested. I informed S of this, and he told me I wasn't asking for too much at all, in fact it was the salary that he was on, and he would help me to push back. S spoke to the managing director of the department I applied for, making a case for me to be paid the amount I requested (the managing director controlled the budget and luckily enough had interviewed me in my final round). The managing director agreed and signed off on this and the following day, the recruiter called me back and explained there has been this change of heart and asked if I would accept the offer with the now updated salary offer. This wouldn't have happened without having a company ally.

### Note: Not all advice is good advice

Everyone's experiences with recruitment agencies can differ, but several times I have found when they have presented me with a job opportunity and I have discussed the salary with them, they've told me I was asking for too much 'for someone at my level' and I should be 'realistic'. They've tried to humble me. Sure, these agencies interact with organisations all the time and they bring their own knowledge based on what they're used to. But if I had taken their advice as gospel, I would be on a far lower salary than I am now. Be wary of taking that type of advice, especially where you're not provided with a good reason.

## During the negotiation

### Relax
Asking for more money is nerve-racking, but keep in your mind, you are asking to be paid your worth and you have all the receipts

to back up why. Try your best to be calm, collected and present your points with confidence. If you're worried about your confidence being mistaken for arrogance, make sure you convey enthusiasm and communicate that you're grateful for the opportunity to have that conversation.

### Get the language right

When we think about negotiation, we often think about what we 'need' and 'deserve'. While that language is okay when talking amongst ourselves, when having a discussion with your manager or a company recruiter, we need to reframe the context. It's not about you, it's about what you can do for them. What value can you add to the role, the company? How can you make a difference? How have you contributed to the company goals?

### Don't make any rash decisions

There might be a lot of things covered in that discussion, but don't feel pressured to make any decision on the spot. If you need time to think, then say so. That might be better than accepting an offer in the heat of the moment which is far lower than you wanted.

## Post-negotiation

### Reflect and regroup

If your negotiation didn't go as well as you hoped, reflect on it. What went well and what didn't go so well? Was there anything you could've done better or was there too much resistance to overcome? We will always have to negotiate in our lives whether in the workplace or outside so it's a skill worth developing.

## Make sure you receive documentation

Whatever the outcome, but especially if it was a positive outcome make sure this is documented and you receive an email or a letter with everything that was agreed in the discussion. Check this closely for any discrepancies and follow up if you don't receive it or if something doesn't look right.

Any type of negotiation can feel a little daunting, especially salary negotiation but no one is going to fight on our behalf to ensure we are being paid fairly, only we can do that. We have to ask. The way I think about it is either I negotiate now, or I struggle later, and I'm not trying to struggle! We also have to question if we really want to work somewhere that doesn't see our worth. There is no guarantee that negotiating your salary will result in a favourable outcome, but we have to use our better judgement to assess our personal circumstances and weigh up if that's a risk we can afford to take. Even if you're not planning to negotiate your salary right now, know the numbers and understand what you should be doing to command a certain salary.

# RESOURCE: SALARY NEGOTIATION

Tip: When pitching for a higher salary, make sure you are using words and phrases which are action and results oriented, like you would you in your CV for example, established, implemented, led, increased, oversaw, created, expanded, developed, enhanced, delivered. This is about showing what you did, what you're capable of. In combination with this, you should try to quantify those achievements, the results and outcomes of what you did. If you're not sure of financial figures such as sales or profit generated or your role isn't directly linked to financial metrics, use other details such as the number of people positively impacted by the project you worked on, the number of cities or countries your worked spanned across or anything else which is indicative of scale and impact.

Here are a few different scenarios that could occur when working out the details of your salary for a new job and some and some sample responses which have worked for me.

Scenario 1: You receive a call from a human resources representative at the company you applied to, informing you that the feedback throughout the recruitment process was impressive and they'd like to offer you the job. You express how happy you are and then the representative provides more details including the salary which is far lower than what you feel you are worth.

*Thank you for this great news. I'm so happy to receive this offer as I've heard great things about the company and the role sounds amazing. However, if I'm being honest, this salary is substantially lower than I expected. Based on the research I did around the typical salary for this role, in this industry, in combination with my qualifications, skills and experience (here you want to name these, especially any which are unique), could this offer be increased to (insert range)?*

Scenario 2: You have one or more higher paying offers from other companies, but you really want to work at this particular organisation.

*Thank you for this great news, I'm so happy to receive this offer as I've heard great things about the company and the role sounds amazing. However, I've been successful in another recruitment process and that company is offering to pay (insert number). I really want to accept your offer and join your organisation; would you be able to match that figure?*

Scenario 3: The human resources representative expresses that they are unable to offer you the salary you've requested, even after you have expressed why you think you are worth more. They mention that they do have a great overall benefits package. Despite being disappointed, you really like this company and the role and would be open to accepting the offer if certain benefits were flexible.

*Thank you for your transparency with regards to the salary. You mentioned that the company provides quite a comprehensive benefits package and I would love to know more. Are any aspects of the benefits package negotiable, in particular (insert a benefit of interest to you e.g. holiday allowance, learning and development budget, medical insurance etc). I only ask because (insert reason).*

# ALEXANDRA BURKE

*Singer and Actress*

Alexandra Burke rose to fame after winning the fifth series of The X Factor in 2008 and currently stands as one of the most successful winners of the show selling well over 4 million records in the UK alone. Her debut album, Overcome, debuted at number one in the UK Album Charts and spawned four number one singles. Alexandra appeared BBC One's Strictly Come Dancing, where she made it to the final. Alexandra has achieved great success in theatre and she made her West End debut in 2014 when she starred as Rachel Marron in the highly acclaimed musical, The Bodyguard. In 2016, she stepped into the lead role as Deloris van Cartier in Sister Act, touring the UK in an all-new production, receiving 5-star reviews across the country. In 2021, Alexandra made history as the first black woman to play The Narrator in West End production of Joseph and The Amazing T echnicoloured Dreamcoat at The London Palladium. In the same year she won The Great Celebrity Bake Off for Stand Up To Cancer and Channel 4's SAS: Who Dares Wins. Alexandra will make her movie debut this year (2022) in the BFI/BBC film Pretty Red Dress.

**Tell us about yourself?** *I was born in Islington, Caledonian Road. I went to Copenhagen primary school and then Elizabeth Garret*

*Anderson school in Angel, Islington. All the girls in my family including my mum went to that school, so we kept the tradition going. That school really helped me with regards to choosing a career within music and the arts. I used to attend after school clubs such as drama classes, dance, and I was also a member of the choir. I also used to go to another place called St Mary's which was a youth club and I'd go there after my after-school club to do further sessions to enhance my singing, dancing and acting.*

*When it came to choosing my GCSE's, the government changed the rules on how many you could select, it went from 3 choices, to only 2 and I really wanted to pick music, dance and drama. I remember my school doing a massive petition for me to be the only child in my school to have 3 choices, but the government wouldn't let me. My point is that my school really believed in me, and knew how dedicated I was to singing, dancing and acting. They really did everything in their power to help me.*

*Another massive thing for me when I was younger that helped me make my decision even more solid, was when I was 12 years old, I was part of a TV show called Star for a Night which Jane McDonald used to host and the school allowed her to come into a music lesson and surprise me on camera which then went on tv. That came with its own highs and lows and when I say lows, I mean it came with a little bit of bullying in school. It was extremely nerve racking but I'm super grateful my mum encouraged me to do it.*

**What was your motivation to pursue music? Where did the interest come from and how did you secure your first opportunity within this space?** *My mum was in a group called Soul II Soul,* *she was their last leading lady, their last lead singer and she is the reason I wanted to sing. I remember seeing her on Top Of The Pops when I was much younger and she was performing with Jazzie B and I remember thinking to myself this is what I want to do with my life, this is who I want to be. It was wanting to be my mum; she's been the inspiration behind everything I have chosen to do in my life. When I was a teenager, she also got me to do gigs on the weekend, sing in pubs and clubs, perform at Bar Mitzvahs, weddings, funerals every single weekend. My mum also ensured I performed at open mic nights. She'd make me go there during the week after school, and weekends, I'd perform at pubs. That was to perfect my craft, teach me how to perform live, how to work an audience, mic technique etc. My musical schooling was all done through live performance and that was hard as a child because I just wanted to hang out with my friends sometimes, and there were other things I feel I missed out on, but I have no regrets because it's made the woman I am and the artist I am today.*

**How did you find the transition from being relatively unknown to winning The X Factor, the biggest talent show on TV?** *Coming from a family that was pretty well known because of my mum and seeing her with all these TV commitments felt very normal. However, when I went on The X Factor, it felt weird because the cameras are always in your face, it was nothing like my days singing in a pub, it was so different and the only way I could get through it every week was imagining that I was in a pub. Seeing my mum receive attention was pretty normal but now that it was directed at me, it didn't feel so normal and wasn't something I was used to. I have to give thanks to my mum because she really* helped me form a thick skin during that period of time and taught me the importance of being myself. I wouldn't say the transition was difficult, but it wasn't easy. At nineteen, I don't think I really understood how big the show was at all. I just thought ok here I am performing on this TV show, hoping I would do really well but in my head, I thought I was going to be voted out by week 2. I remember I sang Whitney Houston in Week 1 and I was like I don't want to sing Whitney, then they gave me Mariah Carey in week 2 and I was like guys I love Mariah but want to perform something that's outside of my comfort zone. They wouldn't let me do it and dictated the songs weekly which is just how the show worked at the time. I really thought I'd be out by week 2 which would help me to generate more gigs, more income to help my mum. I wasn't thinking of the bigger picture, my goal was to try and get to the live rounds as I had got to the judges houses when I was 16 and the exposure from live rounds would mean more weddings, bar mitzvahs to make extra money. I didn't realise how big the show was or the impact it would have on my life, which worked to my advantage because I think viewers at home could see I was just trying to get through each week.

Once I won, my single Hallelujah did amazingly well but my family's business was in the press and it quickly started to feel overwhelming for a young twenty year old. What kept me grounded throughout this time was my family. I'd still go to my mum's house and she'd still make me tidy up after myself, we still did Sunday dinners. Those family traditions still stayed the same, my mum made sure that never changed, so I never changed. I think that's so important because I went through so much at a young age going from pub gigs to big stages, it's such a different *world and it was really important for me to remember where I came from because I didn't want to be that lost child in an industry you can't control. I say that with regards to people who achieved success really young and never really found their way. That is why you need people around you who keep you grounded. It was a mad time just after I won The X Factor but keeping my friends and family close reminded me of who I was.*

**For any talented black individual considering a TV Talent show, what would be your advice to them, what should they be aware of?** *My advice would be to always be yourself. In this industry and on these talent shows, it can be very easy to look at someone else and think 'I wish I had what they had'. No. You are unique and there is only one you and that's something my mum always used to tell me. Going into these talent shows, stay true to who you are, know what you would like to achieve and stick to your goal. Always remember that the sky isn't the limit, it's just the view.*

**The music industry can be a tough space for black women with heavy scrutiny and limitations placed on our appearance, and the type of music we make. Did you experience any of this and what advice would you give to black female musicians trying to find their way in the industry?** *In the beginning I didn't feel like I experienced any of this, maybe my head was a little lost in the clouds. As I've become older, I've realised that there is so much more that I have experienced when it comes down to my colour. I'm also way more aware of it now, compared to when I was 20 years old. For any black artist trying to make it in the industry I think it's so important to not take in everything that people have* *to say about 'black artists', as sometimes it can really dampen some of your most positive experiences. You have to make decisions for yourself, you have to believe in things yourself and go with your heart. A small example I have is there was this one time when I was scheduled for a performance and I wanted to go for a natural look, different to how I would look normally with my weave etc and I was told that my natural appearance (having my hair up in a bun with some baby hairs at the front) looked 'aggressive'. That was the word used. It sounds so ridiculous, even repeating it makes me annoyed. I've also had people come up to me and say if I was white, I'd be so much bigger, and it's frustrating. Like why say that to someone?*

*As a black woman in the industry, I do question myself and wonder if I was in America, would my career be bigger than it is and don't get me wrong, I've achieved so many great things 11 years after The X Factor and I love what I do but I do question things. If I was in America, would there be more opportunities for me and the answer I believe is yes! I feel like America is more embracing, especially of black artists. I've had tremendous support and success here in the UK and Europe and when I weigh up the people that talk about my colour and the people that don't, the majority of people don't talk about my colour. As a black woman, unfortunately sometimes people will make comments and the best approach to take in my opinion is by proving people wrong with your success and talent or proving them wrong with no response. Stay silent, work hard and become successful.*

**Having experienced great success as a singer, you are also making huge waves in the West End! How do the two experiences differ**

**and what have you learnt doing musical theatre?** *I'm a very disciplined artist, person, just disciplined full stop, but theatre is a different ball game. Doing theatre has changed my whole attitude towards keeping a healthy voice, lifestyle, and energy to sustain myself for example 18 Whitney Houston songs a night, for 6 nights a week! Theatre is hard work, there is nowhere to hide, you can't mime etc. The things that I do to keep my voice, for example gargling salt or TCP, and it's vile but I do these things so I don't let the audience down and ensure I can perform at my very best on stage. There is no other discipline like theatre, you can't come off stage and go for a drink. You have to cool down, steam your voice, go straight to bed, get up again, head to the gym and repeat. You don't get much of a social life, you have to fully give yourself to the show but I honestly think it's amazing. I'm not a massive fan of touring which I've always been honest about because I miss my family and being at home, but I love performing and every time I felt frustrated about touring, the moment I went on stage, all those feelings went away because I could see the audience were excited to be at the theatre and really enjoying their experience.*

*It's a bittersweet feeling because when I was younger, we couldn't afford to go to the theatre. The first show I ever went to was The Lion King, which my friend Shaun bought me a ticket to as a first date. It was eye opening because I remember seeing lots of black performers in the show and thinking wow, this is amazing, I could do this one day, it's possible and here we are, I've been part of shows that I could only have dreamt of. My heart is with music, being in the studio is really important to me, but at the same time, theatre has given me so much joy and I can only thank people for coming out to all of these shows. Being a part of shows that have either sold out or sold really well is such a blessing for someone like myself who isn't theatre trained.*

**What challenges have you experienced in your career and how have you overcome them?** *The main challenge I've faced is when people have tried to change me! That's a hard one for me because I don't believe that anyone should be forced to change. I've had people say to me you're not going to sell records until you lighten your skin. That was 10 years ago, and I made sure I would never work with that person again. I got told if I didn't lighten my skin, straighten my hair and appeal to a whiter audience, my music wouldn't sell, because a white audience wouldn't connect with someone too black. Ultimately, I didn't lighten my skin, I wear my hair now how I wish, and people have embraced me for who I am.*

*I've also had people say, 'oh my god, you're actually really nice', or 'you're not a bitch at all' and I just think really?? I've heard that so many times. At the end of the day, people will have their opinions and as long as you know what the truth is, that's the most important thing.*

**What have been some of your career highs and lows?** *A massive highlight was my own UK and European tour which I did back in 2010. Another highlight was definitely singing with Beyoncé, that was a dream and I had less than 24 hours' notice. That was so crazy, 11 years on I still look at the video and shed a tear. I think overall to still be here working and doing what I love, performing 11 years later is a big achievement for me, especially as winning a TV talent show doesn't necessarily guarantee longevity and success, which we see all the time.*

*A low point for me would be seeing my family going through certain things because of my success. For example, their personal business being out in the papers and people selling stories on them. I've had friends who I've grown up with who have sold stories on me for a little bit of cash. Those are the low points, but the main thing is seeing others hurt because of me. I hate the fact that the press digs into other people's lives, because they are associated with me, whether that be my brother, sister, mother, father etc. They put things out there that don't need to be made public and I feel so bad for them. How we've handled it is to come together as a family and work through it together instead of allowing these things to cause family rifts.*

*The press has made things difficult, but then I've come from a show where you needed the press, so it's a catch 22 and you have to pick your battles carefully with them. They have a job to do and papers they need to sell, it's just a shame that it's at the expense of other*

**What has been the best career advice given to you?** *The best advice I was given was learn to say no, learn the power in a no. Being a yes person and agreeing to everything can be detrimental to your career.*

**What advice would you give to black students and professionals starting out and advancing in their careers?** *Don't change who you are. We only have one life, we all have a purpose, there's a reason why we are all here, so if you don't fulfil that purpose, you're doing an injustice to yourself. It's something I struggle with sometimes, but you need to try your best to get up every day and be motivated because no one is going to work hard and execute on your goals for you, only you can.*

# ALEX BOATENG

*Co-President, 0207 Def Jam*

Alex Boateng is the co-president at major label 0207 Def Jam, the newly launched offshoot of Universal UK, where he has worked for over a decade. Prior to this recent appointment, he was president of Island Records' first Urban Division (also owned by Universal) which played an instrumental role in shaping the current and sustained trajectory of UK Black music. After taking the role in 2018 he oversaw UK campaigns for Drake, Tiwa Savage, Buju Banton, Nav, Giggs, Unknown T, Ray BLK, M Huncho, Tekno and Miraa May while also spearheading the campaigns for George The Poet's debut book release, British film *The Intent 2* and UK-based clothing brand Lizzy. Alex is a member of Universal Music's Task Force for Meaningful Change, which was created as a driving force for inclusion and social justice. He joined Universal Music in 2010 in a digital role at Island Records before going on to hold positions in marketing and A&R, working on campaign launches for Tinchy Stryder, Drake, The Weeknd and Nicki Minaj as well as A&R for artists including JP Cooper, Sean Paul, Jessie J, Dizzee Rascal, Donae'o and Big Shaq. He started his music career balancing a marketing degree with DJing, multiple shifts in radio and running his own marketing and promotions company with his then BBC 1Xtra colleague G Money, before moving on to consulting roles with Atlantic Records, Polydor and AATW.

**Tell us about yourself?** *I was born in East London, Newham to Ghanaian parents. I have an older brother, a little sister and a twin brother (Alec Boateng, 0207 Def Jam co-president), which is cool. Growing up, there was a lot of music around in the house – the latest eighties vinyl of Michael Jackson, Luther Vandross, plus highlife and Ghanaian music. With Ghanaian parents, pretty much every weekend we'd be getting dragged to some event from funerals to hall parties, from East London to Elephant and Castle to Broadwater Farm. My parents were really hard-working and emphasised the importance of education. There's that pressure being second generation and representing everything they came to the country for and not wanting to let them down. I felt like I was in two different worlds most of the time, because there's school where I'd be with my friends, playing football and then I'd go home, and it would be like mini-Accra. Even when we were in nursery, because my parents only spoke to us in Twi (a Ghanaian language), we didn't learn English until a bit later than other kids. At the time I found those things a little frustrating but look-ing back now I truly appreciate it, because it really shaped who I am, who we were and gave me a lot of character, value and appreciation for many things.*

*We then moved to Bow and Bethnal Green which had a real mix of different cultures. I went to secondary school in south London, and I noticed how distinct east and south London were culturally. Nothing massive, but little nuances like the language, fashion and influences – it was pretty interesting to be part of both. I did well in my GCSEs and then went to Saint Francis Xavier Sixth Form college in South London and that's when I think I started to get distracted by all the usual things that distract teenagers. I got kicked out and had to go to a college in East London and by this time while education was still important, so was football and music. Most of us back then was massively influenced by the music coming from the US and Jamaica and, at the time our own UK musical identity was starting to form. With house music coming from the States and to my understanding, drum 'n' bass originating from reggae, we saw how this evolved over here into what became known as garage. In my corner of East London, it was all about garage music.*

**Where did your motivation to pursue music come from and how did you secure your first opportunity within the space?** *It started with DJing. In my area, garage was emerging, and everyone was DJing, MCing or had some involvement in music or football. Even then, me and my twin brother wanted to be different, we grew up listening to R&B and hip-hop and that was what we wanted to play at the parties rather than garage, which was good, because I learnt early that differentiation is important, it gives people a reason to specifically call you. Everyone had garage and was spitting, but we used to get loads of bookings because people would call us for when the girls wanted to hear music they could dance to. I remember the first time I DJ'd for a girl's party and got paid, I loved it! It was only £20 but the fact that I got money to do something I enjoyed was a bonus and I was able to use it to buy my favourite records. Around our area Wiley, Tinchy and Dizzee Rascal were coming up and it was mad seeing them become these 'ghetto celebrities'. I went to school in South*

London and So Solid Crew was coming up and members of So Solid were doing sets in East London and the scene was starting to come to life.

While I was DJing, I was also studying in university. I knew I wanted to study something business-related, and marketing felt like the one area which infused business and creativity. It was a subject that I fell in love with straight away and I ended up doing additional reading around it to truly understand what connects products and customers. It was the first time that education really excited me, to the extent that by the end of the degree, I was less than half a percentage off a first class which still burns me! The only reason I think that happened was because in university, I was juggling so many different things. My brother had this idea for us to drop a mixtape as growing up in our area – from Nasty Crew, to Wiley, to Kano – the music scene was really emerging. The idea was unique at the time, in that if you were a grime MC, you would spit on a hip-hop beat, if you were a hip-hop MC, you spat on a grime beat. Kano was one of the people on the mixtape, it was the first time record labels heard him and that's how he got signed. All of this was happening while we were in university and it was crazy because we would be going to our lectures, handing in assignments but also meeting with all these record labels. My brother got offered a full-time job at the Ministry of Sound, so he ended up dropping out of university, but I wanted to finish my degree. We did an interview on a BBC radio station and they loved how my brother sounded, so he was also offered a show on BBC 1Xtra and I got a job there as a producer.

I met a guy called G Money and we set up a marketing company together called Angles Marketing and we were doing campaigns for Dizzee Rascal and Ms Dynamite, again all while I was still at university, so I was able to apply everything I was learning to the real world, in real time. I was also working at a gym at the same time. Looking back, I don't even know how I finished my degree.

**How did you then make that move into working for a record label?** *After university, keeping the marketing company going was difficult in terms of generating substantial revenue, so I got a job at this place called Xtaster which did a lot of music marketing and fanbase management and I was there for a while before deciding that I just wanted to do my own thing. That's when I started to consult for labels and looking back it was quite a brave thing to do at the time. I was initiating meetings with labels and trying to be vocal about what I felt they were missing. It was during that time when Tinchy Stryder, N Dubz and Tinie Tempah were all coming through and Tinchy was coming from an area I knew very well. He was signed to a label, and I felt like there were some gaps in how they were marketing him. My expertise was largely around digital at the time and when I was talking to labels, I was trying to be forthright about what I felt they were missing and what skills and knowledge I could bring.*

*At Island Records, the person who was doing Tinchy's marketing left, and when they approached me about stepping in within a consulting capacity, it just made sense. Island Records was home to some of the biggest artists; it had the Bob Marley history. Working for a major label wasn't part of my plan to be honest. When I first started, I felt a little intimidated, I didn't think it was for me as a young Black guy. I preferred to be at the talent end, in the studio with the artists, but I took the job as I was confident in what I believed I could bring, and I did this three days a week at first. Looking back, this was one of the best decisions of my career. People look at big companies and, in this case, record labels, as big machines, but they are ultimately still about people, expertise and networks which the amazing musical talent that I've worked with and work with deserve. Talent was also something that I saw in the labels across all departments: impressive accounts people, creative, digital, strategic, promotions, legal and so much more. This really helped me to understand and appreciate how important the right teams behind the artists are and how hard they work.*

**You started as a consultant and eventually were hired into a full-time permanent role. How were you able to make yourself indispensable?** *I think it was utilising the mix of marketing skills I had, with the genuine relationships and understanding I had of the culture. Even though I came in as a consultant, I wanted to do more. I saw my role as more than a job and tried to really embed myself in different areas while delivering the basics in terms of marketing and campaigns. It caused frustration at some points, because there were times where I was distracted from the marketing basics because I was involved in other things, but the value I was bringing to the company and the artists was worth it. I wasn't like any of the other marketing managers, whether it was organising events and DJing at them or using the connections I had to bring certain people in or building international relationships in an authentic way. My contributions were truly unique, and it goes back to my learnings from DJing and being the only one playing R&B at a time when the environment was* doing something different and having an area of expertise. My advice to everyone is to always have something that people call you for over anybody else, a USP.

**Has the A&R (artists and repertoire) manager role changed since you started? If so, in what ways?** *The role hasn't really changed but it has more so evolved. Pure A&R is still really important, in terms of understanding what you want to deliver for an artist musically and doing everything around them to make that happen. That can be down to technical conversations around how they sing or deliver certain raps in a way that will connect with the audience to building relationships and using those to put the right things in front of them and even creating the right studio environment. The evolvement of that is now the teams around the artists and the businesses that are being built around that. That involves speaking to artist managers about the businesses they're creating and finding ways to partner with them on top of what you're already doing with the artist musically.*

**Black representation in the business side of music at senior levels is pretty low. In addition to some of the changes that the industry needs to make, what can Black talent in the organisations do to increase their chances of moving up?** *I would say it's important to have a clear, obvious skillset that you are bringing to the business and always deliver on that to the best of your ability. For Black talent, we need to make sure through the unique combination of our skills, expertise and knowledge that we demonstrate that we have a reason to be in those rooms, stay in those rooms, progress and leave the door open for others.*

**What challenges have you experienced in your career and how have you overcome them?** *I would say the feeling of insecurity moving from one environment to another and not feeling like you fit in, especially when you don't have a particular skillset. That feeling takes me back to the early days when I'd be involved in the culture at a street level and then I moved into the business side of things and I felt really insecure because there was no one like me. I went from being in an environment where I was always around people who looked like me and sounded like me to the business side of it, which was the complete opposite and created a lot of negative feelings within me. This is probably why I didn't really like major labels initially.*

*Over time I was able to overcome these feelings by putting myself in environments where I was comfortable, where possible. For example, if there was a campaign going on, I would go and spend time in the studio where the artists were because that's where I felt most at home and energised to go back into the business environment. It's great to see things are really changing and there is becoming more and more of a balance. There is still a lot of work to be done but it's great to be in a position to help make the changes.*

**What have been some of your career highs and lows?** *The high points have always been seeing people journeys up close. I remember seeing Tinchy Stryder spitting in ends then going to one of his shows in Scotland and seeing girls crying for him. Or seeing Giggs bring out Drake at Reading Festival and him being that established that he could bring out the biggest rapper in the world on his own set. It's always the moments that solidify other people's journeys that are highlights and it's a great feeling when* *you realised you've played a small part in that. Another highlight is 0207 Def Jam and how my brother's and my journeys have come together to create a business and partner it with a brand we used to buy vinyl for. It's insane. I always hoped for us to come together but I didn't expect for it to be at this level, it felt like something other people did. Again, when you don't see people who look like yourself at a certain level, you expect to be on the outside of any type of machine, instead of being an influential person within.*

*The low points are times when I've had to make decisions regarding artists and their campaigns, and I didn't make the right ones and maybe tried to think about things too commercially. I definitely look back on these moments as learnings instead of low points, especially with how far I've come.*

**What has been the best career advice given to you?** *The best career advice I've received is always around just being yourself and remaining authentic.*

**What advice would you give to Black students and professionals starting out and advancing in their careers?** *Always fight to be the best version of yourself instead of better than anybody else. This is because I feel like when you are trying to be the best version of you, that never stops, it's something you work on every day. When you are trying to be better than someone else, that can have an end.*

*Your Blackness and your culture are a gift. Despite the challenges, find the spaces where your Blackness is appreciated and immerse yourself there. I love being Black, Ghanaian, British, coming from East London and my upbringing. I could look at that through the lens of all the challenges that it's presented, but I choose to see how that has enriched me and made me who I am today.*

*Boundaries are important. You are you – don't allow yourself to be defined by careers, titles, or successes. So many people attach themselves to companies and roles and then when they end, they have no identity. We all started without these things; these companies existed before us and will continue after us, even the ones we own. We need to be able to exist without them.*

# BEVERLEY KNIGHT MBE

*Singer, Actress and Presenter*

Queen of British Soul, Beverley Knight, has been one of the UK's most consistent artists for over two decades, highlighted by gold and platinum-selling albums, 14 Top 40 hits, sold-out tours, 3 MOBO Awards, several Brit Award and Mercury Music Prize nominations plus even an Olivier Award nomination for her more recent formidable parallel career in musical theatre. Beverley starred as the lead in The Bodyguard (where she was nominated for Best Takeover in a Role), Memphis, Cats amongst others. She also started a 'supergroup' with Amber Riley and Cassidy Janson called 'Leading Ladies' featuring classic female songs from musicals such as Cats, Rent & Beautiful which went Top 10 and Silver within weeks.

Wolverhampton born Knight was awarded an MBE by the Queen in 2007 for services to British music and charity, and her outstanding live performances have seen her also collaborate on stage and on record with the likes of Prince, Chaka Khan, Andrea Bocelli & many other iconic artists.

Beverley released her first ever Christmas single at the end of 2020, which was Radio 2's 'Record of The Week' and heavily Playlisted. The track was also featured in a Christmas movie starring Joan Collins. Recent collaborations include 'Enough Is Enough' with Gary Barlow which reached A List at Radio 2 and performed live earlier this year opening the new Ant & Dec series.

**Tell us about yourself?** *I was raised in the West Midlands to West Indian parents. My dad came in the late 50s and my mum came in the early 60s and they had me and my two siblings. A big influence on who I am in general, and definitely musically, is Wolverhampton itself. It's a real melting pot in a way that I don't think London is. London has a lot of nationalities and ethnicities from all over the world but when I was coming to London during the 80s, they didn't seem to mix with each other like how it was at home in Wolverhampton. Me and my Asian friends used to be in and out of each other's homes, they'd introduce us to Bollywood movies, we'd share the reggae and soul tunes we listened to. I didn't grow up compartmentalising music into genres, apart from gospel, as both my parents were Christian. We couldn't listen to certain songs in front of them, so we'd take the radio from their room to listen to the music we wanted to. I listened to soul, R&B, funk and then later on, hip-hop as much as I listened to rock and indie music. London back then was slightly more tribalist because of the way friendships were formed (people found a tribe, stuck to it, and that tribe listened to a certain type of music), whereas in Wolverhampton you listened to music and saw it as either good or rubbish. I'm grateful for that because it provided me with a broad approach to the type of music I liked and then influenced how I made my own songs.*

**What was your motivation to pursue music and how did you secure your first opportunity within this space?** *I come from a musical family, so it wasn't a massive surprise when I came out* *singing. Within my family group, I had the most unique of voices and what I certainly had which no one else did is the gift of performance. I believe I was born for the stage; I was always performing for everyone. I started to perform to large audiences at church and then during my teenage years, I'd sing for anyone that would listen at my local youth club and that led to me being introduced to lots of Black community leaders and the African Caribbean society at university. This put me on the radar of Pirate Radio, which as a teenager was a big deal. I started performing at the clubs and parties the DJs would throw, and this led to me being offered my first record deal just before I went off to university. I waited until I was in the final year of university to sign that deal because I wasn't going to throw away my degree, my dad didn't play!*

**There is often this expectation of Black female artists, especially those with a strong vocal ability like yourself to make R&B and soul music, even if your sound is pop for example. How easy or difficult was it to navigate these categorisations?** *The short answer is: it's not easy and it wasn't easy. But I knew from very early on that I was very talented and that gave me exceptional self-belief because I don't know if I'd still have a career if I didn't. Women in this industry are expected to look and sound a certain way and when you're a Black woman, this is only reinforced. It's not only white people in the industry that try to put Black female artists in a box, but it also comes from within our own community and the expectations of what type of music a Black artist should make. I knew that breaking out would be hard, but I also knew that one day the world would come around to where I was, and I also had examples of other Black women in the industry who had been able to break out of what others expected musically from them.*

With Whitney Houston for example, the industry executives had never heard an artist who was appealing to a fanbase which was way beyond the Black community. Her fanbase was mostly white folk. When she started to make songs like 'I Want To Dance With Somebody' and all those other pop songs, the Black community initially crucified her. The same happened initially to Michael Jackson and also Prince, who is my idol. However, the world eventually comes around and then they're 'ground-breaking'.

**You've experienced being signed to major labels and also being independent. What do you see as the pros and cons of both?** *The pros of a major label is the muscle. If they have the will, they can really push you out to an audience which is much harder to do when you're independent which is important because then you can make an amazing record, but nobody hears it. However, a major label, in wanting major success, will sometimes encourage you to make the type of music that they would like you to make. You don't have that issue when you're independent, you are creatively free to make your own choices musically and that is a joy for a creative person. But the process of promoting and marketing yourself is very tough, even with social media. It's fantastic when someone has a creative vision and can get there by themselves using the internet and all the tools we have at our disposal today to break through and be heard. On the other hand, if you're on a major label and you're flying, you can really fly. Look at Ella Mai, Rag'n'Bone Man, Billie Eilish as examples. Then you have artists like Moonchild and Tom Misch doing things on a much smaller scale but still making waves or you have a lot of the hip-hop artists that came through in the 2000s, set up their own labels and achieved great success. That's the holy grail right there, we want that.*

In addition to music, you've achieved great success in theatre. What has that experience been like and what have been your greatest learnings? *I did theatre as a child, so it's been a full circle journey for me. Coming back to it as an adult has been wonderful because it's another performance outlet for me, but one that the public didn't know I had. Compared to being a musician performing onstage, theatre is graft. It's much harder work than being an artist. You're doing eight shows, six nights a week; the rehearsal period leading up to it is often five to six weeks, again six days a week, nine till six every day, one day off. For most people in theatre, they don't get paid that much so they really do it because they love it. Most contracts are roughly six months, sometimes they can be a year. If you're on stage performing, you get paid, and if you're not, you don't get a penny. My greatest learning has really been to value your creative gifts.*

You've had a successful career spanning over twenty years. During a time when the career of an artist can seem fleeting, what would you say has been the key to longevity? *A lot of it is making the right decisions creatively, making smart business decisions and still appreciating that you are learning your craft. You can never know everything there is about the music industry because it constantly changes year on year. I remember the days of recording everything on a cassette and then CDs came in and took over cassette and vinyl, then came the internet and the digital era. You have to adapt – adaptation is everything, otherwise you stagnate, and you die. Things change and you have to change with it. Having a talent is important but so is having a passion for it. If you look at artists like Madonna for example, she isn't* known for her vocals, but she's passionate about her performance and that's what she works on constantly.

**What challenges have you experienced in your career and how have you overcome them?** *There's been a few. The perception of what it means to be a female artist, to be a Black artist and both of those things together, the 'double' stereotyping. Especially as a Black artist, there is this perception that you only listen to certain types of music and you're only knowledgeable on particular topics. I remember when I first signed my deal, when I'd speak in meetings everyone around the table would look at me in total disbelief. As a Black person, they don't expect you to come from a middle-class background and a stable home with two parents. It doesn't fit their narrative of what it is to be Black. I remember a journalist writing an article about me at the beginning of my career and through my press officer managed to get a few quotes from me. I remember being so excited about the piece coming out until I read it. The article had a picture of me and my school friend, and the headline was along the lines of I was local girl that had made it. I read that I came from this single parent family which wasn't true, my parents were married until my father passed away, so straight away it was totally disrespectful to my family. The journalist wrote that I grew up in a council estate which again was false, I came from a four-bedroom semi-detached house in an affluent area in Wolverhampton. I didn't fit the stereotype so the newspaper created a story so I did. When I read the article, it didn't sound like it was about me at all. It was a very early lesson in realising that in this industry, as a Black person you're expected to fit this mould and if you don't, they will make you anyway.*

*Being compartmentalised has always been a challenge for me because I don't like the labels and boxes. People, namely journalists, will ask a male artist about a track and very much refer to it as 'their track'. When it comes to a female artist, one of the first questions people will ask if it's a big hit is, 'who wrote it?'. That's something that gets asked a lot, 'who writes your songs?', unless they've done their homework on you and know you're a singer-songwriter. It doesn't happen to me so much now at this point in my career because my journey is well documented, but in the early days of my career, I was asked constantly about who wrote my songs, and questions around fashions choices, my relationships, 'when are you going to get married?', 'when will you have kids?'. This just doesn't happen to male artists.*

*Remaining true to myself throughout is the only way I could handle these things and not being afraid to speak up, especially when correcting things that aren't true.*

**What have been some of your career highs and lows?** *Going to Los Angeles, because Prince flew me there to perform at this Oscars party in 2008, which was nuts and Stevie Wonder turned up as well. It was a Tuesday, and Prince reached out and asked if I could come to LA on the weekend, so casually like LA is down the road. I wasn't feeling well, but suddenly I was feeling perfectly fine and got on that plane, got there, still no idea why he asked me to come. The penny started to drop when all these A List celebrities arrived at the hotel I was staying, it was the Oscars weekend. He flew me over because he wanted me to feature in a party he was throwing for Oscars weekend. I was on stage singing with Prince's band and then Stevie Wonder made his way through the crowd, got on stage and jumped on the keyboard.*

*After Stevie performed a set, Prince then passed me the mic and told me to get ready to perform Aretha Franklin 'Rock Steady', which we had performed the September before when he was on tour in the UK. The whole experience was unreal.*

*With regards to lows, you learn very quickly in the music industry that loyalty is rare, whether it's from your own team or record labels. Record labels aren't designed to be loyal and are only loyal for as long as the money is coming in. Even when the money is coming in, if it's not enough in their eyes, they will simply part ways with you. Audiences aren't loyal, that saying, 'you're only as good as your last record' is so true, people fall away very quickly and that's something you have to accept and get on with. When I released my fourth album and people didn't like the musical direction I was going in (although it was my most successful record to date), it was a bizarre time because my core audience, the people who you think are always going to stand by you and understand your creativity were the first to fall away. A few years later, I walked away from my recording deal at the time because I didn't feel the label was supportive of my creative decisions. From around 2004 to 2007, it was a really tough time but slowly things started to improve. There are peaks and troughs in life, but especially in music and there isn't an artist alive who hasn't had that period where one minute everyone loves them and then the next, they are the worst musician ever. It's about how you come through those times because that shows whether you really have staying power.*

**What has been the best career advice given to you?** *The best career advice I have received is from my husband who really stresses the importance of having multiple streams of income.*

*I've always been someone who has solely focused on my music and the creative process, but he has always reminded me to think about other ways to generate income that I can then invest back into my music and also, so I'm not heavily reliant on music. Look at the current pandemic. If the only way you make income is from performing in front of a crowd, then potentially you were in trouble because everyone was at home in lockdown, there were no festivals or shows. If you look at hip-hop artists such as Kanye West and Jay Z, outside of music, both have numerous other businesses and, if they wanted to, would never have to make music again.*

**What advice would you give to Black students and professionals starting out and advancing in their careers?** *Don't maintain the status quo! If you never take risks, you'll never receive the rewards. Actively encouraging people to never take chances, never take risks and to keep treading water is the worst thing you can tell anyone. Yes, make smart decisions to weigh up risks versus rewards, but don't stand still and stagnate. Also never let anyone make you feel like you can't achieve something or you're not worthy of particular opportunities because you're Black. And I say this sensitively, but if you're not achieving or where you hoped to be, don't immediately assume it's because of your race. There could be a number of reasons and you have to ask yourself 'what could I have done better?'. There will be people that discriminate against you, but you have to use that as a fuel to propel yourself forward.*

# GLYN AIKINS

*Co-President, Since '93*

Glyn Aikins is a music fan who has transformed his passion into a culture-shifting career. Having stumbled into the industry from spending his every spare minute hanging out in record stores, he's been driven by the need to make a positive change by trying things his own way, leading him into paradigm shifting roles in A&R and now as a label president. Glyn has changed the face of UK music multiple times, launching the careers of So Solid Crew, Emeli Sandé and Krept & Konan then launching the label, Since '93 – a joint venture with his friend Riki Bleau – to house some of the country's most distinctive talents including Aitch, Fredo, Loski and Amun.

Glyn was recently appointed to the board of governors at London's iconic Southbank Centre, where he will play a role in overseeing and supporting the executive team of the organisation.

**Tell us about yourself?** *My name is Glyn Aikins and I am the co-founder of Since '93 Records. I grew up in Waterloo, South London and my family is from Ghana.*

**What was your motivation to pursue music from and how did you secure your first opportunity within this space?** *My interest in music started when I was a child, I was given an old record* *player and I used to spend my weekends going to record shops buying seven-inch vinyls and I used to play them and pretend I was presenting a radio show. I was ten years old when I first discovered hip hop; my mum bought me a hip-hop compilation album called* Street Sounds *which was part of a wider series called* Electro, *there was an Electro 1, 2, 3, 4 and so on – Electro 7 was the first record I bought.*

*My friends went to boarding school and when they came back, they played me Public Enemy's It Takes A Nation Of Millions album which I loved and then I remember later on when I heard Wu-Tang Clan's first album and it blew me away.*

*I remember when I first started going out raving and the DJs used to always frustrate me because I didn't think they were playing the music right or they were playing music I didn't want to hear – and that mindset was really the foundation of what has served me throughout my career. This 'I can do it better myself' attitude. So with that, I became a DJ. This was around the time I went to university and there was a group of us that all wanted to be DJs and we knew a guy that had turntables in his house, and we used to go around to practise. Eventually I bought one turntable, a mixer and used an old record player and just lived in the record shops buying vinyl after vinyl. While at university, I joined the ACS (African Caribbean Society) and approached them to host their parties. Me and my friends really wanted to DJ but we didn't know how to get ourselves out there and build a brand so we could get bookings. Something we started to realise was 50% of it will be based on who you know and the other 50% will just be doing it ourselves, so I used to organise these raves at university and we booked ourselves as the DJs, booked the line-up.*

This period of my life definitely shaped my career choice, going into A&R which is what I do now. I was studying accounting which I found incredibly boring, and it wasn't what I really wanted to do but knew it would please my parents.

As a result of going to record shops all the time, I met a lady who worked for a music PR company, and she asked me if I wanted to come and do work experience at her company. I did two weeks' work experience at this company called Media Village and they were based in Leicester square, a stone's throw from all the record shops that were in Soho. They did promotions – street promotions and radio promotions – and their clients were the major record labels for Black music artists. After two weeks' work experience, I was offered a full-time role which came at the time I was nearing the end of my degree studies. I had a part-time job at Boots which I knew I didn't want to continue full time, and I definitely didn't want to become an accountant, so I grabbed that job offer with both hands.

**With your foot now in the music industry, how did you become an A&R (artists and repertoire) manager?** After I graduated, I was always going out, the FOMO (fear of missing out) was real. But because of this, I was always musically in the know of what was popping and what wasn't. I remember hearing Shanks & Bigfoot 'Sweet Like Chocolate', and thinking it was going to be huge. I walked into the office with the record under my arm, thinking this is massive. A big sign for me was the fact it had spilled out from its own scene (garage and house) into R&B and so on, everyone liked it. My managers dismissed my excitement and then it became a number one record.

That summer at Carnival, the song 'Who Let The Dogs Out' was being played everywhere and everyone including the police-men were dancing to it. Again, I thought it was a massive song, many disagreed but then it exploded into the UK charts into the top ten. It was becoming clear, especially to the owner of Media Village, that I was someone who had an ear for music that would do well. Around this time, there were conversations about Media Village doing a deal with Ministry of Sound to turn the company into a record label (which later became Relentless Records).

While this was happening, I was travelling up and down the country hosting parties and competitions with Tim Westwood as part of this activation the company had with Activision computer games. Everywhere we went around the country, the same record kept being played over and over again, it was Artful Dodger featuring Craig David, 'Rewind'. I called the team back at the office and told them that the song was blowing up and we needed to sign it ASAP. We signed the record; it was a massive hit and the first ever release on Relentless Records. That was my first foray into A&R.

Those first few years were an incredible run of just finding these songs that became big hits. We signed DJ Pied Piper and the Masters of Ceremonies, 'Do You Really Like It' which became a number one record and just after that, I signed So Solid Crew and released 'Oh No'. Following this, our next signing was Daniel Bedingfield, 'I've Got to Get Through This' which went number one. Then we signed Lethal B and 'Pow' was a huge song, and then signed Wiley.

**What do you think makes a good A&R versus a great A&R?** *As an A&R person, you're only as good as the artist you sign, so the* *difference would be signing more great artists than not so great artists. The ability to build great relationships makes a difference too, because while we work in music, this business is all about people. Relationships are the key because that's ultimately what you lean on to make things happen. You have to have good relationships, particularly within the creative community with artists, record producers, songwriters, etc., because what you're trying to do is put the best combination of people together to produce the best record for the artist which makes them the best version of themselves to be presented to the world. You have to keep abreast of the changes, as there are always new and talented people coming through. Also, depending on what area of music you operate in, particularly if it's an area governed by youth culture, you have to be close to what is going on, and understand the concerns and trends of the youth today.*

**You are one of a few Black British executives within the music industry. What do you feel that the industry (junior Black employees, Black musicians, etc.) lose out on from not having more Black decision-makers?** *Talking from a major label/corporate space perspective, I feel you miss out on mentorship and guidance. I have had so many conversations with younger executives asking me for advice on various subjects and issues. It made me realise there was no one like me to go to when I was younger. I wish I could have had the conversations I have now when I was coming up.*

**What challenges have you experienced in your career and how have you overcome them?** *I remember when I was leaving Virgin, some people asked me if I was sure? Throughout my career, I've* had people ask me if I'm sure so many times and thankfully I didn't listen to any of them. I'm here because I didn't listen, so why should I start listening now? My view is I'll determine whether I succeed or fail, not someone else's opinion. You need to be quite single-minded in A&R because quite often you are alone with your beliefs, so you learn to grow a thick skin. I read a quote from Amazon founder Jeff Bezos and he said entrepreneurs have to accept being misunderstood for long periods of time and I know exactly what he was talking about. Most people desire comfort, so doing something new or something that seems risky makes them feel uncomfortable. But I honestly don't believe anything great was achieved by playing it safe and, ultimately, I want to do great things, I want to create a great company for creative people who want to create culture. Therefore, it demands we take the path less trodden in order to get there. I believe all of my experiences have led me up this point where I feel super comfortable being alone in thinking 'this is going to be great' even when there aren't many tangible signs that it will be. Being single-minded in this way may not work, but I don't worry about that, because it might work, and I prefer to be optimistic.

**What have been some of your career highs and lows?** *Signing So Solid Crew was a massive high point in my career. I remember we released their first single 'Oh No (Sentimental Things)' and it didn't end up charting because of a chart rule that you could only put a certain number of remixes in a single package and we exceeded the limit, so instead of it going into the single chart, it went into the budget album chart which was a total mistake. It became some sort of happy accident because the media thought it was done on purpose, with So Solid Crew taking an* anti-establishment stance and not playing by the rules, which in many ways drove their popularity, making them seem more 'interesting' and 'cool'. Then came the massive hit '21 Seconds' which has a funny story behind it. There were like ten MCs in the group, and they all wanted to feature on the track. We said that's fine as long as the song doesn't exceed three and a half minutes (this was the length of a radio edit). They went away and did the maths that if they had three and a half minutes and divided this by the ten MCs, then everyone has twenty-one seconds to rap which is how the song came about. When the video first premiered, it was such a moment, people were screaming, there had never been a video in the UK like it. It's only in more recent years that I fully understand the effect it had. So many people have said to me that video made them realise that pursuing a career in the music industry was possible.

Signing Emeli Sandé was also a highlight for me; we sold millions of records. After Relentless Records ended their partnership with Ministry of Sound and entered a new partnership with Virgin Records, I signed Naughty Boy and he played me some Emeli Sandé songs, which blew me away. On that basis alone, I offered her a record deal. A few people weren't sure if that was the best decision and I was like when have you ever heard someone who can sing and write songs like she does? She's a supremely talented songwriter and has a voice which emotionally moves you. For me, that puts her up there with the greatest vocalists.

I'd say my highest point has been starting this new record label Since '93, a Sony music label, and being the co-president. We've only been in existence for just over eighteen months, and we've had an incredible start, working with some talented artists *such as Fredo, Aitch and Morrison. We've had a fantastic run of really great music from artists that people love. We started this label from scratch with no artists and to see where we are now is a great achievement.*

*I don't have a specific low point but I'd saying trying things that didn't work. Part of working in A&R is that you won't always get it right, you will get it wrong sometimes. As long as you have the ability to be honest with yourself and look at the reasons why something didn't work, you'll take the learnings from that to hopefully not make the same mistakes again.*

**What has been the best career advice given to you?** *The best career advice came from Darcus Beese, former President of Island Records US. For context, Virgin Records and Parlophone were part of EMI, which Universal ended up buying. In the end Universal had to spin off Parlophone because the mergers and acquisitions committee wouldn't allow it, due to the view being Universal would have unfair competitive advantage with its purchase of EMI. Virgin moved under the Universal system and Darcus was the President of Island Records and I remember asking him, 'how does it work here?' and he said to me, 'always make sure you're in a position where you have artists releasing records, because you don't know where the success is going to come from but you won't be able to be successful if you're not releasing the records'.*

**What advice would you give to Black students and professionals starting out and advancing in their careers?** *Have some patience. As long as you're serious and focused on your goals, your time will come. There's no need to be in a rush. What I've seen often is* *people at the beginning of their career coming into an organisa-tion and wanting to be CEO. It's not impossible to progress quickly but I'd say it's important to learn and understand the business you're in, in its entirety because as you move forward, it will provide you with a strong foundation and context. Progress with patience and make sure you manage your relationships well. As I mentioned before, the music business is massively about people, and the relationships you have are your most important assets. Protect them and manage them like your life depends on it.*

# JB GILL

*Musician, Farmer, and Presenter*

JB Gill is a musician, farmer, and presenter. JB rose to fame as a member of one of the UK's biggest boybands – JLS. Four years ago, JB set up a farm in the Kent countryside, where he lives with his wife and two children. Their smallholding successfully produces award-winning KellyBronze turkeys and free-range Tamworth pork. JB has used his success within the entertainment industry to highlight his passion to educate children about the origins of their food and he is the lead presenter on CBeebies' BAFTA-nominated television series *Down On The Farm* (created for children aged zero to six years, teaching them about life on the farm and in the outdoors). JB's enthusiasm for farming life and knowledge of countryside issues has seen him regularly contribute to BBC's *Countryfile* and *Springwatch*. In 2016, JB became the first ambassador for the Mayors' Fund for London, an independent social mobility charity linked to the mayoral office that's seeking to empower young Londoners from all walks of life in their journey onto London's career ladder.

**Tell us about yourself?** *I'm JB Gill. I'm thirty-four years old, a husband and father of two. I was born in West London. My father is from Guyana, West Indies and my mother is from Antigua and Barbuda, West Indies and I have a younger brother* *who is thirty-three years old. I spent my early years in Antigua and Barbuda as my mother worked as a nurse there, while my father was involved in construction and carpentry. We moved back to the UK around the time I started school at five and we lived in Brixton. I have always lived in South London and although my home is a little further out nowadays, we are still South as that's where I'm most familiar with.*

**What was your motivation to pursue music from and how did you secure your first opportunity within this space?** *The first instrument I ever played was the recorder (which was most people's first) but I was able to play pretty much all the songs given to me really well. My teacher caught on to my ability and I was offered the opportunity to take up flute lessons. I did really well with the flute and that led to me auditioning and securing a place at the Centre for Young Musicians. I was about nine years old, and I was there until I was roughly twelve years old. That was really the foundation for the music. During my teenage years, I also became good at rugby, playing for the county, going for trials at London Irish – I was doing that at a high level which took over my classical musical training. I first realised I wanted to have a career in music when I got injured during a rugby tour in South Africa and I realised my chances of going pro was slim. With more time on my hands, I started writing songs, using instrumentals I found online, reaching out to people on MySpace for beats, really developing my craft. Before I went to university, I started working with a company called Major Music, and met my first vocal coach through them. I studied theology at university as that was truly a subject I loved and I told myself, I would either be working full time in* music within six months after graduating or I'd have to leave my studies to pursue a career in music. Fast forward two years, I met the other JLS boys, we were together for around a year and half and then we auditioned for The X Factor, and I left university after my second year.

**As a member of JLS, not only are you colleagues, but you're also friends. How are you able to navigate those relationships?** *People naturally look at JLS as one entity because we are a group, but we are also four individuals with different personalities, mindsets and ambitions. The secret to us maintaining good relations is to always remember those things. Very early on we said if three of us want to do something, then majority rules. With some groups, everyone has to agree, but we found that counterproductive as when you're in a group of any number, you're going to have people that see things differently and it doesn't necessarily mean they're wrong, but in order to keep things going you have to reach a consensus.*

*Being on the same page is also key! From the beginning we were super professional, always being on time for events, making the effort to remember the names of people we had met, equally putting in the effort to secure additional contacts that would help us advance musically.*

*Another thing is you have to take things with a pinch of salt. If we do have a disagreement, we have a discussion about it and then move on. This is an approach I've always taken with my family, and JLS are an extension of that.*

**Post JLS, you've successfully transitioned into presenting and farming. What made you move in a direction that was so far**

**from your comfort zone of music?** *There was a year and half between when we announced that we were going our separate ways and our last day, so you'd think I'd be in planning mode, but I was still discovering what it was I wanted to do. I didn't want to put out any solo music and a few people suggested presenting, but again I wasn't 100% because the only professional career I ever had was music. I left university and went straight into it. While I was in JLS, I moved into a new house and where we live now has approximately thirteen acres of farmland, I was thinking about what could be done with it as any type of farmland needs to be well-looked after and maintained. A few people mentioned farming, especially as we had wildlife here too and I decided to give it a go. I would say I went into it a little blindly and with the success of JLS, I did have resources financially and in other ways which meant that I wasn't necessarily starting from scratch.*

*My wife encouraged me to use my existing profile and platform to talk more about my newfound love for farming. Not long after, CBeebies approached me and asked if I'd be interested in presenting a TV show called* Down On The Farm *and I was like 'let's do it!'. I was also able to incorporate music into this by singing the theme song for the show, and I try to incorporate music where I can.*

*As I started to talk more about farming, I was invited onto TV shows to discuss the importance of healthy foods, understanding where food comes from, etc., and built a profile around that. This was during a period where I was learning a lot about farming, as it's not something I grew up with and even though we have thirteen acres of land which sounds like a lot, in farming terms it wasn't, so we had to be sensible and innovative about how we used our space. That's how we got into pig and turkey farming. Keeping my entertainment and TV work at the forefront was really important because that is what people knew me for. While it's great to do something different, if I didn't use my existing platform then the impact wouldn't have been the same. I love music, but I didn't want to limit myself to just that, especially as I have other passions.*

**Farming and music are so different! What have you learnt from both experiences that you believe are valuable?** *In the music and wider entertainment industry, there are more opportunities than what you see. For example, you might see me as the presenter on a show but there are so many people behind the scenes making things happen such as an executive, a series producer, a runner, someone responsible for the lighting, the sound, etc. I'd encourage people to think more broadly about a career in the industry. JLS, for example, couldn't exist without a team of people. As big as you might think you are, you're nothing without the help of others and you need to respect and remember those people. The saying that comes to mind is 'the people you see on the way up, are often the people passing you on your way down'. I remember a situation where one of the runners from my time on* The X Factor *was the executive producer and a key decision-maker on one of the shows I was up for presenting. If I have treated that person badly during* The X Factor, *I wouldn't have been selected to present this particular show.*

*Also, I always knew that our JLS journey would come to an end at some point which takes a lot of adjustment, so I always encouraged the boys and even myself was to establish a business away from the music. The thing about the entertainment* industry is that one week (relative terms) you're the flavour and the next week, you're not. That 'week' can last for a year; it could last for a month. Think of all the nineties R&B groups, how many of them are still having number ones now? Resurrections can happen and they do, but not for everyone. For anyone who wants to become an entertainer in any capacity, I would highly recommend having another income source, whether that is setting up a business or utilising other skills they may have. It's easy to end up in a predicament where you don't have any work because someone doesn't like you or how you look and so much else, and you want to make sure that if or when that happens, you still have a sense of ownership and value.

Farming has really taught me to be patient and understanding, that there is a season for everything. Being able to cultivate and look after something, whether it's an animal, crop, fruit and vegetables, takes roughly a year of work. You have to be on it every day but there is something so rewarding when you achieve success, especially with our turkeys which are our biggest commercial enterprise. Every single year, we get emails from customers complementing our turkey which makes all the hard work worth it, especially when we've had to deal with foxes eating the turkeys throughout the year and birds eating the fruit we've grown – those struggles that no one sees.

**What challenges have you experienced in your career and how have you overcome them?** *I've been working on several shows, funded some of my own shows and I'm planning to bring out my own books. I feel like I'm finally at a point where people think of me and my name and make the connection with farming but that has taken four to five years. I've approached*

*management companies to discuss the brand I'm trying to build
and they just didn't get it and the ones that did, didn't know
what to do next. I didn't want to present game shows, I wanted
to travel the world talking about my passion for farming, nature
and food creation and that was difficult for some people to
comprehend and take seriously, especially as I came from a
boyband. Typically, our community is represented as only being
successful in either sports or music, and it's like why can't we be
farmers, engineers and astrophysicists? There are Black people in
those careers, but my point is we shouldn't allow society to limit
us. We can be successful in sport and music, as well as science,
farming, and anything else we put our mind to. I've had to persevere and really be committed to my goals as it can be easy to give
up if you keep hearing 'no'. All it takes is one opportunity and
that normally leads to several more.*

**What have been some of your career highs and lows?** *Musically,
when JLS won two BRIT awards, that was huge as it was something growing up I had dreamed of. Winning Best Single which
was unheard of and so hard to win as well as Best Newcomer
(now Best Breakthrough Act) was great. It's great to be recognised on platforms like that because typically artists from* The X
Factor *didn't get any recognition.*

*As I mentioned before, I went into farming a little blindly. I
had huge aspirations to create this business where we could
welcome visitors to the farm and I invested quite a lot of money
into a project that would enable us to do that, but it didn't work
out. It was really exhausting, as up until that point I had never
experienced putting so much time, energy and resources into
something that doesn't amount to anything. Recovering from*

227

*that situation wasn't easy, especially financially as I was no longer working in music. It made me realise just how cyclical life is, you have good seasons and not so good seasons and during these times surrounding yourself with loved ones, in my case my wife and kids, is important and helps put things into perspective. Tough times don't last forever, and one opportunity normally leads to several more.*

**What has been the best career advice given to you?** *The best advice I ever received was from Seal, who said that the boys and I should enjoy every single minute of what we are doing because life is so short, and we never know when it might end.*

**What advice would you give to Black students and professionals starting out and advancing in their careers?** *There are so many words of advice I could give; we might need another book but I'd encourage people to do what they love. Love is a foundation that cannot be broken, it allows you to work longer and harder than anyone else, it enables you to give when you have nothing left to give. It helps you to push through difficult times because it gives you hope. All these things are important when it comes to a career in anything. Also, I would encourage them to nurture their relationships. Relationships are what life is built on, not just in your career but every aspect. And when things get tough, which invariably, they will, it is often family and friends that are by your side to help you get through it and pick up the pieces so cherish those relationships above anything else.*

# MENTORS AND SPONSORS

'It takes a village to raise a child.' – African Proverb

Have you heard of the phrase 'it takes a village to raise a child'? It's an African proverb and basically means that a child needs the guidance and support of many to truly thrive. This can be applied within a career context too. Throughout our career journey, we will require the input, guidance and support of many people, especially those who have been in our shoes before, in order to accomplish our goals and reach our potential. No one gets to the top alone and without the help of others.

## Mentors

When I joined the corporate workplace, I had these weekly catchups with my manager where we would talk about my progress, team news and prepare for the review period. It was useful, but I wasn't receiving wider career guidance and support. Our conversations were mainly around the day to day.

I didn't know I was missing anything until the Vice President (VP) of my team asked me if I had a mentor, and I said no.

Sidenote: When I think about it, it feels commonplace for my white peers to have mentors and sponsors. Over the years, I've heard 'just going to catch up with my mentor', or 'my mentor advised me to . . .', 'my sponsor put me forward for this opportunity where I . . .' and similar comments much more frequently from my white colleagues than my Black peers. Even among my own friendship group of Black women, we only very recently spoke about mentors and sponsors and our relationships with them. It feels like we got the memo late regarding the need to have mentors and sponsors . . .

But anyways, my VP said he wanted to introduce me to someone who he thought would be a great mentor for me. Let's call him C. C was a Black VP in another business area, who was known for progressing from analyst to VP in six years which was unheard of at the company. From the moment we met, we hit it off! The fact that he was Black and from a similar background to me meant that we skipped that initial awkward phase when you don't really know someone, which helped, but as a mentor, C was amazing! He demonstrated so many traits and characteristics which now I can identify as being incredibly important when seeking a mentor:

**He established trust:** From our very first meeting, C explained that everything we discussed would remain between us, he wouldn't share anything with my manager unless I asked him to. This was good because it meant that I felt comfortable talking to him about everything including the challenges with the job, the things I didn't like and more. I didn't go into our meetings with this false pretence that everything was great because I knew I could be honest without it leaving the room. That trust went two ways. When he provided me with the REAL tea about some of the corporate politics he was dealing with, I told no one.

**He had expertise in something I was struggling to navigate:** While my mentor wasn't from the same business area as me, he was an expert in getting promoted; he had been promoted three times in six years. Although I was smashing my work, I didn't really know what else I needed to do to be considered for promotion. He shared with me the things that he did to get promoted at each stage of his career, and we created a plan with actions that I needed to complete consistently to work towards that. This was also a great way to be able to hold me accountable, which he always did.

He also understood the unique challenges that existed for Black women trying to get promoted, so he connected me with two Black women who had recently been promoted to the level I was aspiring to, so they could provide me with slightly more relatable advice.

**He was a great listener:** My mentor listened to me, asked further questions, took notes, showed empathy and provided responses based on that. This is important because you don't want a mentor that just provides you with the same generic advice they give to everyone else, or they just spend all your catch ups talking at you or cutting you off when you're speaking. A great mentor listens to truly understand you, so they can help you.

**His network was large and diverse:** C was well connected and made a conscious effort to get to know people not just within his business area, but beyond, and people at all levels. This was massively helpful to me because when I started to express my desire to potentially move teams, he sent introduction emails to several people in his network who worked in teams I was interested in. This saved me a lot of time.

**He had a good reputation:** Linked to my previous point, he had a good reputation which is key because you don't want to be associated with someone who people don't like or respect.

**He had time:** One of the things that I've struggled with over the years is mentors being inconsistent with the time they are able to commit, and I get it. It's an addition to their day job which I'm sure is busy enough. C was great in that he made the time to ensure we caught up often and even if there was a period where we didn't catch up in person, we were in communication through email or internal Skype messenger (Slack was not a thing then!).

**He really wanted to be a good mentor:** Maybe this sounds silly, but it's something you shouldn't take for granted. Mentoring is fast becoming a 'tick box' exercise for managers in the workplace trying to progress, and many are making it part of their personal brand. While there is nothing wrong with your mentor seeing benefits for themselves from mentoring you (this should be a mutually beneficial relationship), you'd hope this wasn't their primary motivation. Having a mentor, a genuine mentor, who wants to help you win is important and I found that in mine.

I mentioned C was Black, but I've been fortunate to have a mixture of great Black and non-Black mentors throughout my career so far. The main thing to seek is compatibility – are they in the same business area as you or an area you aspire to be in? Does their career path reflect similar steps you hope to make? For where you are at in your career, and what you're trying to accomplish, is that person best positioned to help you succeed?

**The Benefits of Having Internal and External Mentors**

While my example refers to my mentor within my work-place, having mentors both within and outside of your workplace can provide great value, especially when starting to think about your career in more broader terms. One of my closest friends, Honey is a superstar UX designer, and she shared with me the value she gained in having both.

*I personally believe having a mentor is key to personal growth. I've had two mentors so far in my career and I stumbled upon them at different times.*

*One of my mentors noticed me at work struggling to facilitate a session with colleagues of clashing personalities. He supported me through the session and then came up after to give me some tips for next time. Then we scheduled another catch-up over tea a few weeks later, just to see how things were and the relationship blossomed naturally. I think the success of this partnership was because it grew organically, he noticed someone struggling and did what he could to support. Since then, we have regularly catch-ups every two weeks, and it has been amazing for my personal growth to have a mentor that helps me shape my career and hone my craft. My mentor also holds me accountable to my goals but is also there for pastoral support. As a senior designer he can also share his experiences and advice, which motivates me to reach for my potential and success.*

*My second mentor, we actually met on social media. She mentioned she was a senior designer passionate about helping others grow so I reached out to her for help to grow my CV and portfolio ahead of me starting to apply for new opportunities. (Never be afraid of just sending someone a direct message to connect!) As a senior designer, she was able to give me clues as to how I should market myself, and what other senior leaders would be looking for when hiring. She also helped me articulate my achievements into the industry standard so that I will stand out to employers. She understood my experiences, stopped me from underselling myself and gave me the confidence to go out and look for what I deserve. The support helped me push past those internal thoughts of 'I'm not good enough'. This mentorship was only for a season, as the specific reason for the connection was to support my CV and portfolio design, but I don't think I would have been selected for the opportunities I had without her support. It's key to understand what you're looking for in a mentor as the relationship ended after I completed my goals, but we still check in every now and then.*

## Sponsors

While mentors are great for providing more general career advice, sponsors are typically senior people with influence, power and decision-making authority. Mentors listen and support but sponsors act. When they see your excellence, they open doors for you, clear obstacles which may be in your path, and are willing to put their own reputation on the line to advocate for you.

I remember my first ever sponsor and how we met (let's call him D). It was several years ago at this company event and we both started talking, but not about our immediate work. He was a managing director of a different business area to the one I was in and he spoke to me about his family and his teenage daughters mainly, and I shared with him my background and my career journey to date at the time. He expressed how impressed he was and wished that his daughters aspired to women like me and weren't so engrossed in the 'celeb' culture. We spoke some more and then we swapped emails and he asked me to send him my CV which I did. A few days later, he emailed me and said he shared my CV with his daughters because he wanted them to see what a woman can achieve while being so young. I was shocked but it truly meant so much that he thought so highly of me very early on. In our first meeting following the networking event, we discussed some of my career goals and I'll never forget when he said, 'Who do I need to shout about you to?' and boy did he shout! I used to receive emails from senior colleagues across the business which would start with 'D told us about the incredible work you are doing . . .' or 'D shared your CV with us and WOW!'. D would occasionally reach out to my managers to make sure that I was being given the right opportunities to truly show my skills in front of the right people. There was this one occasion where the US CEO for the company came to London and did a Q&A session with a small group of people and D managed to get me in. I was definitely the most junior person among the group, but I raised my hand to ask a question and the CEO laughed and said it was a great question before proceeding to answer. Even if it was only for one minute, I got onto the radar of every single person in that room, and it paid dividends during the networking sessions after. When promotion conversations were happening, D sent an email to my managers, their managers, and other stakeholders (which I screenshotted and still have). A few things he said:

'I was impressed with Rene from day one, especially when she shared her CV with me.'

'I have introduced Rene to a number of senior stakeholders across the business and the feedback has been excellent and consistent.'

'Rene is not only great at her job as you are aware, but her passion and energy is infectious, and I would have zero hesitation in recommending her progression in the organisation.'

D was a great sponsor because he:

- Connected me to other senior leaders
- Connected me to new opportunities
- Advocated for my promotion
- Promoted my visibility
- Provided me with career advice – beyond my day-to-day career and helped me to believe in myself and self-actualise even greater goals for myself

A sponsor is critical for career advancement and can propel your career by advocating for your promotion, championing your name and work in rooms you're not in and recommend you for opportunities that may not be publicly available. For Black employees, this is even more necessary because current organisation processes for progression are not working for us. Research from the *Business In the Community: Black Voices* report revealed that Black employees are the most likely to have to wait for three years or more for a promotion, are most likely to have never been promoted, and are more likely to have never been put forward for a new role by their manager.[*] For Black women in particular, despite wanting to be promoted, the research shows that we are not being promoted into leadership roles at the same rate as other groups and many of us don't feel supported by managers or that promotions are fair and objective.[†]

A well-invested and committed sponsor can offer us a lifeline and help us break through the 'concrete ceiling' if they are able to advocate on our behalf when these decisions are being made regarding our career.

---

**The 'Hype Man' Effect**

According to research by the *Harvard Business Review*, having a sponsor also positively impacts our own actions in the workplace.[‡] Both men and women with sponsors were more likely:

• To be satisfied with their rate of career advancement
• To ask their manager for a career stretch assignment
• To ask for a pay rise

---

* Bitc.org.uk. 'Race at work: black voice.' (23 August 2020). Retrieved from: https://www.bitc.org.uk/report/race-at-work-black-voices-report/
† Lean.org. 'The State of Black Women in Corporate America.' (2020). Retrieved from: https://leanin.org/research/state-of-black-women-in-corporate-america/section-1-representation
‡ 30percentclub.org. 'The Sponsor Effect: Breaking Through The Last Glass Ceiling.' (December 2010). Retrieved from: https://30percent-club.org/wp-content/uploads/2014/08/The-Sponsor-Effect.pdf

Having what I call a 'hype man' (not necessarily a man, by the way) in your corner fighting for your career advancement, letting the world know just how wavy you are can give you that much needed confidence boost to take more ownership of your career. When I think of a hype man, former Arsenal legend and football pundit Ian Wright MBE aka Uncle Ian comes to mind. The way he gasses up young Black footballers, heaping tonnes of praise on them often when others don't, having their backs in rooms they're not even in is just everything. We all need an Ian Wright in our career. Period.

## The politics of sponsorship when Black

Although Black employees want sponsors, recognising the value that having one can bring[*], according to research, Black women, are significantly less likely to have sponsors compared to other groups.[†]

Securing a sponsor as a Black employee can be difficult because leaders often tend to support and advocate for those that are like them in many ways, which makes sense right? On a human level, we do gravitate more to people who are like us. Known as the Similar-to-me bias, in the workplace, hiring and promotion decisions tend to be impacted by the fact that those in positions of power overvalue and prioritise those who look like them, think like them and share other similarities. In most workplaces, leaders and decision-makers are white men, who tend to then

* Bitc.org.uk. 'Race at work: black voice.' (23 August 2020). Retrieved from: https://www.bitc.org.uk/report/race-at-work-black-voices-report/
† Mckinsey.com. 'Women in the Workplace 2020.' (30 September 2020)

sponsor other white men, at the detriment of Black employees who miss out on that much needed support. Over three quarters of sponsors select individuals of the same race or gender to sponsor.* It's the reason why we see the same type of people again and again at the top of most industries.

Something that I noticed when I first started working (and it's changing a bit now) is I never felt like the few Black people who were in positions of power were outwardly advocating for other Black employees. I would see white leaders rave on about how amazing other white employees were and sometimes minority employees. I didn't see this energy from the few Black decision-makers there were, and I didn't get it. My thoughts were 'why would you not want to be seen to help and uplift us in the same way your white peers are unapologetically uplifting their people?' But over time, I realised that many of the Black people we see in positions of power in our workplace are still navigating the exact same issues that we are: the racism, microaggressions, the pay inequality and more. Their senior status doesn't make them exempt from those things. A study found that when minorities in leadership positions advocate for other minorities, they receive lower performance ratings.† The researchers believe that this is because they are potentially seen as 'selfishly advancing the social standing of their own low-status demographic groups'. Black people are punished for doing the same thing their white peers do.

* Coqual.org. 'The Sponsor Dividend.' (2019). Retrieved from: https://coqual.org/reports/the-sponsor-dividend/
† Journals.aom.org. 'Does Diversity-Valuing Behavior Result in Diminshed Performance Ratings for Non-White and Female Leaders?'. (3 March 2016). Retrieved from: https://journals.aom.org/doi/full/10.5465/amj.2014.0538

A report from PayScale also revealed that the race and gender of your sponsor can hugely impact what you earn. Black women with Black sponsors earn nearly 12% less than those with white sponsors.[*] Not only do we need sponsors, but who our sponsors *are* is also important.

## Seeking mentors and sponsors

Seeking mentors and sponsors doesn't necessarily need to be a strategic exercise. Often these relationships happen organically and over time without it being anything too formal, however some things you may want to think about are:

*What are your career goals?*
This doesn't need to be five to ten years ahead and could even be your career goals in the short term. Are you trying to pivot into another area of your business or wider industry, acquire certain skills, or move up? These questions will help you identify the type of sponsor or mentor you might like.

*What type of mentor or sponsor can help you achieve your goals?*
Based on your goals, you can now start to identify potential mentors and sponsors which will help you meet them. These can be individuals with a certain skillset, with a network you'd like to tap into, or individuals with a certain level of influence and

* Paycale.com. 'Sponsors: Valuable Allies Not Everyone Has.' (31 July 2019). Retrieved from: https://www.payscale.com/data/mentorship-sponsorship-benefits

decision-making power. A key thing to note here is that especially with regards to sponsors, they don't need to be really senior, they just need to have power and influence. Seniority doesn't always equate to power and vice versa.

*Reaching out and establishing the relationships*

As I mentioned previously, these relationships are often formed organically and sometimes spontaneously (not planned for) like how I met D, who became my sponsor. However, if you do have specific people in mind to be your mentor or sponsor, feel free to reach out to them via email or a platform like LinkedIn if they don't work at your company. If you know they're going to be at a certain event, maybe go along so you can speak to them in person. One thing I will say is whether you're reaching out in person or online, don't immediately ask for that person to be your mentor or sponsor, especially if it's someone you're engaging with for the first time. Start by introducing yourself, share why you're reaching out to them (try to refer to things you may have in common here, and a little flattery always helps) and then ask to catch up. Build that relationship over time.

You may also find that your workplace has a mentorship and sponsorship programme. In the last few years, a growing number of companies have started to create these programmes for their minority employees. In one company, I was part of a mentorship programme specifically for Black employees with less than five years' experience and in another company, I was part of the team creating a mentorship programme for Black employees. Do I think these programmes are always effective? Unfortunately, not:

- Sometimes organisations copy and paste these programmes that worked for other underrepresented groups e.g., white women, without tailoring them to address the unique issues that Black employees face in the workplace.
- Some mentors and sponsors only participate to elevate their own career, fulfilling the minimum requirements of the programme, but not providing you any real value (they probably got some feedback that they don't do enough to nurture talent, and then signed up).

However, I still believe they are worth a try especially if you are finding it difficult to connect with a mentor or sponsor through your own efforts.

## Attracting sponsors

If a sponsor is going to advocate for you and put their neck on the line to help you get ahead, you have to be excellent. You don't just 'get' a sponsor, you have to earn one. When sponsors take great people under their wing, it also bolsters their own reputation as someone cultivating the next generation of talent. When I met D, he was impressed with everything I told him about my career journey at that point, and therefore he wanted to keep in contact with me. As he got to know me more, my career goals, heard great feedback about my work and from the stakeholders he connected me with, he wanted to do everything he could to elevate me. To attract a sponsor, you should:

- Have a track record for delivering great work consistently and make sure you amplify that. Share your wins and successes – potential sponsors want to support outstanding individuals.

- Do things that will increase your visibility and increase your exposure e.g., speak at an internal or external event or volunteer to lead an initiative, as this will help you to get on the radar of a potential sponsor.
- Ensure there are other stakeholders that can speak well of you and your work.

## Maintaining these relationships

How much value you derive from your mentors and sponsors massively depends on how well you manage and maintain these relationships.

- Be clear about your aspirations and goals and any issues you're struggling to navigate as this will enable your mentor and sponsor to understand the best ways they can help and support you.
- Make things easy for them, for example, meeting at their preferred time or location (if it doesn't put you out too much) as it shows thoughtfulness, especially as they are the one helping you mainly.
- Establish up front how often you plan to meet, best channels for communication, anything which will provide your relationship some structure.
- Ensure the relationship isn't one-sided and you're not just reaching out when you need something. Even if you're relatively early in your career, it doesn't mean you don't have anything to offer, which is something I always used to think.

Ask them if there is anything you can help with no matter how small. There have been times when I've signed up for certain initiatives because my sponsor was short of people to get involved and I had the free time. Those things don't go unnoticed.

- Be accountable. If your mentor or sponsor gives you feedback or advises that you do certain things that will ultimately help your career, show that you've acted upon this.
- Be proactive, follow up with them, provide updates. Don't always wait for them to reach out.

There are some that say that having a sponsor is far more important than a mentor but I disagree. They both serve different purposes and become more important at different points in your career. For example, at the very beginning of your career when you're learning the ropes, you probably won't need a sponsor then, upward progression may not be your priority just yet, but a mentor who can help you navigate the day to day of your career, is probably going to be more valuable. As you get more experience under your belt, start to excel and think about moving up, a sponsor may be better placed to accelerate your upward progression.

Relationships are at the heart of everything we do at work and so putting in the time to build and maintain them is key and not just the relationships you think you can gain something from. Give that same energy to your work husbands and wives, your trusted peers who you can lean on for advice or cry to when things aren't going so well. As a Black woman in the workplace, those are the relationships which have enabled me to function daily because those people are in the trenches with me for better or worse. Also, when you feel that you are able to, make sure to throw the ladder back down. Whether formally or informally, support those that are coming up next. Few of us get through the door and even less of us get to the top, so we need to make sure that we share all the things we are learning with each other.

# RESOURCE: MENTORS AND SPONSORS

Knowing the differences between mentors and sponsors can help to identify when you need them and what you should be looking for. I have provided a non-exhaustive summary of what I see as the main differences between them.

| Mentors | Sponsors |
| --- | --- |
| Mentors are individuals at any level with your desired expertise and experience | Sponsors are often (but not always) senior level individuals invested in your upwards progression |
| Mentors provide advice on how to navigate certain aspects of your career that you need guidance with e.g., how to attain certain skills, how to get promoted | Sponsors utilise their power, influence, and networks to directly connect you to opportunities |
| Mentors play a more supportive role, helping you in the background | Sponsors promote and champion you publicly, using their platform to help get you visibility |
| Mentors provide support to those regardless of performance | Sponsors typically support those who are already high-achieving performers |
| Mentors help you to plan out your career vision and goals | Sponsor actively partake in driving your career vision and goals |
| Mentors often mentor several different people | Sponsors are very selective about who they sponsor. They sponsor few people |
| Mentors invest their time and knowledge | Sponsors invest their social and political capital |

# ANU ADEBAJO

*Senior Investment Manager, British Patient Capital*

Anu is a Senior Investment Manager at British Patient Capital focusing on investments into venture capital funds and sitting on fund advisory boards. She is also a venture fellow with early stage fund The Fund London. Prior to this Anu spent five years investing with the Angel CoFund, an early-stage venture capital fund.

Anu is an advocate for the representation of ethnic minorities in the venture capital (VC) and private equity (PE) industry and is on the advisory board of Future VC. She previously ran an award-winning online hair and beauty business and has an undergraduate degree from the University of Nottingham.

**Tell us about yourself?** *I was born in Nigeria but moved to the UK before I turned one. We moved around a lot before finally settling in Sheffield in the north of England when I was seven. I've ended up staying in Sheffield and studied Finance, Accounting and Management at University of Nottingham.*

**What was your motivation to get into investment management and how did you secure your first opportunity within this space?** *During university I knew that I wanted to be in the private equity industry. I loved the idea of helping several companies grow and develop at the same time. I get bored focusing on just one thing.*

247

*I tried cold emailing a few partners at PE firms who obviously didn't reply (I've since got to meet one of those partners and have told him this story!). The 2008 financial crisis happened just as I was graduating, and job prospects suddenly became scarce.*

*I started my own business in the Black online beauty space which gave me an insight into what founders go through but decided that it wasn't for me as ultimately you have to be obsessed about a singular thing – your company. I wanted to do something completely different, so I moved to Nigeria to do my NYSC which is a one-year programme where you work and do charity work at the same time. I honestly thought it would be a permanent move and I started interviewing at accounting firms and PE firms, but unfortunately, I didn't get any offers (the first time in my life I'd been for an interview and not got the role). I moved back to the UK and happened to see an analyst role for a venture capital fund in Sheffield which is incredibly rare. By that time, I knew that I wanted to be in the VC side of private equity, so this was perfect for me. I applied online, got a response from the recruiter, and ended up getting the job. There were people with more experience than me during the interview, but the feedback was that I had shown the most passion and knowledge about the area. Don't underestimate the power of doing your research and showing enthusiasm even if you don't have the technical qualifications of other candidates!*

**The venture capital and private equity industry has become an attractive space to work. Why do you think this is? Also, what would you say are common misconceptions about working in VC?** *People in general are more aware of the tech world and its impact. Not everyone can be or wants to be an entrepreneur but* *working in the VC industry gives you the chance to contribute to the success of disruptive, world-changing companies and many of the companies we interact with most today are VC-backed.*

*It's good to be realistic though, for most it isn't a glamorous role. At the junior level especially, there is a lot of work without the external recognition. Not every firm can be a top firm, and it's a very competitive industry. The real power of a VC is in networking like crazy – with Limited Partner investors as potential investors for your next fund, with other VCs to share deal flow and provide follow-on investment for your companies and with founders to find the best ones early. You also need to be able to add value to founders usually beyond just capital. This can be anything from operational skills you picked up elsewhere to a useful network you can plug them into. Or maybe you have amazing people skills and can build such a great rapport with founders that you are always their first point of contact. Either way, being able to spot good companies isn't enough, the real work starts after the investment has been made.*

**For Black students and professionals looking to get their foot into the industry, what are some of the things they should be doing, how can they stand out?** *Traditionally, many VCs have networked their way into the industry, being able to bring contacts and wealth with them. Most Black people aren't networked in that way, so it helps to be creative. The first step is to do your research, sign up to VCs' own mailing lists and follow them on Twitter to see what subjects they're talking about. Decide what interests you and start to dive deeper into it. Once you build a point of view, start interacting with people already in the VC space. I presented at an online event and had a flurry of LinkedIn requests* *afterwards. Most contained a standard message, but one person passed on a diversity article that I hadn't seen before. It made them stand out and is likely to make me more responsive should they reach out to me again in the future. Finding ways to be helpful is always appreciated and is more likely to elicit a response when most people are inundated with requests.*

*Another way to stand out is to show, don't tell. If you can make angel investments, your portfolio is a great sign of your picking ability and an insight into the way you think and analyse. Even if you can't invest in the company, you can write an investment note on why you would have invested. Why not post it to yourself, so you have a timestamp showing that you formed your view ahead of the hype.*

*Finally, those looking to enter the industry are fortunate that several groups exist to try to increase diverse entrants, such as Future VC and Included VC. I'm also part of Black Venture Collective, a group of UK Black VCs that hold events for aspiring Black VCs and supports the Black VC community. We want to see more Black VCs entering the ecosystem, becoming decision-makers, and getting more Black businesses funded.*

**You're one of a few Black VCs in the UK and more generally, Black representation in the VC space is small. Does this present any challenges? If so, what impact would having more Black VCs have in the space?** *One of the biggest challenges of being one of the few Black VCs in the UK is finding balance between representing Black people in the ecosystem and looking after myself. I passionately want to see more Black representation at the decision-making levels. I want to see more Black founders receive significant investment capital. I try and use the position*

*I'm in to make this happen, but it can be emotionally draining when you put so much effort in for what looks like no change.*

*I still have my day job to do and summer 2020 was particularly hard. I was being asked to speak at many events and help organisations with their Black Lives Matter statements while still having investments to make. As one of the more senior Black people in the industry I didn't feel like I could turn things down. Not everyone feels able to be vocal for fear of how their firms will react and so I often put myself forward in acknowledgment of my relative privilege.*

*I'm fortunate that I have a great Managing Director who I could be honest about the impact of this on me with and who encouraged to me ease off my day-to-day work, knowing how important it was to me to speak on diversity in VC. As Black people in VC, we are just trying to do our jobs well like everyone else, but we often feel additional pressure to do everything we can to improve our industry. There aren't enough of us at the moment to shoulder the burden or to remove the need for the shouldering in the first place. First and foremost, we need to take care of our own wellbeing or else we'll burn out trying to solve systemic issues that we didn't create in the first place!*

**What challenges have you experienced in your career and how have you overcome them?** *I was in a role where it became clear that there wouldn't be any opportunity for progression. I had to take responsibility for my career, so I identified a team that had the kind of culture I wanted and shadowed one of the team for a while. When a role came up within that team that would have represented a promotion for me, the director strongly encouraged me to apply which I did and successfully got the role. Sometimes* *you have to know when to cut your losses and being part of a team with a great culture has a huge impact on your experience.*

*Given my position, I feel a responsibility to speak on diversity in VC but there was a point when I started feeling typecast. A recruiter once said to me that I should be careful that I don't just end up being the face of diversity and not being able to showcase my work. I've made an effort to be more selective of the diversity-related events I do speak at, signposting to other Black speakers in the industry where appropriate. I prioritise high-impact activity or where the audience is young Black people. I've also made sure my work and expertise can speak for itself and speak on non-diversity-related industry topics too. Don't let anyone make you feel like your only expertise is speaking about diversity. Being Black doesn't make you an expert on the entire Black experience, only your own. You should also be allowed to showcase your sector expertise and interests.*

***What have been some of your career highs and lows?*** *I was able to help my industry body organise a series focusing on ethnic minorities, the first of its kind in the UK VC ecosystem. Early on we decided that the launch should be a breakfast event as we weren't sure whether there would be sufficient demand for it. On the day the venue was packed! I also got to give a speech which I could tell surprised a lot of people and opened the door for me to talk more at other events about diversity and inclusion. I've also got to meet and spend time with people in my industry who I admired growing up.*

*Another high point is seeing the number of Black people enter the VC industry. When I started in 2012, I didn't see a single Black face at any events. I remember scouring LinkedIn trying to find someone who looked like me and they just didn't exist.*

*Every time someone joins the industry or gets promoted; I cele-*
*brate. I'm so happy that the next generation will never have the*
*feeling of being the only one.*

*With regards to low points, I had a role where I was the most*
*junior person in my team. For years I had to "pay my dues" but*
*wasn't really given an opportunity to prove myself. In our shared*
*inbox, I found an email between a colleague and our director where*
*the colleague asked if I should join a call. My director had replied*
*that I should "remain focused on areas where I add value". They*
*didn't know that I had seen the email, but it was a knock which*
*ultimately motivated me to show them that they had underesti-*
*mated me. I learned that not everyone can see the potential in you,*
*so you have to be your biggest cheerleader. Proving people wrong*
*can be a huge driver but I don't think it should be the main one and*
*prefer positive motivations like proving your potential to yourself.*

**What has been the best career advice given to you?** *Build your*
*personal profile. It's a great way to meet people within your indus-*
*try and also get on the radar of potential employers and peers.*

**What advice would you give to Black students and professionals**
**starting out and advancing their careers?** *The world really is your*
*oyster (as clichéd as that sounds). Don't allow yourself to believe*
*that a particular career isn't possible for you. You just need to*
*work out a way to get there which may include several steps that*
*don't necessarily appear sequential. If you asked me ten years*
*ago where I would be today, my response would not have been*
*the place I actually am in today. I've allowed myself to be open*
*to possibilities that are outside of my plan and I'm allowing my*
*values to drive me in ways I couldn't have anticipated.*

# JUSTIN ONUEKWUSI

*Head of Retail Multi-Asset Funds, LGIM*

Justin is Head of Retail Multi-Asset Funds at Legal & General Investment Management (LGIM) and part of a team managing over £50 billion for pension schemes and savers globally. He leads on the management of the award-winning multi-Index fund range for LGIM.

A member of LGIM's Global Diversity Leadership Council, Justin co-chairs the Legal & General Inclusion Team (LEGIT), which aims to create a culture supporting LGIM through networks and events. Externally, Justin is an adviser to the board of City Hive Ltd, which focuses on driving diversity within asset management. In addition, he sits on the steering committee of the industry-wide Diversity Project and is co-founder #talkaboutBlack, a movement which focuses on creating more senior Black corporate leaders. Justin featured on the 2020 EMpower Senior Executive Leaders list, was a finalist in the 2019 Black British Business Awards and in 2020, was awarded the honour of the Freedom of the City of London.

**Tell us about yourself?** *I am a fund manager working at Legal & General Investment Management (LGIM) working in the multi-asset funds team. The team manages approximately £50 billion for pension funds and savers across the world.*

Growing up in a single parent household with my mother and younger brother just north of Manchester city centre in the Crumpsall/Cheetham area, times were often tough. I remember getting our house repossessed in the early nineties' recession, being evicted from our house in my GSCE year, living in temporary accommodation infested with cockroaches and working in fast food restaurants until the early hours of the morning to pay for a household computer to help with sixth form assignments. That said, as the sole breadwinner, my mother always provided me with everything I could have asked for and more. As a teacher, she ingrained in me the importance of education.

That, and a solid foundation of friends and wider family network, played a significant role in my life. I am proudly state school-educated, going to Catholic schools from the age of four to eighteen years old. Outside of my inner circle of friends, many of those who grew up around us were not as lucky. They didn't really get the chance of having a good education, many got sucked into the wrong circles, many got in trouble with the law . . . this unfortunately is the reality of growing up as a working-class person in an inner-city area in Britain. This is only exacerbated when you are Black.

Originally part of the Windrush generation, my mother was born in Grenada in the Caribbean and was one of nine children. Now I am a parent myself, I often wonder just how she managed to balance a full-time job, the upkeep of the house and bringing up two boys. My father was born in Nigeria in the Igbo region of Anambra. My father lived on the other side of the world in Los Angeles in the USA when I was growing up. I also have another brother who lives in California.

*Outside of work, I am a married father of two where my experience growing up means that family means everything to me. It is so important to me that I give my children better opportunities than I had. Finally, and very importantly, I am a season ticket holder at Manchester United and I try to get to as many games throughout the year, which is less and less these days!*

## What was your motivation to get into asset management and how did you secure your first opportunity within this space?

*Always having a passion for numerical subjects, I studied mathematics, politics and economics at A Level, with the objective of becoming an actuary. My passion for becoming at actuary was driven by a maths teacher telling me how great this 'unknown' profession was and that I needed to work hard to even have a chance in becoming one.*

*Following my A Levels, I managed to get into the University of Warwick to study Economics. During my final year, I managed to secure my dream role of becoming an actuary, at Aon Consulting (now Aon Hewitt). Well, at least I thought it was my dream job at the time. However, once I started the role as a pension actuarial consultant, I quickly realised that it wasn't for me.*

*In fact, the first six months were deeply depressing for me. Not only was I deeply unsettled moving from Manchester to London, but I also didn't enjoy the job and really disliked the content of the actuarial exams. While I liked numerical subjects, I realised there were people who liked the theory of mathematics a lot more than I did. However, I was trapped on a graduate program. I began looking for other roles externally within the first month. Then came a glimmer of light ... following a presentation by the Aon's investment consulting team, I felt I had identified a role which suited my passion and importantly, my skillset. I made it my mission to try and seek out a role in that team. I started to email the Head of Investment Consulting directly (and maybe quite naïvely) asking him to understand more about the role. Before I knew it, he called me for a very informal interview with him and one of the team leaders. Very quickly after, I secured a role within the investment consulting team.*

*After a few years in the Aon role, I felt I wanted to understand more about the investments I was recommending so I wanted to focus more on the research of fund managers and the selection of different investments in portfolios. Aon Consulting didn't really have any roles in the research team therefore I had to move on. I found a role at Merrill Lynch Wealth Management as a fund researcher. Working at an American bank, the culture was completely different: longer hours, a more intense working environment, and less leeway for mistakes.*

*Again, though like my time at Aon, it was a hugely enjoyable three and half years. I oversaw the US equity portfolios and also the selection of alternative investments. Here, I worked at one of the banks most affected by the financial crisis, where many extremely smart people I worked with lost their jobs. It is here I learnt that no matter how talented you are, financial markets can make even the brightest people humble.*

*After the global financial crisis, when the job market had started to pick up, one of my colleagues went to head up the multi-asset funds team at Aviva Investors. After a few months, he called me up and asked to meet me for a coffee, asking me to interview for a vacancy to help him manage a £70 billion range* of funds. *While wealth management sits within asset management, it wasn't until the Aviva Investors role that I got exposed to institutional fund management. I suppose in many ways I accidentally fell into an asset management role but having interviewed fund managers for previous seven years, moving to the other side of the table was appealing and it fell into my lap in a fortunate way.*

**According to research, only 1% of the fund management industry identify as Black.**[*] **Why do you think Black representation is so poor, especially in the more senior positions?** *This lack of representation at the top of organisations is not confined to the savings and investment industry where I work. It spans across finance, law, insurance, professional services and the entire corporate sphere. For a better future, we need talent that represents our clients' interests. While we know it's the right thing to do, clearly the current methods we are using to get more Black people into the asset management industry are not working. Within #talkaboutBlack, we have identified a series of structural barriers – or 'kinks in the hosepipe' that prevents Black talent from reaching their full potential. These are:*

*1. **Community**: The socio-economic situation in which many UK-born Black people find themselves means this demographic experience higher rates of unemployment, crime and mental health challenges.*

* Diversityproject.com. '#TalkAboutBlack Workstream.' (2020). Retrieved from: https://diversityproject.com/talkaboutblack

2. **Pipeline:** *These socio-economic challenges result in an under-performance in education when compared to white counterparts and other ethnic minority groups.*

3. **Entry:** *Should these individuals achieve a good education they are unlikely to want to work in an unrepresentative industry, and less likely to be successful in securing their preferred roles.*

4. **Career progression:** *When these Black individuals do break into the industry, they typically end up in support functions, have higher rates of attrition and rarely progress to leadership or revenue-generating positions.*

5. **Taboo:** *Discussions about race remain a taboo subject in the workplace and more broadly in society.*

*Previous attempts to resolve these challenges have been piece-meal and have treated ethnic minorities as a homogenous group, hence the term 'BAME'. A wholesale approach is necessary with a specific focus on single minority groups. To resolve issues in the workplaces requires resolving issues in society.*

**What does life look like as one of the few Black fund managers on a day-to-day basis?** *It is a real privilege to be investing other people's savings and pensions. I have become a respected and well-known fund manager in the UK and Ireland.*

*Microaggressions do exist and at times can really wear you down. Whether it's being mistaken for a security guard, taxi driver or janitor in the building where I work as a fund manager. It's being presumed to be a tea boy or tech support right before a big presentation, which I am leading. Maybe it's being followed around the sports shop during my gym break at lunch or being called by one of my mentees on how to respond to office situations. They might seem like small things, but they all add up. They become draining and simply reinforce the message: You don't belong here.*

*This is why I am dedicated to progression in the workplace and am the founder of the EnCircle Mentoring Circles where Black role models provide group mentoring for corporate professionals. The mentors share their experiences and discuss the tools required to navigate the barriers the have faced throughout their career, leading by example. Being a fund manager and Head of Retail Multi-Asset Funds in a successful team managing over £60 billion means that I can help and encourage others to do the same. I can empathise with having been told constantly you are not going to succeed at school and at work, having a work review and the feedback being that you are lazy or questioning whether investment is the right career for me given that nobody on the investment floor looks like me. These are just some of the themes from these mentoring circles that me and the other mentors can relate to directly.*

**You've been vocal about the need for more ethnic diversity within asset management and co-founded the #talkaboutBlack campaign. What advice would you give to Black professionals when navigating or starting conversations about race in the workplace?** *Many people have contacted me over the last couple of years saying how #talkaboutBlack has helped to progress their careers and to have conversations within their businesses. Having these conversations within the workplace are emotionally draining and can be unfruitful especially at the beginning, particularly if you have few senior Black people in your organisation. The difficulty is often that it can be hard to truly* *empathise with somebody's perspective if the person has not experienced the same struggle. Telling stories about our own journey and how we have felt allows other ethnicities to empathise and start to really understand.*

*Yet while it is important for Black people to be involved in the initiatives that create better representation, they should not feel it is their responsibility. Indeed, Black people did not create the structural barriers that have led to the lack of representation, so it is impossible for them alone to break them down. Engaging with senior Black people outside of your own organisation can also help. Indeed, one role of #talkaboutBlack is to engage with corporations about what they should do to have better representation.*

**What challenges have you experienced in your career and how have you overcome them?** *I think the one of the biggest challenges for Black professionals is to try and establish what you want to do. Even if you are not sure, focusing on a particular area is important as it allows you to focus your efforts and become knowledgeable when prepping for interviews. It is an extremely competitive job market therefore being able to focus will give you an advantage at the recruitment stage. The statistics show that Black candidates are less likely to get jobs than those from other backgrounds. Indeed, I am dedicated to create a fairer and more level playing field, but we must also do everything we can to give ourselves every chance of succeeding. While we can of course complain about bias and being disadvantaged in the current system and we must work to break down structural barriers, change, measured by fairer representation will take a generation. Yet, it's not enough to simply talk or even just action initiatives. In order to make the change required, we also have to* *be successful in our day-to-day roles – we have to strive to win. Focus can help to provide that foundation.*

**What have been some of your career highs and lows?** *There have been a number of high points in my career, and they centre around getting recognition for the work that I have done:*

- *Voted by my colleagues 'CIO team member of the year' at Merrill Lynch in 2009 – this was important to me as it was the first time I had been recognised as doing well in my role so openly and publicly.*
- *Recognised in the EMpower Ethnic Minority Executive Role Model list for 2018, 2019 and 2020 due to my work in diversity and inclusion.*
- *Winning the 2018 Future Role Model for the Invest in Ethnicity Awards.*
- *Winning various awards for the £7 billion Legal & General Multi-Index Funds that I have managed since 2013, which today are one of the most popular and best performing funds in the UK.*
- *Evening Standard 2019 (Project 1000): Voted one of the 1000 most influential people in London.*
- *Being awarded the Freedom of the City of London for my work in diversity and inclusion in 2020.*
- *Being recognised by my home city in the Manchester Evening News during Black History Month in 2020.*

*As a fund manager, I have worked in teams that have generally delivered strong performance and a barometer of this are the flows into my funds. However, they are periods of time when every fund manager underperforms. These periods are generally pretty disheartening, lonely and tend to be characterised by constant soul-searching – where one constantly questions the robustness of how they came to make decisions. Of course, with experience you learn how important communication and visibility is at these times to clients and internal teams. It also does get easier though as over time, those investors that have historically experienced long periods of strong returns are much more likely to maintain confidence in you and the team during shorter time periods of underperformance. Still, periods of weak performance are difficult to deal with and always feel like a personal attack on your competence.*

**What has been the best career advice given to you?** *The best career advice to me has been from my boss at Aviva Investors, Head of Multi-Asset Funds, Yoram Lustig. The advice was simply 'you can do it'. By the confidence he showed me in everything that I did, he constantly challenged my insecurities and self-doubt and by doing so taught me the importance of continuously pushing ourselves to the point that we feel uncomfortable in order to keep on achieving.*

**What advice would you give to Black students and professionals starting out and advancing their career?** *Focus and work hard. There is no substitute for focus. I'm a big believer that while many people are naturally talented, in order to specialise and harness that talent, focus, and lots of it, is necessary.*

*Hard work does not start and end in the office. It is developing softer skills by attending functions, networking, after-work reading, getting professional qualifications out of the way early and volunteering for wider team and company initiatives outside your day-to-day work. LinkedIn and social networks make it easier these days to find other Black people starting out in the industry – it is important to reach out to them, share your experiences and learn from each other. Humility is extremely important. I remember a new graduate saying to me that she will never work harder or learn more than she did during her degree. Three years later she had quit her job stressing how difficult it was. Everybody makes lots of mistakes particularly early on in their careers. What is important is how you learn from those mistakes.*

# TANGY MORGAN

*Senior Advisor, Bank of England,*
*Prudential Regulation Committee*

Tangy C. Morgan is a (re)insurance industry expert and senior advisor with over thirty-five years of experience in the US and global markets. Her executive career includes senior leadership roles at Chubb & Son, TIG, Guy Carpenter, AIG and Lloyd's of London. She currently serves as a Senior Advisor to the Bank of England's Prudential Regulation Committee and Strategia Worldwide, Ltd. Prior to her insurance career Tangy was an Oil and Gas Production Analyst for Conoco Inc (ConocoPhillips Inc).

Tangy is a member of the advisory boards for InsureCore and Cachet (Estonia) and member of the Boston University Alumni Board and Tennessee State University College of Business Alumni Board. She advises technology start-ups in financial services and has been a mentor on accelerators which include Techstars London.

Tangy frequently speaks internationally on topics such as board governance, implications of technology on traditional business models and sustainability, algorithmic bias as well as diversity and inclusion. She is a graduate of Boston University (MSc) and Tennessee State University (BS). Tangy is a member of several philanthropic organisations and holds dual citizenship status in the UK and US.

*Dear Reader,*

*Something I am often asked is how I managed to go from a career in petroleum to working as a Senior Advisor for the Bank of England. As I look back over the years since I graduated from Tennessee State University until now, some forty years later, I too ask myself – how did this happen? Could I have envisaged or planned for this?*

*I grew up with parents that were both successful in their professional careers as a business owner and educator. They demonstrated and expected me to achieve as they had, regardless of my gender, race, or southern US roots.*

*They were able to send me to private schools and taught me to be proud of my heritage and be an ambassador for my race to others. I was told that I could do anything that I set my mind to and because I respected them and saw them live according to this, I believed them!*

*Everyone may not have the same family situation, but we must believe in ourselves and not limit our possibilities based on our origins. I also believe that we must be prepared to step out of our comfort zone and be willing to be the 'first' and bring others along with us.*

*After my graduation from Tennessee State University, I accepted a position with Conoco, Inc. as an Oil and Gas Production Analyst that required me to complete a six-month offshore training program in the Gulf of Mexico. I was one of the first women and women of colour to accept this role and successfully complete before being assigned to positions in offices in Louisiana.*

*I then changed careers after the US oil and gas market downturn and started over again in the (re)insurance industry where* my executive career spanned various global organisations in the US and Bermuda. I ultimately accepted a senior executive role in London in 2002.

Relocating to London brought many challenges and career highlights being a woman of colour as I was the 'first' and 'only' in my roles. As Senior Vice-President of Starr Excess International (AIG), I was the first woman of colour to hold such a global remit within the company. Subsequently, I was asked to join the Corporation of Lloyd's of London in a senior executive position making me the first African American to hold this role. Currently, I am the first African American appointed as a Senior Advisor to the Bank of England's Prudential Regulation Authority.

Throughout my journey the following three pillars have been key:

1. **Confidence**: I have not chosen to focus on the fact that I have been the 'only one', I have actually used it to my advantage to dispel perceptions of tokenism.

2. **Risk-taking**: I started my career in petroleum and then started (re)insuring petroleum companies. Now I advise the Bank of England's Prudential Regulation Authority. The diverse career path has been both rewarding and challenging, but I have been willing to take roles that I knew would stretch me intellectually. Don't be afraid of this stretch.

3. **Relationships**: Many people use the term networking, but, to me, that sounds clinical. I can honestly say that all my jobs since university have come about through someone passing my name on for opportunities that were not on my radar. Be your best possible (and honest) self with everyone in your network and they will think of you when opportunities arise.

*Over the past few years with the benefit of hindsight, I have added* **resilience** *to the above three pillars. As you can imagine, over the last four decades I have had ups and downs personally and professionally. However, I have come to understand that it was important to reach out and not be too proud to ask for help, advice or guidance. The professional relationships I cultivated over the years have been of value during these times.*

*I believe that my life pillars of confidence, risk-taking, networking and resilience have been the threads that have allowed me to focus and not waste energy on negative comments, situations, or colleagues. I have focused on the lessons learned and used those to inform my next role or opportunity.*

*Although I believe that this letter will provide you with insights on navigating your career, technology will play a key role in your career. This will bring about the need to be adaptable and continue to hone skills for opportunities that will come about through innovation and new jobs that will be created. Like me, you may find yourself in a totally different career, but the journey will be all the more enjoyable for it.*

*Wishing you much success in your career!*

*Tangy C Morgan*

# MAKING A CAREER PIVOT

Jenny Blake, the author of *Pivot: The only move that matters is your next one,* defines a career pivot as 'doubling down on what is working to make a purposeful shift in a new, related direction'. Pivoting is an intentional, methodical process for nimbly navigating career changes.

I've pivoted twice so far in my career, changing profession and company each time. When I made my most recent pivot, I thought it would be pretty smooth. I thought that with my experience at a reputable firm, several other big names on my CV and all the skills I had gained, graduating from a top university with a good grade, it would be relatively easy to make the switch. However, I couldn't be more wrong, it was really difficult. I completed over twenty applications, and I wasn't even getting past the application stage. I wasn't being invited for interviews or group assessments. However, after four months, I finally broke the cycle and got to the final round interview stage for the two biggest companies on my list and managed to secure my current role.

Career pivoting and changing jobs still relatively early in your career can feel slightly daunting and there has typically been a stigma around career pivots and job hopping more generally, which stemmed from people having typically stayed in one profession or company for pretty much their entire career.

**Famous Faces that Made Career Pivots**

Career pivots are more common than we think. Did you know:

- Prior to becoming a successful comedian Gina Yashere (who is one of the amazing contributors to his book) was an engineer, helping to build lifts in one of London's best-known buildings.[*]
- Before Whoopi Goldberg became an Oscar-winning actress, she worked at a funeral home applying makeup to the deceased. She was a licensed beautician, having attended beauty school.[†]
- Actor Terry Crews, best known for shows such as Everybody Hates Chris and Brooklyn Nine-Nine played in the NFL for five years before quitting to pursue a career in acting.[‡]

[*] Metro.co.uk. 'Comedian Gina Yashere reveals she faced horrible misogyny and racism while working as an engineer.' (2 June 2018). Retrieved from: https://metro.co.uk/2018/06/02/comedian-gina-yashere-reveals-she-faced-horrible-misogyny-and-racism-while-working-as-an-engineer-it-was-a-horrendous-baptism-of-fire-7600158/

[†] Huffpost.com. 'The Spooky Experience Whoopi Goldberg Had Whilst Working At A Funeral Home.' (15 April 2015). Retrieved from: https://www.huffpost.com/entry/whoopi-goldberg-funeral-home_n_7062388

[‡] Businessinsider.com. 'How Terry Crews went from sweeping floors after quitting the NFL to becoming a transcendent pitchman and huge TV star.' (18 January 2018). Retrieved from: https://www.businessinsider.com/terry-crews-sweeping-floors-to-huge-star-silence-breaker-2018-1?r=US&IR=T

There was an article written by AdAge about Netflix Chief Marketing Officer Bozoma Saint John that highlights this. The headline read 'The CMO most likely to change jobs,' which received backlash as many expressed that instead of celebrating her, it appeared to diminish her accomplishments because she was changing jobs.[*] AdAge accepted the feedback and updated the headline to 'The most in-demand CMO of 2020'.[†]

## Why pivot careers?

There are many reasons why we make career pivots. When I made my first career pivot, it was because I felt that the path I was on didn't offer much growth and I felt like I wasn't reaching my full potential. My second career pivot was due to realising that the skills I was acquiring could be better placed elsewhere. Other reasons may include:

- Our current career isn't what we thought it would be like
- Lack of progression opportunities
- We have acquired skills that we think could be better used in a different career
- The earning potential in our current industry and current role long term just isn't cutting it

[*] Essence.com. 'The Internet is outraged by a piece AdAge wrote about Bozoma Saint John.' (31 December 2020). Retrieved from: https://www.essence.com/news/money-career/the-internet-is-outraged-by-a-piece-adage-wrote-about-bozoma-saint-john/
[†] AdAge.com. 'The most in-demand CMO of 2020.' (28 December 2020). Retrieved from: https://adage.com/article/year-review/most-demand-cmo-2020/2298436

- We work in a dying industry
- We require greater work-life balance
- We want to work in a profession closer aligned to our values
- We seek greater flexibility
- Life circumstances

The list goes on and on. Although on both occasions I changed companies as well as my career, I did first try to pivot internally, however opportunities were not available and also when they were, they were framed to suit the organisation's needs rather than my own career needs.

Making a career pivot is not like a typical job search. I read a Forbes article where the writer summed it perfectly: 'A career pivot is not the same as a job search where you stay in the same role and industry. You know fewer people in the field, and fewer people know you. You don't have exact experience. You don't have insider expertise.'[*] This means you have to be willing to put in a lot more work to fill those gaps.

According to research by The City and Guilds Group and labour market trends experts Burning Glass Technologies, 34% of Britons wants to change their careers.[†] In the US, a survey conducted by Harris Poll for Fast Company revealed that 52% of US workers were considering a career pivot and 44% actually

* Forbes.com. 'Later in your career? How to make a career pivot.'(31 July 2018). Retrieved from: https://www.forbes.com/sites/carolinecenizalevine/2018/07/31/later-in-your-career-how-to-make-a-career-pivot/?sh=12a19ca17215
† Cityandguildsgroup.com. 'Building bridges towards future jobs.' (February 2021). Retrieved from: https://www.cityandguildsgroup.com/research/building-bridges-towards-future-jobs

have plans in place to make it happen.* I didn't realise how many people were considering a career change until I made a Twitter thread about my own experience and had so many people reach out, with many like myself still early into their career, seeking advice. Making a career pivot is a risk and the uncertainty of it can hold us back. The City and Guilds Group research found that 32% of those surveyed expressed concerns about starting all over again, 25% were worried about the salaries of other careers, and 23% expressed lack of knowledge about other roles and industries.

While staying in one industry, organisation and career may at one point have been seen as career goals, many Black employees don't have that luxury. In addition to the career specific reasons I've mentioned, the added layer of discrimination, which is rife in certain industries and organisations, the lack of progression opportunities and pay inequity makes you question if a certain career or working for a particular company is even worth it. Also, I think in the case of Black millennials and Gen Z, while there were some of us who always knew what we wanted to be when we 'grew up', there were also those of us who didn't and just aimed to achieve the best grades, to attend a good university and secure a well-paid job at a good company, in a bid to keep the parents happy. It's common for African Caribbean parents to want their children to become doctors, lawyers or engineers. Our parents aspire for us to have the security and stability they didn't. However, as the time has passed, some of us realised that the

* Fastcompany.com. 'Is now a good time to change careers? More workers are feeling good about it.' (23 February 2021). Retrieved from: https://www.fastcompany.com/90607167/is-now-a-good-time-to-change-careers-more-workers-are-feeling-good-about-it

career we started in didn't fulfil us in the way that our other skills and talents do leading us to pivot, start our own businesses or do both – launch side hustles alongside our nine to five. Research from the Centre for Talent and Innovation has revealed that over 30% of Black employees are planning to leave their companies within two years and Black employees are almost four times more likely than their white counterparts to pivot into starting their own ventures, as a way to have more autonomy over their career outcomes.[*]

---

✓

**Dismantling Career Pivoting Myths**

**'Changing career would mean I'd have to start again'**: This isn't always necessarily the case but it really depends on what the career change is. For example, if you are a primary school teacher and would like to become a lawyer, you would have to start again because to become a lawyer you would have to study and complete training and exams to become qualified. But you have to take a holistic view – is 'starting again' so bad if you're transitioning into a career that will bring you more fulfilment, a higher income and other benefits long term?

**'I'll earn less money if I make a pivot'**: If you pivot into a career where you have little to no previous experience,

---

[*] Talentinnovation.org. 'Being Black in Corporate America.'. (9 December 2019). Retrieved from: https://www.talentinnovation.org/_private/assets/BeingBlack-KeyFindings-CTI.pdf

then you may earn less initially, however in the medium to long term, you could end up earning much more than if you stayed in your old career. Something which I did to avoid this when I made my second career pivot was highlight my transferable skills throughout the recruitment process and the skills which weren't an explicit requirement, but I was able to frame as bringing value to the role. By doing this, you are showing that you already bring a lot to the table.

'It will look really bad on my CV if I make a career change': If your CV is just constant career changes then that may send alarm bells to potential new employers but generally a career change shows that you are motivated to learn, grow and contribute to something new. It can indicate that you are adaptable, having worked in different environments with different teams and you have a diverse and flexible skill set, acquiring a variety of skills in your previous roles. The main thing is to highlight in your CV all the significant achievements in your previous role.

'It's too late for me to change my career': If you've spent a number of years in a particular role, you can start to feel like you're trapped in that role forever and no one will give you the opportunity to try something new, but it's not true. Yes, it will be clear that you have a strong skill set and knowledge base in a particular area but often skills can be transferred and subject matter knowledge can be learned on the job. Don't count yourself out without trying.

Something I want to emphasise is that when it comes to making a career pivot or any career decisions you make, don't allow people to scaremonger you or project their own failings on to you. There's a big difference between individuals that show genuine concern and those that purposely instil doubt into your mind maybe because their own career isn't turning out how they hoped, or a pivot did not work out for them. You will know when it's time for a change and hopefully with the tips I provide below, you will put yourself in the best possible position to do so. When I made the pivot from banking to technology, there were people that tried to put me off saying things such as, 'You don't even have a background in technology', 'Are you sure? Maybe wait a few years.' Then guess who got recruited by one of the largest technology consulting companies? Me! Now imagine if I had listened. In the wise words of Skepta and Wizkid, 'Bad energy stay far away'.

## Tips for a successful career pivot

When I was navigating my career pivot, these are the things that I thought about which worked for me.

### Understand your 'why' and your 'what'?

Why are you changing your career? What is it about your current career that you don't like / wouldn't want to replicate in your new career? Write that down. Why have you decided upon this new career? What makes it appear better / more lucrative than what you currently do? Have you researched this career path thoroughly (different paths to entry, day-to-day responsibilities, opportunities to progress, future earning potential, other careers it closely aligns with if you wish to pivot again in the future?). Is it really a change of career you want or a change of company? There's probably a lot more things I have missed out but ultimately your why and what will really drive and motivate you during that period when it's really hard to make the switch. If you keep them front of mind, you won't give up, no matter how hard or how long it takes. Or you might realise that you don't want to pivot.

### Current skills – required skills – addressing the gap

Probably the most important thing you need to do when changing career is a skills and experience assessment.

*1. Required skills and experience:* What skills and experience does your new career require? Look at job descriptions, find people in those careers on LinkedIn to reach out and ask. If they have put those details on their profile, that should also help. Document this information.

*2. Current skills and experience:* Update your CV. What skills have you gained from your current role, previous ones and extra-curriculars? If you had to categorise your experiences into a few key themes, what would they be?

**Now look at the required skills again for your new career.** Do any of your current experience and skills align? Where are their points or similarities? **HIGHLIGHT THESE.**

**KEY POINT:** What **specific** experiences and skills do you have that could **significantly bring value** to your new role / organisation? For example, in my previous organisation, I was an Adobe Experience Manager subject matter expert, which wasn't a required expertise for any of the product roles I applied for. However, I knew that this particular expertise I had, around a platform that was all about delivering digital user experiences in mobile and web would be highly valuable in a product role, where I'd be building features for mobile app users and in doing so, create great experiences.

3. *The gap: What does your new career require that you don't currently have?* Can this be obtained in the short term (e.g., doing a short course / taking on a responsibility in your current role for a few weeks / months where you could learn those skills) or long term (e.g., a specific degree / qualification). Another way you can address this gap (on paper) is in how you tell your story. For example, some of the roles I applied to named all these very specific data systems that I had never used. But in my CV, I made sure I highlighted all the times I had used data and analytics to drive decisions, outcomes, and results.

### Start building a network in that space

One of the best ways to navigate a career pivot is to build up a network in that new space. You could come into contact with someone who may provide you with introductions to others in that space or help you with the recruitment process for a firm and role you're applying to.

- Add people on LinkedIn and see if they'd be happy have a call or meet for a coffee
- Attend events and strategically network
- Join community groups via Slack, Facebook, WhatsApp
- Reach out to people in your immediate friendship circle or family to see if they know anyone or can even refer you

Both times I changed my career, I reached out to people on LinkedIn who worked in the industries and at the companies I was applying to. Looking at their LinkedIn profiles, I tried to find people who had also pivoted, had a similar amount of experience to me and were in the role or a similar role to the one I was applying for. This helped me massively. One person helped me adapt my CV and cover letter for the application process and spent two hours on the phone preparing me for the final round interview and assessment centre, which led to me getting the job. Another person I connected with provided me with some great career advice and sent several introduction emails to help me grow my network in this new space.

**Redefine your brand**
Publicly showing an interest in this new career area is important, especially when you don't have prior experience. Whether it's writing blogs, sharing relevant content, updating your social media pages, these can all help shape and redefine your new interest and where your personal brand will be heading. Make sure you are also putting your skills on show, especially the ones which will be transferable into the industry you're trying to pivot into.

At a time when we are seeing industries that have existed forever perish and new industries emerge, making a career pivot is fast becoming essential for your growth and development. It may not happen overnight and will take thorough preparation as I learnt, but the trick is to leverage as many of your transferable skills for your new career. Your ability to repackage your experiences and update your career narrative will be key.

# RESOURCE: MAKING A CAREER PIVOT

When making a career pivot, and even more generally when I think about how I want my career to look in the future, I've found it useful to do a mini audit of my skills, experience and expertise. This is a great way to identify the gaps I need to fill to reach my future career state.

It's so easy to be disillusioned by the skills and experience you have (I definitely was). You may have all these amazing experiences, qualifications and a tonne of knowledge on a subject matter, however, and most importantly, is this what your new career requires?

I created the below table which should act as a mini-skills audit, to outline your current skills, experience and expertise and what is required for your new career.

| Current skills, experience and expertise | Required skills, experience and expertise |
|---|---|
| Experience overview<br>Qualifications + certifications<br>Soft skills<br>Hard skills and tools<br>Subject matter knowledge | Experience overview<br>Qualifications + certifications<br>Soft skills<br>Hard skills and tools<br>Subject matter knowledge |

After completing the above table, you should be able to identify what the gaps are in your skills, experience and expertise. In the below table, you can break this down and identify the steps you need to take resolve for them, how long it will take and a target for when you hope to do it by.

| Skills gap | Steps to resolve | Time commitment | Target completion |
|---|---|---|---|
|  |  |  |  |
|  |  |  |  |
|  |  |  |  |
|  |  |  |  |

# GINA YASHERE

*Comedian, Author, Actor and Executive Producer*

Gina was born and raised in London UK, of Nigerian parents, and previously worked as an elevator engineer for Otis.

Gina has been a stand up and TV star in the UK for numerous years, with appearances on iconic TV shows such as Live At The Apollo and Mock the Week, as well as creating & performing the hugely popular comedic characters, Tanya and Mrs Omokerede on The Lenny Henry Show.

She broke onto the American comedy scene with her appearances on Last Comic Standing (NBC), where she made it to the final ten, and then never went home! Gina went on to be named one of the top 10 rising talents in the Hollywood Reporter, and is the only British comedian to ever appear on the iconic Def Comedy Jam.

Gina has four stand up specials currently streaming on Netflix, three of them which she self-produced. Gina has performed for audiences all over the world and currently resides in Los Angeles where she is producing, writing, and acting on the new sitcom Bob Hearts Abishola, which she has co-created with Chuck Loree and is currently airing on CBS.

**Tell us about yourself?** *I was born and raised in London, England. I spent the first eight years of my life in Bethnal Green, East*

London so I'm cockney by birth. My parents are from Benin City, Nigeria. They didn't meet in Nigeria, they met in London, got married and had us all here. My dad went back to Nigeria and my mum stayed here in the UK with me and my siblings. In terms of education, I am a qualified electrical electronics engineer and I have a degree in this.

**What was your motivation to pursue comedy and how did you secure your first opportunity within this space?** *Funnily enough, I had no motivation to pursue comedy, I was always funny as I was an African kid in the 70s and 80s when it wasn't cool to be African, so you'd get teased a lot, called all types of names people would laugh at your clothing, make jokes about your mum's accent, so I used my humour (I didn't know it was comedy at the time) to get out of situations. I was constantly fighting and got into too many fights at school, so I started to use humour as a way to get out of confrontation. I was always told that I was funny, I was the typical class clown, and I was always trying to divert attention from the fact that I was an African kid, and I wasn't seen as cool. I remember a drama teacher once told my mum that she thought I should be an actor, but coming from an African family, my mum thought I should be a doctor, so my mum responded, 'oh no, she can ACT like a doctor when she becomes a doctor.' I didn't watch comedy as a child or have this encyclopaedic knowledge of comedy, I just fell into it by accident.*

*I spent four years as an elevator engineer with Otis where I suffered horrible misogyny and racism (at work, there would be pictures of monkeys above my coat and banana skins put in my jacket pockets) and once I left, I was looking for another job. It happened to be the summer and I had been given redundancy money and thought I'll take the summer off and start looking for work again in the winter. I used that summer to try all the things I had been told I was good at which was acting and making people laugh (comedy), the fun things my mum didn't let me pursue earlier because she wanted me to focus on my academics. That's how I got into comedy.*

*My first opportunity doing comedy came when this comedy duo called Jefferson and Whitfield who were famous on the Black comedy circuit in the 90s did a workshop on how to be a stand-up comedian. They borrowed a book from another comedian/ promoter John Simmit who wrote about how to do stand-up comedy, and they were charging people £50 each to attend the workshop. I had already been performing in talent shows at that point, but I wanted to do stand-up comedy, so I turned up to this workshop with a ten-minute set already written because I knew at the end of the four-week workshop, you'd have the opportunity to perform at a theatre in front of Black comedy royalty who came to the show. That was the reason I did that workshop for four weeks and it was my first ever stand-up gig, performing into front of Black British comedy greats such as Angie Le Mar, Roger D and so on. I started doing stand up that summer of 1995 and it just went on from there, and I never went back to another engineering job. My career as a comedian started to progress, people were paying me, and then I ended up on TV and I thought 'I want to do this'.*

You've achieved great success doing stand-up comedy but most recently you've written and produced your own hit sitcom Bob Hearts Abishola, which is the first American Sitcom to feature a Nigerian Family. How did this opportunity come around?

*I had no plans to stop doing stand-up comedy, my dream was to sell out theatres and arenas as a stand-up comic I thought I'd be doing it for the rest of my life and maybe play the best friend in someone's sitcom if my career went exactly how I wanted it. How Bob Hearts Abishola came about was when Chuck Lorre who is behind Big Bang Theory, Two and a Half men, and several other shows, wanted to do a show which starred a Nigerian woman because he had come back from a trip to Africa and had an epiphany that he could make a sitcom which featured African characters. I was living in New York at the time, and they flew me over to Los Angeles and they wanted me to consult on the show as someone who was African. That annoyed me immediately because I thought how can these white men want me to consult on all things African?? I called my agency and manager after the meeting and said tell them thanks but no thanks. During that meeting, I asked them how they found me, assuming they had seen all my Netflix specials, my Tonight Show appearances, I assumed they had done their research on me. This was not the case at all. They explained that they searched 'Nigerian female comic' into google and I was the best one that came up. They flew me all the way to Los Angeles having done no research on me, the level of white privilege in what I heard really annoyed me.*

*I almost turned the show down, but luckily Lila Rowe, my best friend and Edwin, my younger brother called me up to scream at me, so I decided to stay and consult on the show, and once I was in the room with the guys, I realised they were genuine and really wanted to make a great TV show and they really listened to me. I was honest with them about all the things I found abhorrent in the way that Africans were depicted on TV, and I wanted us to do things properly. We were going to have a*

Nigerian woman in the lead role, a dark-skinned woman at that, and were going to book as many Nigerian actors as possible to make the show authentic, and they all listened. I liked the way they worked, I fell in love with Chuck and the rest of the team, and I started giving them good intel, I started creating characters for them, helped them to write the show, and then they called my agent and said they no longer wanted me to be a consultant anymore, but needed me to make the show, and wanted me to be a show creator and producer on the show. As a stand-up comedian and a performer, I wrote myself into the show as the funny best friend which has always been my dream gig alongside stand-up comedy.

Social media has provided a platform for budding comedians to grow a following and raise their profile. What advice would you give to those trying to transfer that online buzz to a long-lasting career? *Social media is a double-edged sword! It's wonderful for creating your own audience and buzz, but then you have many who are great online but are unable to transfer this offline. Doing two-minute or thirty-second sketches online won't necessarily translate into captivating an audience live for anything between 15 minutes to 2 hours. My advice would be to really put the work into perfecting your craft as a comedian, get out there and really study it, don't just rely on your internet buzz.*

You've successfully cross-over to the US market, how easy / difficult was it to navigate this move? What have you learnt and what advice would you give to those who aspire to do the same? *It was not easy making that move to the US. I left a very successful career in England, sold my house, sold my new Mercedes and came to the US starting again from scratch. The first seven years were a struggle because America is an insular market, they don't care how successful you have been elsewhere. If you want to make it in America, you really have to want it and be prepared to work hard because you will start from nothing. It happens very quickly for some people and not so quicky for others, it didn't happen quickly for me. I was in America for thirteen years before I hit it really big with this show. Over the last few years, I have been making my own specials, managed to get onto Netflix but it was a slow uphill battle. However, I have enjoyed the journey and I knew that I could do it.*

**What challenges have you experienced in your career and how have you overcome them?** *Misogyny and racism mostly. When I started out, I was young and hungry and many of the older comics didn't like that, they felt threatened and so they weren't very nice to me and wanted to keep me in my place. Once I realised that was happening, it made me work even harder to be even better. In this industry working in England as a Black female comedian, you're not afforded the same opportunities. I used to travel with a now super-successful comedian who used to open shows that I would be the headline of, and I remember one time we were on our way to do a show in Japan, and he was so broke, he couldn't afford the taxi fare, so I got a mini cab to his house, picked him up and paid for the cab to the airport. A year and a half later, he was a multi-millionaire selling out arena's whilst I was still struggling to get those bigger opportunities here. This is one of the reasons why I ended up going to America because I thought at least if I fail there, I'll still be a multi-millionaire failure.*

**What have been some of your career highs and lows?** *A career low was when BBC 3 (when it was called BBC Choice) were looking for comedians to host a talk show and they tested several comedians, and I was one of them. They told us that the host with show which got the most viewing figures and was the most liked would get a permanent spot. Everyone hosted their show for a week or two on BBC Three, I did my week, and it blew everyone else's show out of the water. There were queues of people who wanted to be in the audience, who found the show really funny and entertaining. My viewing figures were higher than everyone else's. The feedback was so great that I was given an additional two weeks to host my show. I did that and it was called Up Late with Gina Yashere and by the end of it, I expected to get my show because they told us that whoever's show was the best would get a permanent spot. This didn't happen. In the end, they gave the show to a young white guy called Ralph Little who was on the Royal Family, which was a popular sitcom at the time. The excuse was that he was the 'right fit' for the demographic they were targeting, despite the numbers I had achieved. This was a low point for me because I realised that no matter how much work you put in, no matter how good you are, no matter how any hoops you jump through, nothing is really guaranteed. That was one of the first lessons I learnt about working in TV.*

*There have been a few high points. I made my own stand-up specials which aired on Netflix, HBO and all those TV platforms. As successful as I was in England, I'd never had a stand-up special play on any channel in England, I was never given those opportunities. When I went to America, I decided I wasn't going to wait for those opportunities to come to me, so I rented theatres, sold tickets and booked a producer, a director and shot my* own stand-up specials and then sold them to the major US networks and platforms such as Showtime, HBO, Netflix which means I own all the rights to my stand-up specials.

My highest point is my show *Bob Hearts Abishola*. The fact that I have been able to create a sitcom which features the first Nigerian family on prime-time TV in America and is doing extremely well (we're currently filming our third season) and enabled me to learn new skills and create opportunities for others that weren't created for me is great.

**What has been the best career advice given to you?** *'Think not of yourself as the architect of your career but as the sculptor. Expect to have to do a lot of hard hammering and chiselling and scraping and polishing.' – B. C. Forbes*

**What advice would you give to Black students and professionals starting out and advancing in their careers?** *Love what you do and learn your craft, study it inside out. Be prepared to work harder than everyone else and don't let the gatekeepers tell you what you are and are not capable of. If they shut a door in your face, you build a wall and put your own door in and go in that way, which is what I've always done.*

# KWAME KWEI-ARMAH OBE

*Artistic Director, Young Vic Theatre*

Kwame Kwei-Armah OBE is Artistic Director of the Young Vic theatre. He was Artistic Director of Baltimore Centerstage (2011-18) and Artistic Director of the Festival of Black Arts and Culture, Senegal (2010), where he wrote and directed the opening ceremony at Senghor stadium. As a playwright, Kwame was the first African Caribbean to have a play produced in London's West End (*Elmina's Kitchen*). His triptych of plays was produced at the National Theatre, where he later created the online resource The Black Play Archive. Kwame was Chancellor of the University of the Arts, London (2010-15), is patron of Ballet Black and The Black Cultural Archives, Chair of Warwick Arts Centre Advisory Board and Fellow of Lady Margaret Hall, Oxford University. Kwame was awarded an OBE for services to drama in 2011, and in 2020 was listed as one of 100 Great Black Britons.

**Tell us about yourself?** *My name is Kwame Kwei-Armah, and I grew up in West London. My childhood and my life were absolutely influenced by my rather brilliant mother and her dedication to me and to our loving home. Contrastingly, growing up in a cold and racist Britain undoubtedly also shaped me. The challenge that faced the immigrant generation of improving our* environment, and therefore our country, through our contributions and advocacy for equality, was a major factor in why I chose to do theatre. And ultimately, I do theatre because I wish to serve the community.

From the age of seven, I went to a stage school called Barbara Speake Stage School. I left there at sixteen, to go to college and do my A Levels, and from there I became an actor. When I was older, I went back to university and did an Open University degree and following that I did my master's in screenwriting at the University of the Arts.

**What was your motivation to get into acting and how did you secure your first opportunity within this space?** *My first job came about because Mrs Collins – a mother of a friend of mine – saw an advert in the back of* The Stage *(the theatre industry paper) for a role in the play* Clashpoint *at the Westminster Theatre in London. At the time I was working in McDonalds, and I remember really enjoying climbing the slippery pole of that process – moving from doing the bins to all of a sudden becoming a training manager. I think Mrs Collins was worried I was missing out on my vocation, so when she saw this advert in* The Stage, *she encouraged me to go for the job, and I got it. The play was set in the aftermath of the Brixton Riots of the early 1980s and focused on a racist incident in a school and the terrible ripple effects that followed. I didn't know that you could be involved in theatrical work that was about something so political. But after every show we would hold a post-show discussion, and I think that really set my career and mind in motion. I was a bit like, 'Oh, I can* discuss things that are interesting to me as well as perform!'. *I saw that theatre could be a place for social action.*

In parallel to your acting and TV career, you started to write and direct your own plays. Why? What led to that transition from TV to theatre? *I started to write and direct because I didn't want to have to wait forever for other people to write the work I felt addressed the subjects that I really wanted to engage with. That was my primary reason for writing. And similarly, I got into directing because I wasn't going to wait on other people to do that work for me. I wanted to contribute in that way.*

*I don't think I have ever rejected TV; it has never been a full transition. I was doing theatre while I was doing TV, because I was a writer in residence at Bristol Old Vic Theatre while I was filming Casualty. My first plays were performed at Bristol Old Vic when I was still in Casualty, and then I wrote plays that were performed at the National Theatre in London. I think I really made more of a transition firmly into theatre when I moved from London to Baltimore to become Artistic Director (AD) of Centre Stage, and then I suppose something had to give. So, I had to decide that I was dedicating my main energy to theatre. However, I have continued to write for screen and TV throughout my time as a theatre AD.*

What does the process look like for writing a play and then getting a play staged in a theatre? *I find the idea, or the idea finds me. Then I sit down and just press that idea until I get through to the end of a first draft. Once I get through to the end of that first draft, I then realise, 'Oh, this is what I wanted to say'. Then, really, the writing is about rewriting. I have to ask, 'How do I refine it so that this play says that thing that I want to talk about and make it actually what the play is about?'.*

*I would say before I became an artistic director, I thought that the process of getting a play staged was that you wrote a really good play, you hand it in to a theatre, and then someone says, 'Yeah, I want to put this on'. Quintessentially, this is still true. But once I became an artistic director, I realised that it is an act of God to get a new play produced. There are so many variants that contribute to why a play gets produced – for example, what's happening across the theatre's season, the size of the company in your play, where the company is in the world . . . I now say to playwrights I'm working with: 'There are a thousand reasons why your play might not be produced, just don't let your writing be one of them.'*

You've written and directed plays which encompass universal themes but equally focus on Black characters and Black historical figures. Do you ever garner criticism for this (e.g., Kwame does too much 'Black' stuff) and how do you respond to that? *Yeah I've heard it, I've heard it. I have paid it very little attention. That's how I deal with it. If I grew up in a country like Nigeria, where the population is over two hundred million, then actually you know you're not writing a Black play, the word 'Black' doesn't mean anything there. There are two hundred million of you, so what you are doing is you're trying to write something that speaks to something specific and to a universal theme. And so, when I write now, even though my characters may be Black, I'm writing a universal story. I don't see the box that is Black. I never have done, and I ignore those who think that there is a box.*

In 2005, you were only the second Black British playwright to have your play staged in the West End. As Artistic Director at The Vic, you are the first African Caribbean director to run a major British theatre. What are the challenges or barriers to

**entry for Black playwrights and aspiring artistic directors? What advice would you provide to navigate this?** *On playwrights, the first thing I'd say is that I think now is a really brilliant time to be a Black playwright because people actually want to listen to what you say. But I think one of the issues one had to negotiate is actually how Black is defined. If Black is defined through a really narrow bandwidth of Black trauma stories – in terms of assigning a Black story to the story of how you negotiated 'the hood' or how you negotiate knife crimes, or if you're a woman, how you negotiate being oversexualised – while all of these things are hugely valid, I would say that if the commissioner or the people giving your play the green light only see you through that lens, that means that if you present something else, it becomes very difficult for them to go, 'Oh, this is valid'.*

*Another problem is telling the Black version of the white story or the European story. Again, that's the trope and that's something that has to be negotiated with. So, I think that the difficulty is you are often seen through the lens of what is contemporary and Black, and trying to negotiate your way through that takes some thinking through.*

*As a director, I think the issue is what kind of work are you offered. If it is only work that is seen through the lens of what is perceived to be Black as opposed to what is perceived to be universal, then that becomes problematic. So, you must concentrate on what you are picking, and importantly why you are picking a piece of work. Ask yourself if you are picking something because you see the universality in it and because you see an opportune moment opening up for you to tell any story, or are you using Blackness as an access tool as opposed to a universal tool?*

**Is the theatre world aware of these disparities? If so, what is being done to change this?** *I think they are aware of it. I think Black Lives Matter has made it so you can't avoid it. But the way to help is to continue to advocate, and to continue to create work that pushes the boundaries of what Black is. The way to challenge ourselves is to constantly be asking ourselves what work we are programming, why we are programming it and who we are programming it for. And we should always point these questions in the direction of artistic directors.*

**How did you adapt to the role of being an Artistic Director where you have to manage funds, budgets, staff and much more?** *I used my playwriting template, which is: have an idea, put it through the drafting process, think about it a minimum of four times – because there's no such thing as being finished by a third draft. In fact, just continually redraft and once you've finished redrafting the idea then make sure you understand what it is you are saying. Then this process can be applied to your staff, to your board and even to yourself. And the aim is to be absolutely clear in your intention.*

**How important do you think it is for creatives to have a strong grasp on the business side of things as well as the artistic?** *Very important. If it's not in the budget, it's not on the stage. I would advise ensuring that you understand the budgeting process, so that when you turn around and say, 'Hey, this is the thing I want to produce', nobody can pull any wool over your eyes.*

**What challenges have you experienced in your career and how have you overcome them?** *This is hard for me to answer because* *once my brain has dealt with a challenge, it tends to immediately forget about it. But I suppose that's maybe the advice I would give: don't dwell on challenges, move on and try not to let them consciously shape you.*

**What have been some of your career highs and lows?** *Directing the opening ceremony of the World Festival of Black Arts and Culture in Senegal was an absolute high point. Also directing* Twelfth Night *at the Public Theatre at the Delacorte in Central Park will always be a real highlight for me. And finally, I think opening* One Night in Miami *at Centre Stage in Baltimore was also a highlight. A low point would be the controversy around the development of my show* Tree.

**What has been the best career advice given to you?** *The best career advice I think I've been given is, 'Don't be afraid to ask.' It was given to me by a film and stage director called David Leland, and I've never forgotten it. I hate asking for things. I'm a little too prideful in that way . . . I mean I don't even like asking my staff to do things for me, I keep apologising and apologising.*

**What advice would you give to Black students and professionals starting out and advancing in their careers?** *I would advise you to understand why you have chosen your profession. Understand why you want to use this space and use your voice. And then stand for something or you will fall for anything.*

# KAYODE EWUMI

*Actor, Writer and Producer*

Kayode Ewumi is an actor, writer, producer, and the star of *#HoodDocumentary* (originally made and self-published on YouTube and picked up for a second series by BBC Three). He is also the creator of BBC Three's <u>*Enterprice*</u> which was a BBC Three Comedy Slice pilot in 2018 and picked up for a full series. He recently founded Wolverton House, a faith-based production company.

**Tell us about yourself?** *My name is Kayode Ewumi, and I'm now a writer/producer but I trained to be an actor at Coventry University. I grew up in south-east London and was raised on the Aylesbury Estate. I still live in south-east London, around the Elephant and Castle area. I went to primary school at English Martyr's Primary School, secondary at St Thomas the Apostle, college at City and Islington and university at Coventry. I grew up with my two siblings (Lola and Mary) and my mum and dad (Samuel and Yemisi). I had the best childhood I could imagine. My community was multicultural, and we all helped each other in so many ways.*

**What was your motivation to pursue acting and how did you secure or create your first opportunity within this space?** *My* motivation to pursue a career in acting stemmed from a film I watched called The Mask. I was mesmerised by the way Jim Carey could take me into another world and different emotions through a memorable performance. I then decided that this is something I wanted to do. I created my first opportunity within the space when I co-created an online mockumentary called #HoodDocumentary *which opened up many doors for me. After that, my next role was in the reboot* Are You Being Served? *on* BBC One, *which was an amazing experience.*

**You achieved great success with the #*HoodDocumentary* and your character Roll Safe is a legend. Where did the idea come from?** *The idea came from a vine that I created with a friend of mine, Tyrell Williams. Tyrell made a suggestion and shot a vine for me and RS was created. It was very spontaneous, and the main aim was to make a short and funny clip but little did I know that this would be my door into the industry.*

**Creating viral content is an aspiration for many due to the opportunities it can lead to, with great examples within the Black British comedy space. Based on your experience, how best can Black online personalities capitalise and get the most from virality?** *This is very simple. Have smart, transparent and innovative people around you. Your surroundings are everything. Don't let money lead you, you will find smart and innovative ways to capitalise from virality.*

**BBC Three went on to commission six more episodes of the #*HoodDocumentary* and then the *Enterprice* series – what was the transition like from doing something independently on**

YouTube to creating something for a corporation? What advice would you give to creatives when engaging with corporations for the first time? *The transition from YouTube to a full TV series was fairly simple. Things move a lot slower within a corporation like the BBC as there's so many more people and so much money involved. EVERYTHING has to get signed off in order for moves to happen. I see making work online or independently is like playing Connect Four, while making work for broadcasters is like playing chess . . . The advice I'd give to those working with a broadcaster for the first time is: speak up and believe there are some things the bosses also don't know. Don't always think you have to say yes, you don't.*

As a creative, when do you know that it's time to move on? How do you balance that personal need to do something different, with the external pressure to keep doing what everyone knows you for? *Knowing it's time to move on can always be a difficult thing to gauge. However, you have to know why you got into the industry in the first place and stay true to yourself. Once you always stay true to yourself and no one else, you will be fine.*

It sometimes feels like there is this pressure for Black storytellers to write about things which are race related. Have you had to navigate that and how important do you think it is to have diverse Black narratives? *Tell the stories you want to tell. I don't think any Black storyteller should feel the pressure of having to tell a story that is specifically about race. I have always told myself that it's always about the story first, everything else comes later on.*

**What challenges have you experienced in your career and how have you overcome them?** *One recurring challenge that comes up a lot is learning how to manage time. The industry can be overwhelming at times, and you soon realise that you haven't got as much time on your hands than you thought. However, I'm learning to overcome this by waking up early and going to sleep early. I used to go to sleep late but I soon realised I was less productive. However, during writing season, I work through the night. I like the stillness.*

**What have been some of your career highs and lows?** *Some of my career high points were definitely during the season of RS being birthed. Also writing my own full TV series (Enterprice) was a great career high for me.*

    *Some lows were realising that the industry wasn't as motivational as I thought it was. You could feel like your work was terrible but then you just realise that if you get it, it's fine. Stick with it until you find someone else who gets it too! This is when the magic happens!*

**What has been the best career advice given to you?** *It was advice my mum gave me, she said: 'Don't aim to work twice as hard because you're Black. There's no competition. Just work hard. That's it.'*

**What advice would you give to Black students and professionals starting out and advancing in their career?** *The advice that I mentioned my mum gave to me!*

# ASHLEY WALTERS

*Actor, Producer and Musician*

Ashley Walters has been acting professionally since childhood, winning his first television role in *The Young Indiana Jones Chronicles* at the age of ten. His acting career has been varied and prolific across film and television. He is perhaps best known in film for his roles in *Get Rich or Die Tryin'* and *Bulletboy*, for which he won a BIFA Best Newcomer Award in 2004, and in television for his starring roles in *Top Boy* and *Bulletproof*.

'Asher D' is also a well-known name in the music industry, where he played a pivotal role in the UK garage scene in the early 2000s, both within the collective So Solid Crew and through his work as a solo artist.

As well as being the lead cast on both *Top Boy* for Netflix (originally a Channel 4 production) and *Bulletproof* for Sky, Ashley is the executive producer on both shows. In 2017, Ashley established his own production company SLNda, through which he is now producing film and television content that will champion new talent within the UK industry, and better represent the Britain that he sees. In 2021, he made his directorial debut on the short film *Boys* which premiered on Sky Arts.

**Tell us about yourself?** *I grew up in Peckham with my mum and stepdad, as my mum's only child, I have half-siblings on my dad's* side. I was a creative child and into music from an early age, listening to my mum's old school records. I liked to entertain but I was also shy at the same time. That need or want for a creative outlet took me to Sylvia Young Theatre School. I didn't enjoy the experience that much because there was no one really like me there; it was predominantly middle-class white kids and I stood out like a sore thumb. I resented a lot of the people in that environment because of what they had and what I didn't have but I quickly realised that it was better to focus on my own journey. That was the beginning of my journey into realising that I wanted to work in the entertainment industry.

Behind the scenes, I had a stepdad that I didn't really want to connect with, although he brought me up but I longed for my real dad and I knew he was out there but had other things going on in his life. My mum played the role of mum and dad essentially. She was a strong woman, who backed me all the way, supported my ambition to work in entertainment, and spent a lot of time travelling around the world with me filming. She gave me a really good start in life despite the bad things that were sometimes happening around us.

I was leading a double life to some extent because back then it wasn't cool to be an actor and to work in theatre. I would be at Sylvia Young on the weekend performing and when I came back home, I wanted to be out on the road with the guys in my area. I didn't talk about my acting life with them, I tried not to mix the two.

**What was your motivation to get into acting, as you started with this before music? How did you secure your first opportunity within this space?** *Growing up, I used to try and find ways* to entertain myself and this was mainly through creating my own monologues, imitating what I saw on TV and it became a hobby. When I was around the age of six, my mum made me go to Sylvia Young as I already has a cousin that attended, and my mum used to take him often. That was where acting started for me. I went to Pimlico School near Victoria for secondary school as my mum didn't want me to go to a school in our area due to the community violence. It was a great decision because I ended up meeting other like-minded people, I really found my tribe there. The school was really good for music and drama; it was what they prided themselves on. I had a brilliant relationship with my drama teacher and music teacher. I found a youth club nearby where I was doing a lot of music performance and at the same time, I was able to acquire an agent from Sylvia Young as I was still on their books. That brought a lot of work and I was doing musical theatre from the ages of eleven to fifteen, performed in Oliver at the London Palladium, and all the major theatres in the West end. This progressed into me doing TV work, making appearances in a few TV shows here and there. My first major opportunity came in 1998 when I landed a role in the BBC Two screenplay Storm Damage. That came through an open audition, an agent at Sylvia Young sent me the details for it.

So Solid Crew are pioneers in the UK music scene. When you guys came out, there had never been anything like you guys before. What advice would you give to young Black people navigating spaces where they might be the first to do something or there is no clear blueprint to follow? It's a catch-22 because when you're doing it, you don't think about being the first or a pioneer, *you don't know what you're doing. With So Solid, naturally things just progressed with different groups and individuals coming together and making their contribution. There was a blueprint for us, not genre-wise, but with regards to success and the level we wanted to take it to. We looked at Soul II Soul as they were an international collective and we based our model on them.*

*I'd say when navigating spaces where there aren't many other examples to follow, never forget that your individuality is key. Yes, everyone has to have a foundation and some form of talent, but always celebrate your differences. That was our objective with So Solid.*

**You have achieved great success as an actor and musician. What are some of the greatest lessons you've learnt from both experiences?** *In regard to acting, your experience is key. Drama school, in my opinion, can't prepare you for being on a real set, so get as much experience as possible. Remember as much as you can and always practice vulnerability and humility. Ask yourself, what would a kid do? I say this because kids are super imaginative and fearless. With music, integrity is everything. The ability to connect with the masses, like* 21 Seconds *did and most recently* Top Boy, *was due to honouring the people and staying true and authentic to the time. Wear your heart on your sleeve with your music, be true to yourself.*

*A really important lesson to call out is the importance of knowing the legal side of the business. It's just as important if not more so than the practical and creative side. When you're signing contracts at a young age, be brave, don't be in a rush or desperate. Take your time to be comfortable and familiar with all the fine details, seek advice and don't be tempted by someone dangling money in your face.*

**You've started a drama school (Kingdom Drama school) and production company (SLNda). What inspired you to start them?** *I was producing before I officially opened a production company, however I didn't feel like I was being properly credited or paid for my time and I realised that I could create stories for minorities coming from London that truly represented them in the right way.*

*With Kingdom Drama School, I wanted to provide a place for up-and-coming actors to sharpen their skills, hone their talent and provide them with a point of entry into the market they're trying to get into. I was seeing so many young people finish drama school and not land any opportunities after, there was and still is a clear disconnect. Kingdom Drama School is trying to bridge that gap, by connecting the school with the industry and giving the industry access to the students.*

*I want the industry to keep growing, for talent from minority backgrounds to have access to some of the best opportunities, and I'm fortunate to have enough experience to try and influence that.*

**What challenges have you experienced in your career and how have you overcome them?** *In my industry, 80% of the time you're being told 'no' and that you can't do something, so I've always been that person who tries to make the impossible, possible. The 'no' spurs me on to do better, to pioneer and change things. The worst thing you can tell me is 'no' because I'll often find a way to do it.*

*I would say the lack of diversity is probably the main one. In this game, there's huge disparities between me and my white male counterparts and it's been that way for a while, although slowly but surely things are starting to change. I just want things to get to a place where the best person gets the job and it's not because of a lack of representation. Even with everything I have accomplished, I still have to battle on a daily basis to get the same opportunities as my white peers. I stay in it and stay fighting to try and influence positive change where I can.*

**What have been some of your career high and low points?** *In terms of high points, my first film* Storm Damage, *which was a BBC screenplay with Lenny James, who also wrote it, and Adrian Lester. Industry-wise, that put me in a really good place. Playing the lead in* Bullet Boy *was an unforgettable experience and what it did for my career – I was seen as one of the newcomers to watch – gave me that momentum.*

*Starring in* Get Rich or Die Tryin' *was also a big moment for me, as was* Top Boy *which has been going for ten or eleven years now.* Bulletproof *on Sky is my new baby and, as one of the creators and producers, to see it do really well is a proud moment for me.*

*Low points have always been when I've not been able to do what I love doing, not being able to work, whether I physically can't or, majority of the time, the work not being there. I had a period of time when I wasn't working, I went through bankruptcy, I went to prison, I lost a lot. When I came home from prison, I had nothing and had to start all over again. I keep pictures of those moments in my mind, they push me to make sure that whatever it is I do, I do it to the best of my abilities.*

***What has been the best career advice given you?*** *Take it slow. At the earlier part of my career when I wanted leading roles, my agent told me to hold back and focus on surrounding myself with great people and that's what I did in the beginning. I worked with big names and maybe only featured in one scene or half a scene in a TV show or film, but I was able to shine in those small appearances without taking on the full responsibility of having a leading role. This gave me the time and space to really learn and perfect my craft.*

**What advice would you give to Black students and professionals starting out and advancing in their careers?** *Something I tell everyone is your time will come. Don't focus too much on the destination, focus on the journey and embrace it, because you will be learning throughout. Never see a loss as failure, see it as a win if you can learn from it. When you are inevitably told 'no' during you career, think of it as a 'yes'. You need to find a way to figure out how to turn that 'no' around into a yes if possible.*

# PREPARING FOR THE FUTURE OF WORK

## Evolve or be extinct

When I initially had the idea for this book in 2017, I had no intention of writing this chapter. But a lot has changed since then, most noticeably the recent global Covid-19 pandemic.

The resulting lockdowns have led to companies and entire industries and skills becoming obsolete. On the other hand, some industries have thrived and we're seeing demand for new skills and jobs. The industries which adapted have been able survive and those who were stubborn to change have perished. This has led to significant shifts in the labour market and accelerated the need for a new type of workforce.

For the Black community, we need to be alert to these changes because we have seen time and time again that when there are adverse events with significant economic impact, we are nearly always the most disproportionately affected. Using the Covid-19 pandemic as a recent example, research in the UK showed for the period of October to December 2020, unemployment rate for BAME employees rose to 9.5% from 8.5% compared with 4.5% unemployment rate for white workers, rising from 3.1%.*

* ONS. 'A09: Labour Market status by ethnic group.' (23 February 2021). Retrieved from: https://www.ons.gov.uk/employmentandlabourmarket/peopleinwork/employmentandemployeetypes/datasets/labourmarketstatusbyethnicgroupa09

Specifically, Black employees had one of the highest employment rates of 13.8% in this period, where we are overrepresented in low-wage, insecure jobs.

**The Future of Work**

In 2020, The World Economic Forum created a report titled The Future of Jobs 2020 providing insights into the key jobs and workplace trends they see emerging over the next five years in a number of industries.[*] Understanding these trends will enable us to pivot, adapt and position ourselves to take advantage of these changes.

**Some of their key findings:**

**Due to COVID-19, companies are pushing to:**

- Scale remote working
- Accelerate digitalisation
- Accelerate automation

The World Economic Forum predicts that the most in demand skills by 2025 will include:

- Analytical thinking and innovation
- Complex problem solving
- Critical thinking and analysis

[*] World Economic Forum. 'The Future of Jobs 2020.' (20 October 2020). Retrieved from: https://www.weforum.org/reports/the-future-of-jobs-report-2020

- Technology design and programming
- Resilience, stress tolerance and flexibility

With companies looking to accelerate automation and digitisation, this may lead to a growing demand for some jobs and a reduction in demand for others.

*Jobs with a growing demand include:
- Data analysts and scientists
- Digital transformation specialists
- Digital marketing and strategy specialists
- Business developments professionals
- Software and applications developers

*Jobs with a declining demand include:
- Date entry clerks
- Accountant and auditors
- General and operations managers
- Business services and administration managers
- Client information and customer services workers

*For context, these were the findings across the industries of advanced manufacturing, agriculture, food and beverage, automotive, consumer, digital communications and information technology, education, energy utilities and technologies, financial services, government and public sector, health and healthcare, manufacturing, mining and metals, oil and gas, professional services and transportation and storage.

## Remote working

The COVID-19 pandemic has meant that many of us have been working from home or some form of hybrid working arrangement (between home and the office) for a year or two. Research from Future Forum, a research company developed by Slack Technologies, found that only 3% of Black knowledge workers were happy to go back to work in the office full time, compared to 21% of white knowledge workers who were looking forward to working in the office.* This is not surprising considering that their research also found that only 53% of Black knowledge workers agree that they are treated fairly at work vs. 74% of white knowledge workers).

Remote working has provided a level of freedom and flexibility that those of us who work in office-based jobs haven't experienced in a while. Freedom from the white gaze, freedom to just be ourselves without having to constantly explain, defend or tuck away aspects of our Blackness. Do you know how refreshing it has been to have ackee and saltfish for lunch without 'what's that smell?' comments or rock my afro without the fear of a colleague shoving their dusty hand in it? What a time to be alive!! Working remotely has also enabled us to exercise control over our environment, our daily routines and the factors that cause stress and burnout. We are no longer forced to physically share the same space or engage in conversations with colleagues that may have caused us harm, directly or indirectly and some of us

* Futureforum.com. 'A new era of workplace inclusion: moving from retrofit to redesign.' (11 March 2021). Retrieved from: https://futureforum.com/2021/03/11/dismantling-the-office-moving-from-retrofit-to-redesign/

have been able to structure our days in a way to incorporate healthy practices such as working out which has reduced our stress and anxiety.

The research also revealed that many Black people felt micro-aggressions and discrimination had drastically reduced since working remotely as well as the need to constantly code switch and whilst I agree for the most part, I also think these behaviors have evolved and shifted to online channels.

For example, something I've observed is that it's only really the Black and Brown people at work (myself included) who often don't turn their cameras on for meetings or typically use an alternative background. Many of us are going to great efforts to position our camera's in a certain way to avoid our home space from being in view or finding a space where a blank wall is our background. For Black women, although working remotely has afforded us with the opportunity to be experimental with our hair and feel comfortable rocking our natural hair within the safety of our homes, we're still going for hairstyles which are seen as more professional and would generate less questions. My 'dash my wig on five minutes before the meeting starts' game is strong! These are all examples of how we code-switch in the remote working world. Why do we do this? Because digital microaggressions are real. Now that colleagues have a window into our personal space, a space that has typically been our refuge and sanctuary, we want to protect ourselves, not giving them anything that can be used to further marginalize us. Whether it's the artwork on our walls, to a glimpse of our family members in the background, to the noise coming from the next-door neighbour's house; the supposedly harmless 'banter' that can arise from these things is not something any of us want to endure or expose ourselves to. It's one thing when the bad vibes were in the office, but who wants that in their home? Not me, that's for sure.

The language around working remotely typically centres around working from the comfort of your home and how this should in theory boost productivity and reduce burnout, but in reality, this idea of 'comfort' isn't a shared universal experience. Research commissioned by People Like Us revealed that Black, Asian and ethnic minority workers are almost twice as likely to be using their bedroom as office space, with no desk and chair set up and 58% of professionals are working in a home that is shared with two people and more.* I can relate to this because I've a spent a significant amount of time working from my bedroom and although it was lit at first, after a while it does your head in when you realise you are working and sleeping in the same room. Where the lines are blurred between home and work, it becomes nearly impossible to switch off and you even feel bad to, because you don't want your colleagues to think you're not working hard or slacking. The number of times I have responded to emails late at night (even though there was no expectation to) because I didn't want there to be a perception that I'm not on job working from home. For those of us that still live at home or in a flat share, there might not be enough space to create a separate office. Also, not all companies have provided home office equipment or an allowance to make those purchases, which would mean the expense would fall on us. This is exasperated by those colleagues who are desperate to show off their fancy home office set up during meetings, without realising they are further highlighting

* Metro.co.uk. 'Black and ethnic minority professionals twice as likely to be using their bedroom as a home office – without a proper desk.' (11 August 2021). Retrieved from: https://metro.co.uk/2021/08/11/Black-workers-twice-as-likely-to-be-working-from-bedroom-with-no-desk-15072823/

the inequalities which puts certain groups of people at a disadvantage when working remotely.

Remote working has also presented challenges regarding how we build, maintain and foster new relationships, since in-person networking and social interactions have reduced significantly. Don't get me wrong – it's possible to maintain your catchups and network with people virtually, but online fatigue is real and let's not pretend that meeting people in person doesn't add another dimension to a relationship (unless you physically can't due to location differences). For Black employees, we know that a massive part of our ability to succeed at work rests on the relationships we build, our visibility and how present we are. Working from home has made this trickier and I think we might be even more susceptible to online fatigue because we feel the need to join all the online events and initiate all these meetings.

As conversations about remote working and hybrid work become more prominent due to companies starting to outline their post pandemic work models, have a think about what this means for you and how you manage your career going forward. Don't be afraid to ask your employer questions, for example, if you work for a company that is moving to a remote working model, find out if this will impact how your performance is reviewed, the feedback process, if there will be any changes to pay and your benefits package?

## How can you prepare?

**Do your research:** Start to research the future trends within your industry or the industry you plan to move into. Some of the key themes that emerge should point to certain skills and knowledge areas that are going to be required. For example, within financial services, blockchain and machine learning have been discussed for years as technologies that will disrupt financial services as we know it. It therefore makes sense that there is a tonne of data scientist and machine learning engineering roles popping up across the major financial institutions.

**Identify your gaps and upskill:** Once you've identified the skills you will require, make a list of your own existing skills and expertise. Once you've placed these next to each other, it should be easy to see what gaps you have (take a look back at the table I provided in the Career Pivot chapter of this book [include page number]).

Search online for courses and qualifications which will enable you to upskill in the areas. Try and persuade your current employer to pay for any which have a fee (create a pitch highlighting the value you can bring to your role and the organisation by upskilling in this area).

The websites below contain a mixture of courses (free and paid) which should provide a good foundation to get started.

Coursera: https://www.coursera.org/
Future Learn: https://www.futurelearn.com/
Skillshare: https://www.skillshare.com/
Udemy: https://www.udemy.com/
Udacity: https://www.udacity.com/
LinkedIn Learning: https://www.linkedin.com/learning/
edX: https://www.edx.org/

**Think holistically about your future – beyond work:** When I graduated from university, my priority was securing a graduate role at a prestigious organisation that paid well. When I did, I didn't mind working long hours, I thought the stress and occasional breakdown was totally normal and wore it like a badge of honor in many ways. I'd post selfies on my snapchat at midnight still working in the office, thinking that all these long hours I was working made me tough in some weird way and that's just what you did if you wanted to progress. However, I didn't progress quickly, and I wasn't happy. Fast forward to today and things couldn't be more different. When I think about my career, I think more holistically about the life I'm trying to create for myself— my career must supplement and support that. When thinking about the future of work and what that means for your career, consider all the other aspects of your life too. Work takes up a significant part of our life but it is not our life and it's important we never lose sight of that regardless of what the future looks like.

# BLACK AT WORK: UNDERSTANDING THE LEGAL CONTEXT

# CHARLENE BROWN

*Co-founder and Managing Director of Howlett Brown*

Over the last few years, hundreds of Black employees across a variety of industries have been publicly speaking out about their workplace experiences and, in some cases, have taken legal action against their former employers, revealing racist, toxic work cultures and organisational processes. As we seek to hold companies accountable for their actions, at a time when they are making promises and commitments not only to do better by their Black employees, but the Black community, understanding the legal context has never been more important.

I spoke with Charlene Brown an employment lawyer and the co-founder of Howlett Brown to get more insight. Howlett Brown is a people intelligence business working with organisations to manage their people risk whilst ensuring their inclusion, integrity and purpose thrives at the same time. They specialise in investigations, culture, diversity and inclusion, communications, workplace training and people advisory solutions. Their unique set up means that they are able to advise their clients on the law as well as their culture, strategy, training and communications.

Why do you think over the last few years we have seen so many Black employees publicly speaking out against their former employers?

*Discrimination is something that Black employees have faced in the workplace for a long time, but the murder of George Floyd and the video of it created a visceral reaction which made us reflect on how we have been treated and for some, a reality that the world is not equal for all as much as some might like to believe. George Floyd's murder triggered a worldwide awakening. It is true that people live their lives in a vacuum which is a perception and experience of their own environment shaped by life, choices and circumstance. For non-people of colour their silos can include not realising that what happened to George Floyd happens daily and so for some, it was a realisation that racism is alive and well despite people sharing their experiences of racism for so long. For some Black people, it was an 'enough is enough' moment. We can't continue like this; something must change. With there being an increased spotlight on race-based discussions, people have felt a little braver to speak up about their experiences and call out racism more than ever before. However it's important to note that not all organisations and environments have made it safe to be so vocal and not everyone in society is willing to speak up about their experiences or acknowledge that there is an issue of racism at all.*

With many Black employees being more open about their workplace experiences, there has been a lot of discussion around Non-Disclosure Agreements (NDAs), with some saying that Black employees shouldn't sign them due to their restrictive nature. What are your thoughts on NDAs and things to consider if or when signing them?

*NDA stands for non-disclosure agreement and can have multiple purposes. It can be a standard part of an employment contract in the form of a confidentiality clause or it can be an agreement. The main purpose of confidentiality clauses and non-disclosure agreements are to describe what information is sensitive or confidential to one party (say the employer) and what the other party can use that information for and what it must not do with the information it has access to or knowledge of.. Such clauses can also be used when an employee exits an organization through redundancy or other means. Imagine that I worked at an organisation, and I decide to leave and talk about my experiences; I could do that. There is nothing really preventing me from doing so based on standard confidentiality clauses and approaches to NDAs. However, if I am in a negotiated exit state with my employer and I'm due to receive an exit payment of sort, then confidentially terms are often included in settlement agreements. There is also often a non-disparagement clause in a settlement agreement too, which prevents you from speaking ill of your employer following your exit from the organization.*

## Changes to the legislation

There have been numerous cases that have come up in the last few years where there have been challenges that clauses in settlement agreements can be abused. These have been called in the press as "gagging clauses" which mean that they prevent an employee from revealing the reason for the settlement agreement which can include the circumstances which led to the termination of employment. There are plans by the government to further regulate the use of such clauses and NDAs to prohibit them from limiting people disclosing information to individuals in certain professions, in certain circumstances (such as the police) in the form of new legislation. This legislation will also introduce enforcement measures to deal with clauses that do not comply with new legal requirements. This does not mean that such clauses won't still be used in settlement agreements and in such circumstances it's certainly mandatory in the UK that an employee has a lawyer sign off on their terms of settlement and advise them of what the agreement means. Therefore, employees have a choice to make; whether they want to exit in this quid pro quo situation or they don't, and they want to speak out.

I think it's important for bad conduct to come to light and that organisations learn from those situations. But I also recognise that if used correctly and in the right circumstances settlement agreements and confidentiality clauses can be useful and as such, people must look after themselves and have personal decisions that they need to make. You asked if Black people should agree to confidentiality terms preventing them from speaking about their experiences with an employer. In these circumstances, no one Black person should feel like they must fight on behalf of all Black people, it's a lot to carry and the pressure and strain that can come from exiting an organization that requires a settlement agreement is enough to bear alone.

I understand why NDAs exist, but they should not be abused. If you're signing an NDA, the most likely reason for that is because you are getting something in return and that is an individual choice to make.

Many Black employees who have spoken out mention that they did speak to their human resources department first and were dismissed or nothing was done. When working with organisations, what gaps do you see when it comes to their processes for handling people issues?

## The Law as an Institution

The laws in the UK aren't readily equipped to deal with a lot of the workplace issues we see arising. If we use the UK as an example; it is unlawful to discriminate against nine protected characteristics. However, in the workplace, discrimination does not occur in the traditional forms described in the Equality Act 2010. In a direct discrimination situation, you must have a comparator to show that if it wasn't for that person's colour or nationality for example, they wouldn't have been treated a certain way. In an indirect discrimination situation, you must show that a particular criteria or practice is affecting a group of people who share a protected characteristic. When you consider microaggressions and how they manifest in the workplace, they do not fit easily into current legislation. The law doesn't clearly and comfortably align with issues like microaggressions. I think we will start to see some cases where microaggressions will start to qualify as harassment or bullying but the point is, when the laws were created, they didn't account for unintentional behaviours which could be harmful. From an educational perspective as a society, unless someone teaches you these things at home or through other forms of education, you're not likely to know or understand. The Law hasn't adapted to the social climate that we live in now, but case law is trying to change that.

## Allay (UK) Ltd v Mr S Gehlen

There was court of appeal case in February 2021 where Mr Gehlen accused his employer Allay (UK) LTD of racially harassing him. There were numerous incidents where the alleged perpetrator had classified their comments as banter, but racism is not banter. In a racial harassment case, an employer can be liable for the acts of their employees, and they must be able to demonstrate that they took all the reasonable steps to prevent the harassment from occurring. In this case, the employer said they had delivered diversity and equality training and the judge reviewed the training. There were no informational top ups, no regular refresher sessions and there hadn't done the training for some time. The judge said that the training was 'stale' and the employer lost the appeal.

## The Current Challenges [with/for] Employers

### Organisation structure

All policy and procedures within the workplace are based on employment legislation which means that they are not fit for purpose in this current climate we are living in. At Howlett Brown, we do a lot of work with our clients on assessing their policies and procedures, checking best practice in law, culture, wellbeing and accounting for issues which from a legislative standpoint aren't addressed such as microaggressions, tokenism, gaslighting. Not even Acas reference those in sufficient detail in the UK, although I suspect this will change over time. Our work includes assessing an employer's tone of voice in respect of its culture - as an organisation are the terms and descriptions you're using representative of the culture you want to present?

## Technical expertise

Most people are hired to do a technical job e.g., being a lawyer and advising on the law, being a trader, buying or selling some form of financial asset or instrument. Rarely when individuals become people managers are they trained to the technical level that they should be about being managers; about people. Society generally treats the skill of managing people as an 'add-on', not a fundamental.

**We're now in an environment where our policies and procedures aren't right, which guide managers, who have never been supported or trained to understand what microaggressions and gaslighting are and don't understand that 'banter' can become a massive problem and verge on the edge of harassment. The line between banter, bullying and microaggressions wears thin.**

Many of these gaps are no one person's fault, but there is this expectation that because diversity and inclusion has become a well-known concept, everyone should've woken up as experts which isn't the case as we are seeing today.

**Apart from the human resources function, what other business areas play a key role in helping to remediate and address people issues within the workplace?**

There's this misconception that human resources are there to just look after employees and that's not true. I think human resources are meant to be the bridge between managers and employees, whether that's to resolve issues or allow functional activities such as people being paid on time, getting access to the right benefits etc. Human resources is only as effective as its leadership allow it to be. Ultimately, they can give a recommendation to the business, and the business can choose to ignore that. They advise but they are not the main decision makers. There are a few other groups that play an advisory role, but ultimately, the decisions are made by the managers.

## Beyond human resources

### Employee Relations
They tend to be a division that works in partnership and support of human resources and are specifically skilled in dealing with disputes, and people related complaints and issues, whereas human resources include talent strategy, recruitment, benefit and is much broader.

## Risk and compliance

In certain industries such as financial services, insurance, people have regulated roles which means their conduct is scrutinized even further by regulators.

## Legal

There is always a power structure within organisations and depending on how much power a lawyer has, they can advise and direct how a matter should be handled. Similarly, to human resources, legal traditionally advise and decisions rest with management.

---

**Collecting data on employees**

Part of the reason why organisations don't know their data is because data collection has not been around for very long, especially collecting data on people. Generally, organisations have never collected data on their people in the way they are expected to now and they need to figure out how to capture the data of their current employees and those who are joining them. Then they need to think about:

- What information they need to collect?
- How do they collect it?
- What's legally permittable to be able to collect that data? (The introduction of GDPR adds additional legal obligations)

---

In order to collect the data, employees need to understand why their organisation wants data on them and how it will be used. Developing a culture of trust and communication is not an easy task.

When working with organisations, I advise them to start collecting the data now, before they are legally mandated to, because they will need time to understand the data, learn from it and make improvements within the workplace if the data shows that improvements are needed. Time to establish a plan and put processes in place and to establish a culture of trust so employees will share their data.

The things I've mentioned aren't excuses; companies should be doing better. But if we think about the end goal of getting to a point where companies are declaring their data and we are seeing the ethnicity pay gap decrease, and more diversity at leadership levels, I think it's important to acknowledge the challenges that need to be addressed to get there.

## If a Black employee wants to:

**1. Publicly speak out about their discriminatory workplace experience what should they be aware of and consider**

They should ask themselves what the purpose is of them speaking out. If it's about drawing attention to workplace issues, there are many ways that can be done. I'm not suggesting a person shouldn't speak out, but I am saying that the why, and the responsibility that comes with it, is important. Speak with a legal advisor before doing so to understand what the implications may be for you. In many organisations, there is an internal process that people should exhaust before they move to a claim. If you don't want to go through that process, is that because you don't see a resolution, or would you prefer to name and shame your employer or are you keen to raise a profile and draw attention to the bigger issue? If the latter is the goal, then you have to ask yourself what are you trying to change and how your contribution will move towards that.

I said it earlier and I'll say it again; no one Black person should be carrying the fight against racism on their back alone, for the entire Black community. Everyone has a part to play in a way that matters to them most and in a way that they feel safe being a part of it.

I would also say be clear and reflect deeply on what happened that you had an issue with. This is not to diminish anyone's experience but understand the full picture of how a situation unfolded. Sometimes I meet people who are far too placid about their experiences, and they almost normalise certain behaviors as acceptable when they are not. On the other hand, I've come across people who exacerbate the impact and their experiences.

One of the topics we discuss in our trainings is intent. Intent is often irrelevant where racism is concerned because the impact is still the same. Not meaning to crash into someone's car doesn't erase the crash, or the resulting damage. Even though intent doesn't change the outcome of whether something was discriminatory or not, intent can help us understand how an issue happened. It doesn't diminish your experience, but it provides context. In being able to understand how an issue arose, you might be able to find a different way to resolve it.

Regarding speaking out, I think it is important and necessary for change and I respect and commend the bravery of people who do.

**It is important though that those speaking out understand what it means for them personally before doing so from a personal wellbeing perspective but also a professional one. Some employers may pay attention to it if a person is looking for a new role in a positive and negative light.**

This doesn't mean you shouldn't speak out, but it's about understanding the implications that can arise and making an informed choice.

**2. Take legal action against their employer, what should they be aware of and consider?**

For the most part, you should try to exhaust all your internal processes first before getting to that stage. There is a conciliatory service here in the UK called Acas and you have to go through Acas to get a certificate before you are able to issue a claim against your employer. They will work with you to see if there is another solution before pursing the tribunal route.

You should also be aware that your legal action is time limited. For certain claims, there are limits on how long to bring a claim. It's usually three months. For things like personal injury, you have a much longer period of time to bring a claim through a different route.

You can take legal action and win or you could lose but regardless, you have to endure that process which can be extremely stressful. Employers need to be held to account but don't forget the impact that can have on you as a person. Witness statements have to be taken, you have to show up in court and relive traumatic experiences, plus court cases can last weeks. My words in this chapter are not to detur you from taking action. They are to prepare you if you decide to.

---

Are there any resources that Black employees may find useful in learning more about the legal context as it pertains to their employment?

---

There are legal podcasts and podcasts specifically about Being black in the workplace. Acas (Advisory, Conciliation and Arbitration service) is also a source of information too. I think it is helpful to read law firm updates that are designed for employers but it can provide an insight into how an employer may respond in certain circumstances around law, cases where there has been a determination or regulation.

# BLACK AND NOT SO GREAT

*'To be Black in the workplace is to truly suffer.'* – anonymous

In June 2020, I co-created the #Blackintheoffice. Following the unarmed killing of George Floyd and the resulting second Black Lives Matter uprising, I saw numerous Black people speaking out against former employers on social media, revealing the poor treatment they had been subjected to. There were also a lot of Black people that alluded to issues within their current workplace but felt scared to reveal too much in fear of a backlash. So, myself and my friend Adesuwa created the hashtag and asked Black employees to anonymously share their workplace racism and the companies they work at. Very little space is made for Black voices to be heard, especially when it pertains to us highlighting the ugly realities of systemic racism which is truly ingrained in our society. When we do have the opportunity to speak, we are gaslighted, our experiences being minimalised and reduced to being nothing more than a mere overreaction, misunderstanding or, at worst, a lie. We've seen this time and time again, one example being the Harry and Meghan interview with Oprah. They expressed the racial undertone of the constant attacks on Meghan, and Meghan even revealed that there were 'several concerns and conversations' about how dark Archie's skin might be when he was born. *Loose Women* presenter Jane Moore was quick to brush this off as a case of casual racism.[*] Erm what is casual about racism?

Creating this hashtag was our way of giving Black people a platform to speak their truth.

We received around one hundred submissions from across pretty much every industry you can think of and it was hard to read. Traumatic even. The idea that racism doesn't exist at work and that as a community we are being 'oversensitive' or 'imagining' these things just isn't true. Many called the hashtag 'shocking', 'triggering' and 'uncomfortable', but an 'insightful' and 'important' read.

---

#Blackintheoffice

'One day I came to work to work with cornrows and I was asked if I had joined a gang.'

'I had a manager say to me that they went on holiday and wanted to tan and get dark so that we could look related.'

'I once overheard a colleague someone that they were scared to forward me an email for my file in case I "beat them up" . . . I've never had a violent altercation in my life!'

'We were asked to change our actual names as they sounded too Black and customers wouldn't want to speak to us.'

'Every day I would beat my sales targets and I would be met

---

* Chroniclelive.co.uk. 'Loose Women's Jane Moore slammed for casual racism response to Harry and Meghan baby claims.' (9 March 2021). Retrieved from: https://www.chroniclelive.co.uk/news/tv/loose-women-jane-casual-racism-19990198

with a look of frustration and given more work to do, while my white colleagues would do the bare minimum and get all the praise in the world.'

'There was a Halloween costume competition where one of the white execs came as Barack Obama in Blackface.'

'He often made comments about Black people and anytime I said he was being offensive he'd say I have a chip on my shoulder.'

'When I finally decided to leave, I found out the junior hired to replace me was offered eight thousand more than I was on.'

'One day before a meeting, he told me I was useless, and this was why the company hardly hired Black people in general apart from the cleaners.'

I thought long and hard about writing a chapter which shines a light on the not-so-great aspects of being Black in the workplace. I'm one person, a Black female that can't speak on all Black experiences. There are some Black people that may not be able to relate to these experiences and that's great, we want that to be the case for all of us one day. But I have tried to summarise what I see as just some of the key issues when navigating the workplace when Black.

## The recruitment process

Before we even join the workplace, many of us are changing our names and 'whitening' our CVs because we are aware that any inference that we are Black at the application stage could hinder our ability to progress through the recruitment process.

According to research at Nuffield College's Centre for Social Investigation, British citizens from Black and ethnic minority backgrounds have to send an estimated 60% more job applications to receive a positive outcome from employers compared to their white counterparts, despite having identical CV and cover letters.[*] This number rose for certain groups, such as Black Africans who have to send on average 80% more job applications. According to research in the US, 25% of Black candidates who 'whitened' their CVs received callbacks from employers, compared to only 10% of Black candidates receiving callbacks who opted to leave in ethnic inferences.[†] This reminds me of when I was working on my CV in the lead up to my placement year. I was told by a career advisor at the time to remove items such as being part of my university's African Caribbean Society and being named one of the top 100 Black students in the UK in the *Future Leader* magazine because there was 'too much Black stuff' on my CV. At the time, I felt some time of way; I was being told to remove my Blackness and it didn't seem right. It wasn't right but looking back now and knowing how the biases in these processes work, it was probably the right thing to do, even though that shouldn't be the case. If Black candidates progress to the interview stages, studies indicate that employers who perceive the voice of a candidate to be 'Black-sounding' during telephone interviews were more likely to have negative

[*] Csi.nuff.ox.ac.uk. 'New CSI research reveals high levels of job discrimination faced by ethnic minorities in Britain.' (18 January 2019). Retrieved from: http://csi.nuff.ox.ac.uk/?p=1299
[†] Hbswk.hbs.edu. 'Minorities Who Whiten Job Resumes Get More Interviews.' (17 May 2017). Retrieved from: https://hbswk.hbs.edu/item/minorities-who-whiten-job-resumes-get-more-interviews

judgements of that candidate.* A former diversity recruiter at Google revealed that often Black candidates who graduated from HBCUs (Historically Black Colleges) were asked questions about the 'quality of their computer science degrees' during their interviews and several highly qualified Black applicants were denied roles at Facebook after being told they were not the right 'cultural fit' for the roles.† Don't ever get it twisted! Despite the public announcements and commitments to hiring more Black employees, companies can and do continue to find reasons to keep us out.

## We're often the only ones

Once we get into these organisations, we are often the only Black person in our team or department and one of a few across the whole organisation.

- Less than 1% of university professors are Black‡
- Less than 1% of asset managers are Black §

* bbc.com. 'How hidden bias can stop you getting a job.' (7 August 2018). Retrieved from: https://www.bbc.com/worklife/article/20180806 -how-hidden-bias-can-stop-you-getting-a-job
† thehill.com. 'Facebook accused of not hiring black candidates because of culture fit.' (7 April 2021). Retrieved from: https://thehill. com/changing-america/respect/equality/546910-facebook-accused-of-not-hiring-black-candidates-because-of
‡ Hesa.ac.uk. 'Higher Education Staff Statistics: UK, 2019/20.' (19 January 2021). Retrieved from: https://www.hesa.ac.uk/news/19-01-2021/sb259-higher-education-staff-statistics
§ Theia.org. 'Black Voices: Building black representation in investment management.' (June 2019). Retrieved from: https://www.theia.org/sites /default/files/2019-06/20190611-black voices.pdf

- Less than 11% of jobs within the UK Creative industry are filled by Black people[*]
- Only 3.4% of the civil service workforce (excluding the NHS) are Black[†]
- 94% of the British journalism industry is white and only 0.2% of British journalists are Black[‡]

This can make the workplace experience a lonely one at times. It also presents this weird paradox where on the one hand we are hyper-visible due to our physical appearance being different to majority of our work colleagues. We stand out and this means sometimes feeling like you're under a microscope, you're every move being observed, and it makes you afraid to slip up, to fail because we don't always have the benefit of being given a second chance. But we are also invisible, our skills and talents often being overlooked, and we are disregarded when opportunities emerge. This can look like being left of important emails and meeting invites, your ideas and suggestions being ignored, and as a result working longer hours, working harder to prove our worth, to prove we actually exist.

[*] www.gov.org. 'DCMS Sectors Economic Estimates: Employment (2016) and Trade (2015).' (26 July 2017). Retrieved from: https://www.gov.uk/government/statistics/dcms-sectors-economic-estimates-2017-employment-and-trade

[†] Ethnicity-facts-figures.service.gov.uk. 'Civil Service workforce.' (26 November 2019). Retrieved from: https://www.ethnicity-facts-figures.service.gov.uk/workforce-and-business/workforce-diversity/civil-service-workforce/latest

[‡] Theguardian.com. 'British journalism is 94% white and 55% males, survey reveals.' (26 March 2016). Retrieved from: https://www.theguardian.com/media-network/2016/mar/24/british-journalism-diversity-white-female-male-survey

## Racial microaggressions

Racial microaggressions are a pretty standard part of the Black workplace experience. Often, racism is thought of in the more overt sense e.g., being called a n****r among many other words and just outright racial hatred but microaggressions are a lot less obvious, sometimes quite subtle to the extent that you will question if that really did happen? Did he or she really say THAT? Examples include a colleague mispronouncing your name despite having told them the correct way to pronounce it several times, being the only one constantly excluded from meetings and being left off invites for team events. Then there's the comments such as 'you sound so articulate', implying that they don't expect a Black person to be a well-spoken professional or 'where are you really from?' which assumes that being Black, you're not really British. The issue with microaggressions is that you feel them, they hurt, but because they aren't so obvious, you can't prove that someone intentionally tried to cause you harm, and if you gather the courage to try and address it, you risk being called 'oversensitive' seen as overreacting or its often disguised as being a joke, which leaves you feeling even more alienated. Constantly questioning your own reactions and the intentions of your colleagues can chip away at you and overtime significantly impact your well-being which is why psychologists often compare microaggressions to death by a thousand cuts. Whilst some people may dismiss the seriousness of microaggressions, taking a 'you need to grow a thicker skin' attitude, the consequences are very real. In 2017, research by the Centre for Health Journalism revealed there is significant evidence that microaggressions increase depression and trauma amongst minority groups and there is a link between racial microaggressions and suicidal thoughts. *

## Don't touch my hair

Growing up, many of us had complex relationships with our natural hair, especially those of us with tight 4C curls. I remember begging my mum to relax my hair when I was only twelve. All the Black girls on TV at the time has super straight, slick hair and this translated into the school playground, with the Black girls in the older year groups trying to replicate those hairstyles. As a year seven student on the brink of my teens, naturally I wanted to be just like them. Now with more images of Black women wearing their natural hair, more Black-owned hair brands catering to natural hair and increased education on how to style and maintain natural hairstyles, many of us feel empowered to wear our natural hair, and take pride in rocking different natural hair styles, however in the workplace, it can be detrimental to our careers.

A study from Duke University found that bias against Black women with natural hairstyles prevents us from securing job opportunities. In a series of experiments where participants were asked to act as recruiters and evaluate potential job candidates, Black women with natural hair consistently scored the lowest marks on professionalism and competence, and were not recommended for interviews, as much as white women and Black

* Centerforhealthjournalism.org. 'How racism and microaggressions lead to worse health.' (10 November 2017). Retrieved from: https://centerforhealthjournalism.org/2017/11/08/how-racism-and-microaggressions-lead-worse-health

women with straight hair.[*] Where professionalism and competency are rooted in whiteness and more generally western ideals of beauty, anything that doesn't resemble that can often be seen as a threat. This is why the introduction of the Halo code is so important. The Halo code, created by the Halo Collective is the UK's first ever Black hair code, a pledge signed by schools and businesses to ensure employees and school children are not discriminated again or face barriers due to their afro textured hair.[†]

Those of us who do feel comfortable with wearing our natural hair at work then have to deal with the questions about how we did it, how long it took. Then there are the colleagues that go a step further and start touching our hair (often without permission). Then (and here's where it gets juicy) it's having to explain how you managed to transform your shoulder-length braids on Wednesday to twenty-two inches of Black human hair flowing down your back by Thursday.

## Black not BAME

You'll often see or hear the term 'BAME' being used when addressing Black people or Black issues. During the Black Lives Matter movement, many companies said they stood with their

---

[*] Fuqua.duke.edu. 'Research Suggests Bias Against Natural Hair Limits Job Opportunities for Black Women.' (12 August 2020). Retrieved from: https://www.fuqua.duke.edu/duke-fuqua-insights/ashleigh-rosette-research-suggests-bias-against-natural-hair-limits -job

[†] Halocollective.co.uk. 'Hair discrimination in workplace.' (December 2020). Retrieved from: https://halocollective.co.uk/halo-workplace/

'BAME' employees, and with the global pandemic it's been high-lighted that BAME people have been disproportionately dying from Covid-19. The lazy use of the terms BAME to address all Black and ethnic minority people is problematic for a few reasons:

1. It erases and undermines the unique experiences of every-one the label is applied to. The experiences of Black, Asian, and other ethnic minority groups are not the same and shouldn't be treated as such. The Asian community in itself is extremely diverse for example there are South Asian, East Asian and Southeast Asian people all who have differ-ent experiences. This idea that because we are all non-white, we must be the same is wrong and dangerously simplistic. For example, it is Black people who are being unlawfully murdered by police officers, Black people who are over four times more likely to die from covid than white people*, not BAME people collectively.

2. To some extent, the term BAME suggests a type of cama-raderie among the groups, and this isn't the case – there is a high level of anti-Blackness that exists within many ethnic communities towards Black men and women.

3. It's terrible for data collection and research. In the UK, there is little research that purely focuses on the experi-ences of the Black community, nearly everything is BAME

* Ons.gov.uk. 'Why have Black and South Asian people been hit hard-est by COVID-19.' (14 December 2020). Retrieved from: https://www. ons.gov.uk/peoplepopulationandcommunity/healthandsocialcare/ conditionsanddiseases/articles/whyhaveBlackandsouthasianpeople-beenhithardestbycovid19/2020-12-14

and as a result, we fail to, from a research perspective, get a true and accurate picture of the lived Black British experience.

Within the workplace, while the use of BAME may be easy for administrative purposes, grouping people under this umbrella term means that little is done to address and resolve the issues different communities face.

## Battling tired stereotypes

Widely held stereotypes pertaining to Black women such as 'the angry Black woman', and 'the strong Black woman' are harmful because they reduce Black women to being nothing more than a 'sassy', 'finger wagging' caricature, therefore diminishing their legitimacy in the professional working environment.

It can make daily interactions difficult. You express a difference of opinion, push back on something you disagree with, passionately explain your view and suddenly you're seen as 'defensive', 'angry' or 'aggressive.' You might be told to 'calm down', even when you're very calm.

You express a concern, share something that hurt your feelings and you're 'overreacting' or 'being sensitive'. As a 'strong Black woman' and being viewed through the lens of masculinity and not femininity, you are not afforded the ability to show emotion and have your feelings taken seriously. No one sees that being delicate, vulnerable and fragile is not only reserved for white women.

The worst thing about navigating these stereotypes at work is the way in which they are weaponised against you and framed to position your colleague(s) as the victim and you as the bad person. The gaslighting is so real.

## "Chocolate" King privileges

There's a certain demographic in the workplace that sexualise the hell out of Black men. They dream of having kids that look like Kim Kardashian's, and whilst they have all the attitude in the work towards our good sisters Adeola and Ronette, their voice suddenly becomes high pitched, and they go all googly-eyed for Marvin and Jerome. They're the "allies" that went to the Black Lives Matter protests with signs that said "I love Black dick, so you will hear me speak" and "Stop shooting Black men. BBC [big black cock] matters" (this really happened by the way). At the work Christmas party, they become far too touchy feely and blame it on the alcohol come Monday morning. You know the type!

The experiences of Black men and women in the workplace differ on many levels but I think it's important to highlight that desirability politics and the way in which Black masculinity is fetishized in society affords some Black men privileges in the workplace that simply don't exist for Black women who aren't desired in that way. Speaking with other Black women, we all had a tonne of examples of times Black men were provided career opportunities by their white female senior stakeholders who made no attempts to hide their 'crushes' on them. For the Black men who don't take an issue with this, after all you're benefiting from this right – there is a ceiling. Being the office pin-up will only get you so far.

## The unbearable nature of diversity and inclusion

Being a Black employee can often mean working for companies that say one thing but do another. Over the past year, corporate diversity theatre seems to have been at an all-time high. In light of the Black Lives Matter movement, companies posted Black squares and released statements of solidarity with the Black community and donated to Black charities, all while Black employees were still being treated poorly in the workplace. Make it make sense!! The tech sector has been a clear demonstration of this, as Black employees at Pinterest, Amazon, Google and Salesforce last year and at the beginning of this year have spoken out publicly about the discrimination they have faced. The rolling out of unconscious bias training is merely just a box ticking exercise because it doesn't work. According to a report commissioned by The Equality and Human Rights Commission on the effectiveness of unconscious bias training in March 2018, they found little evidence that the training changes any behaviours. At most, they can increase the awareness of bias but any other effect is minimal. This comes as no surprise to many of us who can attest that much of the biases we face are very much conscious.

The performative allyship is hilarious to watch too. The same colleagues that were quick to post their support of Black Lives Matter on LinkedIn, the internal company forums and suddenly acknowledge their white privilege, are back laughing at racist jokes. What happened to being an ally?

Then on top of this, it's the audacity at being expected to fix issues we didn't event create. On top of our day jobs, they're asking us to lead anti-racism initiatives and educate colleagues on racism and our experiences. Known as Cultural Taxation (a term first coined by Professor Amado Padilla in 1994), in effect, we are being tasked with becoming diversity and inclusion consultants to our organisations for free, with no consideration for how taking on the additional responsibility will impact our well-being. More recently, organisations have been recruiting Black people into the Chief Diversity Officer role to clean up all the mess (pretty much the only leadership position they recruit Black people into), however it can be difficult to implement change quickly without the support of other leadership peers, who are often white men that prefer to lend their support to profit-making activities.

## 'What about me?' – Oppression Olympics

Something I've noticed over the last year or two is the way that people purposely try to derail important conversations about the Black workplace experience and Black experiences more broadly with 'what about me?'. As an example, I've been on diversity and inclusion calls where leaders have outlined their plans to improve Black recruitment, retention and in the question and answer segment, a variety of people including those from other under-represented groups ask what's being done to serve them, listing their workplace issues like they're competing in the 'Oppression' Olympic games to show that their struggle is more valid. There is nothing enviable about the position that majority of Black people are in within the workplace.

Everyone in the workplace should be able to highlight the issues they face and hold leadership accountable to making sure they are addressed. But when Black employees speak up or the topic relates to our experiences, that shouldn't be the greenlight to challenge and derail the conversation and in the process, invalidate our experiences. The mere thought of Black people gaining any sort of equity in the workplace truly worries some people.

## We're all the same . . . or are we?

When you're the only Black person in your team or one of a few, everyone acts like you're the sole spokesperson and representative of all Black people because evidently, we are all the same? The concept of intersectionality is understood regarding white people e.g. you can be a white woman, white LGBTQ+, white and disabled, and much more. But for Black people, we're all Black and the buck pretty much stops there. It's a unique pressure to feel, because you don't want to let anyone down or represent us all in a bad light, so you start to overthink everything because you know that any misstep will reflect badly on us all.

## It be your own people

Organisations have created these environments where only one Black person in any given scenario can get the job and secure the promotion even when there's several Black people who qualify. As a result, it can create this unhealthy level of competition and distrust amongst Black colleagues – unhealthy because people will play dirty to bypass you. I've seen Black colleagues move unnecessarily badmind towards other Black colleagues in order to better position themselves for an opportunity and later excuse their actions with 'the game is the game.' Unfortunately some Black people in the workplace thrive on being the 'only one' in the room and will do everything in their power to protect that position. In an environment where you'd hope to foster community with the few other Black people, sometimes it's not possible when the career stakes are so high and ultimately there can only be one 'Black winner'.

## It's not always 'gang gang'

Another reason there is sometimes tension between Black people at work is because surprise, surprise! We are so different. We come from different cultures and upbringings, different socioeconomic backgrounds, different religions, different parts of the world, I could go on. You get the point. With that being said, it's then a little naïve to expect that being Black alone will be the thing that unites us at work when at times, we couldn't be less alike. You may even find that you build more solid relationships with your non-Black colleagues who you share more similarities with (another surprise: they're not all pagans). I remember early in my career being excited when I saw other Black people, almost planning out our potential friendship in my head, but it wasn't always meant to be. As someone from a working-class background, I found it hard to relate to some of the middle and upper-class Black colleagues (the ones that give Kemi Badenoch and Kwasi Kwarteng vibes). Listening to them spew this rhetoric that others who weren't in their position hadn't worked hard enough and laughing off the racist jokes directed towards them and other minorities made me want to vomit. They quickly established a distance between themselves and the Black people at work like me, because they didn't want to seem like THAT type of Black person and that was fine with me.

## The double-edged sword of Black Excellence

On the hand, when I see #BlackExcellence, I love it. I love to see our wins being celebrated and amplified and I think it's important for the younger generation in particular to see Black people achieving success in a variety of spaces as it shows them what is possible. The reason I created my Instagram page Blk & Great was because at a time when I felt the media reporting of Black people was negative, I wanted to highlight the great things being achieved within our community.

But Black excellence doesn't feel so good when it hinges upon white validation because it's something we will never truly have. As an example, every year, we end up disappointed when the Grammys, Oscars, the Brits, BAFTAs and all the major award shows fail to acknowledge us, but why do we crave recognition from institutions that were never created for our empowerment? Are our best talents now not 'excellent' because they didn't get that white stamp of approval?

In some spaces, Black Excellence has also been manipulated to 'other' us. If we look at Sports for example, gymnast Simone Biles and retired sprinter Usain Bolt have both been dubbed as 'freakish', and 'superhuman' on numerous occasions by the media due to their incredible sporting abilities and achievements. So much has been written about Bile's height and body type,[*] Bolt's height and the length of his legs,[†] and less about their

[*] Espn.com. 'How does Simone Biles do what seems impossible?' (13 October 2019). Retrieved from; https://www.espn.com/olympics/gymnastics/story/_/id/27800411/how-does-simone-biles-do-gymnastics-skills-seem-impossible
[†] Bbc.co.uk. 'How does Usain Bolt run so fast?' (29 August 2015). Retrieved from: https://www.bbc.co.uk/news/magazine-34089451

gruelling training regimes and the sacrifices they've made to the best in their sport. Using words which imply that their sheer excellence is a result of some sort of abnormality is rooted in the natural talent myth; the idea that the success of Black athletes is due to their genetics and a physical advantage and not their hard work and dedication, which only further marginalizes us.

In our workplaces, Black Excellence serves as a constant reminder that we have to work twice as hard to get a sniff of success and we don't have the luxury of being mediocre. Black Excellence dehumanises us in many ways, placing conditions on our right to be treated fairly, conditions which many of us will never be able to meet.

## Twice as hard?

Something which becomes more apparent once you've been working for a while is that the advice that our parents and grand-parents gave us to 'work twice as hard' unfortunately won't be enough for us to succeed in the workplace. Despite our efforts, we still aren't being promoted at the same rate or level of our non-Black peers and aren't being paid equally even when doing the same job and sharing similar qualifications. In reality, we need to work twice as smart too, making sure we double down on networking, building a personal brand, seeking out mentors and sponsors and more. At the same time, there needs to be massive changes in the organisations which uphold racism and racist practices which oppress Black employees. Working 'twice as hard' in environments which have systems in place to impede our success won't result in better outcomes for us.

## Sick and tired (literally)

All these things take a toll and have mental and physical impacts which we often don't discuss. According to research, among minorities and people of colour, the increased level of stress generated from experiencing microaggressions in the workplace and discrimination more generally can lead to headaches, high blood pressures and issues with sleeping.[*]

> 'Mental health, especially within our community is really important. Racism can make you sick, so surround yourself with the love of friends and family.' – Sir Steve McQueen
>
> Mental health is a massive issue within the Black community. The findings from an independent report of the Mental Health act found[†];
>
> - Black men are ten times more likely to experience psychosis than white men
> - Black women experience a substantially higher rates of mental health issues than white women
> - Black people are four times more likely to be detained under the Mental Health Act

[*] Pfizer.com. 'Understanding Racial Microaggressions And It's Affect On Mental Health.' Retrieved from: https://www.pfizer.com/news/hot-topics /understanding_racial_microaggression_and_its_effect_on_mental_ health

[†] www.gov.uk. 'Modernising the Mental Health Act- final report from the independent review.' (6 December 2018). Retrieved from: https:// www.gov.uk/government/publications/modernising-the-mental-health-act-final-report-from-the-independent-review

It's not difficult to see how this then translates into the work-place, which in many ways is a microcosm of the wider environ-ment we operate within. According to the BITC (Business in the community) Race and Mental Health report, 47% of Black and ethnic minority workers reported experiencing mental health issues related to work in the last year. Of those respondents, 25% believe that their ethnicity was a factor in experiencing poor mental health symptoms. [*]

There's two layers to this. There're the mental health issues which arise from your actual work. According to the World Health Organisation, causes of this include low levels of employee support, poor communication and management practices, inflexible working hours and limited participation in decision making https://www. who.int/teams/mental-health-and-substance-use/promotion-preven-tion/mental-health-in-the-workplace. Then there's the mental health issues that are caused by racism at work. The code switching and conforming, the overworking to combat negative stereotypes, the gaslighting, the microaggressions, the subtle and not so subtle ways of being told you're not good enough, you don't belong, the socio-economic consequences of not being paid fairly and more can all severely impact our mental wellbeing. According to research, some of the negative mental health outcomes that can arise include depres-sion, anger, hyper vigilance and low self-esteem. [†]

[*] Bitc.org.uk. 'Race and mental health at work.' (8 March 2020). Retrieved from: https://www.bitc.org.uk/fact-sheet/race-and-mental-health-at-work/

[†] Centerforhealthjournalism.org. 'How racism and microaggressions lead to worse health.' (10 November 2017). Retrieved from: https://centerforhealthjournalism.org/2017/11/08/how-racism-and-microag-gressions-lead-worse-health

Conversations about mental health are still quite taboo in our community as mental health related issues are not seen as a 'real' illness and there is a stigma around speaking out and seeking help, with it being viewed as a sign of weakness. This is why it has been so important to see tennis player Naomi Osaka and gymnast Simone Biles speak about their struggles with mental health and make it a priority; both of them withdrawing from a competition within their respective sports.[*]

The Black workplace experience is further compounded by the discrimination we face in all the other institutions we come into contact within society.

- Black women in the UK are four times more likely than white women to die in pregnancy or childbirth[†]
- Black people are nine times more likely to be stopped and searched [‡]

* Thebridge.in. 'World Mental Health Day. Why we should thank Simone Biles and Naomi Osaka.' (10 October 2021). Retrieved from: https://thebridge.in/mental-health/world-mental-health-day-thnak-simone-biles-naomi-osaka-25856
† Npeu.ox.ac.uk. 'MBRRACE-UK: Saving Lives, Improving Mothers' Care.' (14 January 2021). Retrieved from: https://www.npeu.ox.ac.uk/mbrrace-uk/reports#mbrrace-uk-saving-lives-improving-mothers-care-2020-lessons-to-inform-maternity-care-from-the-uk-and-ireland-confidential-enquiries-in-maternal-death-and-morbidity-2016-18
‡ Ethnicity-faces-figures.service.gov.uk. 'Stop and Search.' (22 February 2021). Retrieved from: https://www.ethnicity-facts-figures.service.gov.uk/crime-justice-and-the-law/policing/stop-and-search/latest

- Black Caribbean students are up to six times more likely to be excluded than white students in some parts of the UK *

## Navigating the challenges

'Don't give up. I was studying art and trying to do film at the same time. I made my first film at 28 whilst others made films when they were 23. Your story is important, your ideas are important. If one route isn't available, there will be another.' - Sir Steve McQueen

**Lean on your support network:** Make sure you have a support network within and outside of your workplace that you can lean on when you experience tough days. These can be friends and family, mentors, trusted work colleagues. It's better to talk about and get some advice than to keep it bottled up.

**"Surrounding myself with friends, family and meditation massively help. I'd also say don't be quick to knock religion, and speak to like minded people about things that affect them."** - Sir Steve McQueen

**Protect your mental health:** The past few years has been a pretty heavy one with the coronavirus pandemic, which disproportionately affected the Black community and the Black Lives Matter movement following the unarmed killings. Then we come into work and deal with everything I have discussed. Black fatigue (the adverse mental and physical effects we experience from racism) is

* www.gov.uk. 'Permanent and fixed-period exclusions in England: 2018-2019.' (30 July 2020). Retrieved from: https://www.gov.uk/government/statistics/permanent-and-fixed-period-exclusions-in-england-2018-to-2019

very real and as a community we are more susceptible to mental health issues. For this reason, we must prioritise our health and wellbeing and find ways to safeguard our mental health. This could include frequent exercise and meditation, taking unplanned time off, cutting things out of our routine which trigger negative feelings e.g., social media and feeding our brain more positive content in the form of books, podcasts, etc., or seeking professional health. If your work environment is really toxic, think about leaving.

**Be prepared to leave:** Make sure where possible you're saving money, networking and maintaining those relationships, and keeping your CV up to date, so if it all gets too much and you decide to leave, you have a plan.

**Document everything:** If you are subjected to discrimination at work, document everything. Make sure you make a note of dates, times, witnesses. If this interaction occurred online, try to take a screenshot or save it if possible. This will make it easier to report it if you choose to.

**Know your rights:** Familiarise yourself with your legal rights in the workplace and your companies processes and procedures. It tends to be something which many of us only investigate if and when things go wrong.

# BLACK AND GREAT

Despite all the challenges, and setbacks, we are still here. Young, Black, British, ambitious and thriving. Our greatness truly knows no bounds. We're picking up the baton from those that came before us to continue the race, while creating our own lanes.

We're launching our own professional networks.
We're creating initiatives to serve our community.
We're speaking our truths unapologetically.
We're launching side hustles alongside our jobs.
We're corporate and creative.
We're making money moves (honorary mention to 'Dinner with
    Jay Z' and '100k salary' Twitter).
We're throwing the ladder back down.
We're trailblazers.
We're change-makers.
We're not going anywhere.
We're not giving up.
We're just getting started.
We're Black and what?
Black and Great.
You heard.

# BLACK AND GREAT

## Communities and Networks

As a Black person in the workplace, community and networks are everything. I have provided a list of communities and networks across a variety of industries that not only provide networking opportunities (formal and informal), but many offer mentorship programmes and educational in person and virtual events which address different aspects of your career from getting through the door (CV, application and interview processes) to climbing up the ladder. Many of these communities (but not all) cater solely to Black students and professionals.

All communities are active at the time of writing this book.

### Amos Bursary

The Amos Bursary is an organisation helping talented state school-educated British students of African and Caribbean heritage succeed academically, attend top universities and secure job offers from great companies. They run mentorship programmes, a personal and professional development networking programme and provide multiple networking opportunities in partnership with a number of organisations.

Website: https://www.amosbursary.org.uk/news/

## Black Geographers

Black Geographers is a community created to provide space for Black geographers to network and connect. They partner with employers to run career workshops and events, provide internships and are soon to launch a mentorship programme.

Website: https://www.Blackgeographers.com

## Black in Geoscience

Black in Geoscience is a global community of Black scientists and allies working to drive awareness and support the work being done by Black Earth and planetary scientists from across the world. They are also working to increase the representation of Black geoscientists and scientists from underrepresented communities in STEM.

## Black Creators Matter

Black Creators Matter is both a networking platform set up to connect Black creators and provide them with educational resources, as well as a creative agency which specialises in Black media.

Website: https://Blackcreatorsmatter.com/

## Black Female Architects

Black Female Architects is a network and enterprise founded to support Black and Black mixed heritage females within architectural industry and other built environment fields

Website: https://www.Blackfemarc.com/

## Black Men in Law

Black Men in Law is a community for Black men working in the legal profession and those aspiring to enter it.

Follow them on Twitter: @BMLnetwork

**Black Solicitors Network**

The Black Solicitors network is a non-profit organisation representing the interest of the UK's aspiring and existing Black solicitors. They work with a variety of partners to ensure members are supported at all stages of their career and professional's development.

Website: https://www.Blacksolicitorsnetwork.co.uk/

**Black Barristers Network**

The Black Barristers network is a community which supports practicing Black barristers and pupils both professionally and socially. They work with schools, offer mentoring, run networking events and provide resources.

Website: https://www.Blackbarristersnetwork.org.uk/

**Black Women in Finance**

Black Women in Finance is a community which supports Black women within the financial services, whether they're just starting out or have been in the industry for a few years.

Website: http://www.bwif.org.uk/

**Black Agents and Editors**

Black Agents and Editors is a community for agents and editors of African and Caribbean descent working in the UK book publishing industry. They also run a mentoring programme for Black people aspiring to work within publishing.

Website: https://Blackagentsandeditors.com

**BYP Network**

BYP Network (Black Young Professionals) is a platform and

network which connects Black professionals with each other, employment opportunities, events and Black businesses.

Website: https://byp-network.com

## Capital Moments

Capital Moments are a social enterprise with a focus on enhancing the commercial awareness of millennials as they navigate their careers and make important life decisions. They provide educational content as well as organise events with the aim of providing millennials with the skills to develop both personally and professionally.

Website: https://www.capital-moments.com/

## Colour in Tech

Colour in Tech is a non-profit working to increase the number of ethnic minorities entering the UK tech workforce. They do this through creating informative resources and delivering events and programmes for students, entrepreneurs and experienced professionals.

Website: https://www.colorintech.org/

## Madland Hack

Madland Hack is a community to support people of colour in the marketing and advertising industries.

Join the Facebook group: Madland Hack

## Melanin Medics

Melanin Medics is a non-profit charitable organisation supporting African and Caribbean aspiring medics, medical students and doctors in the UK. They run a number of workshops, events and provide educational resources.

Website: https://www.melaninmedics.com/

## Now You're Talking

Now You're Talking is a community for millennial females, connecting like-minded females to opportunities and resources online and offline. They provide career workshops, networking events and an annual side hustle showcase.

Website: https://www.nytnetworks.com

## Rare Recruitment

Rare recruitment is a diversity graduate recruitment company which connects diverse students with opportunities in leading corporate companies. They run a series of programmes for students interested in pursuing a career in consulting, financial services, law, and the civil service.

Website: https://www.rarerecruitment.co.uk

## Social Fixt

SocialFixt is an online community which connects Black talent to job opportunities within the creative industry. They also run a series of events to equip Black talent with the skills and knowledge to break into the industry.

Website: https://www.socialfixt.org/

## SEO London

SEO London is an organisation which prepares students from ethnic minority or low socio-economic background for careers in leading corporate firms. The deliver a range of programmes in partnership with organisations to support students aspiring to work in corporate law, consulting, engineering, technology, investment banking and more.

Website: https://www.seo-london.org

## WCAN
WCAN is a social enterprise dedicated to the personal development of Black women. They are a network and platform for Black girls still in school to those well into their corporate career. They offer networking with global corporate firms, mentoring schemes, women in leadership workshops, social events and more.

Website: https://www.wcan.uk/

## We Are Stripes
We Are Stripes are a career progression initiative to address the ethnic diversity imbalance within the creative industry, starting with the creative advertising sector. Through content and events, they shed light on the different roles and career paths within the creative industry and provide consultation to organisations looking to create a more ethnically diverse and inclusive workplace for individuals from ethnic backgrounds.

Website: http://www.wearestripes.org.uk/

## We Are Black Journos
We are Black Journos is a community providing a space where established and aspiring Black journalists can come together to share insights and support one another.

Website: http://weareBlackjournos.org

## YSYS
YSYS (Your Startup, Your Story) is a start-up community dedicated to connecting diverse people with opportunities in tech. They run a series of programmes and initiatives for those looking for support with their start-ups or career in tech.

Website: https://www.thisisysys.com/

## Black Mental Health and Therapy Organisations

### Black Minds Matter

Black Minds Matter are a charity with a mission to connect Black individuals and families with free mental health services by professional Black therapists to support their mental well-being.

Website: https://www.Blackmindsmatteruk.com

### Black Thrive

Black Thrive are a Lambeth-based charity working on several projects in collaboration with different partners to improve the health and well-being outcomes for the Black communities in Lambeth. They have also produced several reports which give greater insight into the lived experiences of Black people in Lambeth and the challenges they face.

Website: https://lambeth.Blackthrive.org

### Celutions

Celutions is a Black-founded social enterprise that works to provide tangible solutions to mental health issues through content, resources, events and workshops.

Website: https://celutionsuk.org/about/

# BLACK AND GREAT:
# THE CAREER MANIFESTO

1. Hire more Black people, particularly into positions of power
2. Promote Black employees into leadership and decision-making roles (beyond diversity and inclusion)
3. Pay Black employees, and especially Black women, fairly
4. Publish your ethnicity pay gap data
5. Listen to and believe your Black employees. Period
6. Invest in the development, health and wellbeing of your Black employees
7. Invest in creating a workplace culture that is inclusive of all people
8. Implement a zero-tolerance policy on racism – fire racist employees
9. Stop asking us to fix workplace issues we didn't create
10. Stop asking us to educate you on racism – do the learning, we are tired of explaining it to you
11. Stop trying to touch our hair
12. Stop asking us to do dumb sh*t like rap and twerk and all the other things you think we do
13. Stop assuming we are all the same – we are not!
14. Stop calling us BAME or PoC. We are Black!

# ACKNOWLEDGMENTS

Firstly, I thank God.

Big up my friends, my partner and my family for being so supportive, encouraging and gassing me up on the days when I needed it. BGT, Fantastic Four, nine-man squad full of tens, Destiny's (dutty gyal) Child, Set Pace Crew, love you FOREVER! Special shoutout to my girl Adesuwa, who provided me the plat-form to write my first ever career related articles in 2017 via her blog Bring Me In. Adesuwa was also the first person I ever told about the idea for the book in 2017 and she told me to do it. Sis, thank you.

To the best literary agent ever, Natalie. Thank you for believ-ing in me, my book, my vision and being a source of inspiration to me, as a Black woman and a mother blazing a trail in the world of publishing. The world of publishing is only going to get better, and it will be because of people like you.

To Joelle and the Coronet team, thank you for giving me the opportunity to bring my book to the world. Joelle, you are the most awesome commissioning editor and just the loveliest person. From our first ever meeting until now, it's been nothing but good vibes and you being extremely patient with my annoying writing habits (sorryyy). You can count on me to be a fan girl of all the books you publish because I just know they're going to be LIT!

Thank you to all the amazing contributors who made the time to contribute interviews and open letters to this book. Thank you for leading the way and showing us what's possible. So many of you agreed to be part of this book when it was just an idea, when there was no publisher involved and I was still trying to figure out how I was going to get it out there. Many of you contributed when you had super busy schedules. Your patience and kindness will never be forgotten.

Finally, a big thank you from the bottom of my heart to everyone who has supported the book, from purchasing it, to sharing it on social media, to asking your mum, dad, granny, cousin to show support. It means so much and I am forever grateful.

# PRODUCTION CREDITS

**Commissioning Editor**
Joelle Owusu-Sekyere

**Copy editor**
Natasha Onwuemezi

**Publicity**
Maria Garbutt-Lucero

**Marketing**
Katy Blott

**Production**
Claudette Morris

**Cover design**
Will Speed

**Proofread**
Deborah Balogun